Also by Frank Fitzpatrick:

Worst to First: The Story of the '93 Phillies

And the Walls Came Tumbling Down

Kentucky, Texas Western, and the Game That Changed American Sports

FRANK FITZPATRICK

Simon & Schuster

SIMON & SCHUSTER
Rockefeller Center
1230 Avenue of the Americas
New York, NY 10020

Designed by Deirdre C. Amthor

Manufactured in the United States of America

10 9 8 7 6 5 4 3 2 1

Library of Congress Cataloging-in-Publication Data
Fitzpatrick, Frank.
And the walls came tumbling down: Kentucky, Texas Western, and
the game that changed American sports / Frank Fitzpatrick.
p.   cm.
Includes bibliographical references (p.   ) and index.
1. University of Kentucky—Basketball—History.   2. University of
Texas at El Paso—Basketball—History.   3. Discrimination in sports—
United States.   I. Title.
GV885.43.U53F58   1999
796.323'63'0975251—dc21   98-44995   CIP

ISBN 0-684-83551-7

Acknowledgments

I remember sitting in Mr. Grillo's high school English class one Friday afternoon in March of 1966 when the subject of that weekend's NCAA basketball tournament arose.

As basketball fanatics, my friends and I at that Catholic high school in a Philadelphia suburb argued the merits of the Final Four participants. We all agreed either Kentucky or Duke would win. No one mentioned Texas Western except to disparage the stunning racial makeup of their starting five.

Five blacks! It was one thing for an inner-city high school to start five blacks, but for a major-college team at the Final Four, it was unprecedented.

"All you have to do is get ahead," said one of my friends. "They give up when they're behind."

"Kentucky is too smart," said another. "I'll bet all Texas Western can do is run-and-gun. That's the way they play."

The sad part was I believed it too.

So when Kentucky was upset by Texas Western, with their tenacious defense, disciplined play, and marvelously named players like Big Daddy Lattin and Willie Cager, we were all stunned. My beliefs were shaken as severely as they would be in religion class that same junior year. Maybe I was wrong about the capabilities of black basketball players. About Catholicism. About a lot of things.

I never forgot that game. And when Simon & Schuster editor Jeff Neuman asked me during an unrelated visit to the Philadelphia Phillies' spring training camp in 1994 if I had any book ideas, I mentioned it.

So I must first thank Jeff Neuman, for helping me translate thought into deed. And for sticking with me as I missed numerous deadlines while trying to squeeze this project in between my regular duties as a sportswriter.

I'd also like to thank Jeff's assistant, Frank Scatoni, for his aid and encouragement in this book's completion.

Any book like this, which turns back to an event more than three decades distant, must be a synthesis. This one certainly is. It was only after countless interviews, hours in the archives of both universities, the search for every word written about the game, and the perusal of scholarly studies on the integration of college athletics that I felt I had a halting grasp on this complex story.

There are numerous people to thank for that grasp:

First of all, the players on both teams—particularly Willie Worsley, David Lattin, and Flip Baudoin from Texas Western, and Tommy Kron and Larry Conley from Kentucky—were helpful in giving me a firsthand perspective of the changing times.

I'd also like to thank the staff at the University of Texas at El Paso's Special Collections (particularly Claudia Rivers), and their counterparts at the University of Kentucky's Special Collections and Archives (particularly Frank Stanger), who unearthed not just the papers of Adolph Rupp and John Oswald but found scouting film from a 1966 game, videotape on the coach's funeral, and hours of Rupp's reminiscences taped not long before his death in 1977.

UTEP coach Don Haskins and his secretary Diana Giddens-Lubianski, as well as Eddie Mullens, the school's past sports information director, and his successor Gary Richter provided invaluable information about the once little-known school tucked away in the remote town of El Paso.

Mr. and Mrs. Adolph Rupp, Jr., who certainly will disagree with the book's characterization of Rupp but who were willing to tell their side of the story anyway.

Robert L. Johnson, who even while recuperating from draining chemotherapy, was happy to discuss his days as a University of Kentucky administrator and his recollections of both former president John Oswald and Adolph Rupp.

Charles Martin, the UTEP history professor who has devoted considerable time to the study of athletic integration in Southern colleges and who was willing to share many of his findings.

Mimi Gladstein, a UTEP English professor whose film of the championship game, colorful recollections, and earlier inquiry into questions concerning the academic credentials of Texas Western's players shed light on the subject.

To the dedicated workers at libraries and newspaper morgues across the nation, especially those at the *Lexington Herald Leader* and the *El Paso Times,* thanks for doing what you do.

And, I suppose, to Mr. Grillo, whose passionate focus on literature allowed our seventh-period conversations to take place unimpeded.

To my parents, who instilled in me a love of sports and sportswriting. And to my wife and children, whose patience has allowed me to sustain it.

Contents

A single day is enough to make us a little larger.

—Paul Klee, *The Diaries of Paul Klee*

And the Walls Came Tumbling Down

1965–66 Texas Western Miners

Name	Ht.	Wt.	Class	Home
Willie Cager	6-5	170	So.	New York, NY
Bobby Joe Hill	5-10	170	Jr.	Detroit, MI
David Palacio	6-2	180	So.	El Paso, TX
Jerry Armstrong	6-4	195	Sr.	Eagleville, MO
Louis Baudoin	6-7	200	Jr.	Albuquerque, NM
Orsten Artis	6-1	175	Sr.	Gary, IN
Willie Worsley	5-6	165	So.	New York, NY
Togo Railey	6-0	175	Jr.	El Paso, TX
Dick Myers	6-4	185	Jr.	Peabody, KS
Nevil Shed	6-8	185	Jr.	New York, NY
David Lattin	6-6	240	So.	Houston, TX
Harry Flournoy	6-5	190	Sr.	Gary, IN

1965–66 Kentucky Wildcats

Name	Ht.	Wt.	Class	Home
Louie Dampier	6-0	167	Jr.	Indianapolis, IN
Jim LeMaster	6-2	188	So.	Paris, KY
Gene Stewart	6-2	187	Jr.	Brookville, IN
Bob Tallent	6-1	179	So.	Langley, KY
Tommy Porter	6-3	188	So.	Graley, KY
Tommy Kron	6-5	202	Sr.	Tell City, IN
Steve Clevenger	6-0	185	So.	Anderson, IN
Larry Conley	6-3	172	Sr.	Ashland, KY
Pat Riley	6-3	205	Jr.	Schenectady, NY
Brad Bounds	6-5	207	Jr.	Bluffton, IN
Cliff Berger	6-8	222	So.	Centralia, IN
Gary Gamble	6-4	185	So.	Earlington, KY
Larry Lentz	6-8	217	Sr.	Lakeview, OH
Thad Jaracz	6-5	230	So.	Lexington, KY

1.

Basketball in Black and White

"What a piece of history. If basketball ever took a turn, that was it."
—Nolan Richardson

Adolph Rupp's face would not permit a smile. The legendary basketball coach's eyes sagged as he aged, his eyebrows arched higher, and his chin receded into the expanding fleshiness of his neck. Two creases, widening each year like riverbeds in yielding soil, formed an indelible frown as they descended from his mouth. The result, even in those infrequent moments when he attempted a grin, was a look of perpetual displeasure. It was as if nature had reshaped his exterior to match what dwelled inside.

"Rupp was unique," said Bill Spivey, one of twenty-four All-Americas Rupp coached at Kentucky. "He wanted everyone to hate him and he succeeded."

By December 10, 1977, in a private room at the University of Kentucky's Chandler Medical Center, only that scowl identified the dying Rupp. Family members, realizing he could not long survive the spinal cancer that had hospitalized him since November 9, silently surrounded his bed. The only sound was the buzz of a bed-side radio.

Rupp almost certainly could not hear the broadcast of that night's Kentucky-Kansas basketball game, but announcer Cawood Ledford's voice, familiar and reassuring, comforted the former coach's relatives. Rupp's son, Adolph, Jr., his daughter-in-law, and two grandchildren grew up immersed in UK basketball. Listening to Ledford's broadcasts was nearly a religious ritual for them, as it was for almost everyone in the commonwealth. From Jamboree on the Appalachian Plateau to Linton on the Cumberland River, Kentuck-ians adored the Wildcats. And, for nearly fifty years, they were Adolph Rupp's Wildcats.

At about 10:45 P.M. on this Thursday night, Rupp's relatives heard a great radio-muffled cheer arise from the crowd in Lawrence, Kansas. Kentucky was hopelessly behind. There were fourteen sec-onds left in the game, his son would recall, when Rupp exhaled, shuddered lightly, and died. He was seventy-six.

Rupp, a native Kansan, had transformed himself into a Ken-tucky colonel during his forty-seven years in Lexington. The Baron of the Bluegrass, as the basketball world knew him, owned several farms in horse country—the last a white-fenced, Bourbon County estate where he planted tobacco and called his prized Hereford cattle by name. The drawl Rupp affected deepened annually, as did his de-votion to good bourbon. All that was missing, it seemed, was the standard-issue white linen suit.

He drove his Wildcats to a then NCAA record 876 victories and four national titles before he retired, quite reluctantly, in 1972 at the age of seventy. He made the University of Kentucky college basket-ball's best-known program. Professional teams often tried to lure him away. Politicians asked him to run for office. Businessmen sought his counsel. By the mid-1960s Rupp was so dominant a fig-ure in Kentucky that 83 percent of the state's viewers watched his

Sunday night TV show. "It's on between *The 20th Century* and *Lassie*," he liked to brag.

Yet for all that, he was a solitary man. "He just wasn't a warm person, really," recalled Ledford. "I don't think he had a close friend." A Lexington newspaper columnist who knew and liked Rupp wrote that he "never seemed interested in much except himself and basketball."

Though he had a master's degree in education, he was no intellectual and would not have wanted to be called one. There were few moral ambiguities for him. Life was made to be diagrammed carefully like a basketball play, and that's the way he lived it. Rupp's world was black and white, even if his basketball teams were not.

The circumstances of his death would have delighted him. It came while Kentucky played at his alma mater, Kansas, the two schools that were the great forces in his life. The game took place on Adolph Rupp Night in Forrest Allen Field House, named for his old Kansas coach. And the arena was on Naismith Avenue, honoring Dr. James Naismith, basketball's inventor and one of Rupp's earliest instructors.

It was easy then for those who knew Rupp to imagine his final moments as something melodramatic, like Charles Foster Kane's death at the opening of *Citizen Kane*. In his own world, Rupp's intimidating power had been as immense as the fictional tycoon's, his motivations often as inscrutable. Surely he, like Kane, would have sputtered a farewell that revealed some buried facet of the man. If so, it would have referred not to a lost childhood toy, but to a lost basketball game eleven years earlier.

Rupp hated losing. But that one defeat, number 152 out of 190, stung him the worst. Toward the end of his life, he told visitors, he still awoke at night, wondering what Kentucky could have done differently. It was as if he understood how his reputation would forever be tainted by that one defeat, on March 19, 1966, when mighty Kentucky lost the NCAA championship game to a little-known school from the Southwest. "Rupp carried the memory of that game to his grave," wrote Russell Rice, his biographer.

For those who saw Rupp's death this way, as a symbolic final act to a large and controversial life, there was little doubt what his last words, his "Rosebud," would have been:

Texas Western!

■ ■ ■

Twenty years later, on one of those West Texas mornings that sparkle like a sunlit lake, Don Haskins talks about that same game, now more than three decades distant.

Texas Western's name had been changed long ago to the University of Texas at El Paso, but Haskins still remains the school's basketball coach and that unexpected 1966 championship its greatest monument.

Thirty-six and blond when his Miners shocked Rupp's Kentucky, Haskins is sixty-seven and gray now. He never coached in another NCAA title game, never even reached another Final Four.

The NCAA championship plaque—wood and brass and coated with dust—rests in a bookcase above Haskins' desk, a bookcase with very few books. Mementos from his thirty-six years at the school, particularly of that one game, fill the tiny office in UTEP's Special Events Center. There is a photo of the 1966 team smiling stiffly with that same plaque. Newspaper stories, banners, autographed basketballs all refer to that long-ago night when the school and Haskins leapfrogged obscurity and changed college basketball forever.

Atop a thick pile of papers on his desk this day, the start of another recruiting season, is a North Carolina newspaper story that someone had mailed him. Both its subject and its prominent position on his desk suggest how much 1966 continues to invade Haskins' present. No matter what evasions he attempts, that championship game is always in his face.

That surprising national title, not long after he had been coaching boys and girls at a tiny Texas high school, brought him praise and criticism, honors and hate mail, and, worst of all for this private man, attention. "I'll be honest with you," said Haskins in 1997, not long after he joined Rupp in the Basketball Hall of Fame. "I'm sick of talkin' about the damn thing. Sometimes I wish we finished second."

Now, asked about the clipping, Haskins picks it up. He glances at it, tosses it back on the pile, and, without comment, heads for the parking lot and his red pickup.

One word was prominently underscored in the headline atop the story:

"RUPP."

■ ■ ■

That March 19, 1966, championship game has acquired the mustiness of something stored too long in an attic's corner. The black-and-white film of the game is as interesting now for the basketball relics it portrays—shiny uniforms, laughably short shorts, canvas Chuck Taylor sneakers, and numerous traveling calls—as it is for the game itself.

The filmed record of Texas Western's 72–65 triumph, forty minutes of uneventful basketball on a long-ago Maryland night, appears to contain little of lasting significance. No great drama is evident. The Miners grab an early lead and maintain it with a stiff-legged determination. The game produced no future NBA stars—though Kentucky forward Pat Riley would become the league's most stylish coach—and no memorable individual performances. The shooting is erratic. There's no dazzle or flair. And the pace, certainly by contemporary standards, is numbingly slow.

"I watched that game once on tape and I never watched it again," said Louis "Flip" Baudoin, a Texas Western reserve who didn't play that night. "It was horrendous to watch. Just horrendous."

The NCAA record book is no help either. Texas Western's name there is notable only because it appears misplaced amid the more familiar North Carolinas, Indianas, and Kentuckys. And because 1966 was the only season between 1964 and 1973 when UCLA was not champion.

Nothing hints at why this game haunted Rupp and hounded Haskins. Nothing reveals why it became, in the words of sociologist Randy Roberts, "the most important NCAA championship ever played." Nothing suggests why it came to be regarded as one of those moments when past and future, sports and the real world, collided with historical and sociological impact.

Nothing seems out of the ordinary until the film is examined more closely.

As the camera pans the University of Maryland's Cole Field House, a Confederate flag can be seen amid the tightly packed rows of mostly white shirts. The crowd appears to be entirely white. So are the two officials and all the reporters on press row. After Kentucky's three white coaches wrap up their final instructions, the Wildcat starters, five white players in white uniforms, walk toward midcourt.

And then, moving casually toward them with the slow stride of history, come the Texas Western starters, their orange uniforms a dull gray on film. All five of them are black.

Black basketball teams are so commonplace today that the Miners' racial makeup does not even register initially. Not until it's viewed in the context of the opponent, the surroundings, and, more important, the era, does their blackness become notable.

In 1966, even at the most liberal colleges, basketball coaches observed strict racial quotas. The whispered motto for many of them was: "Two blacks at home. Three on the road. And four when behind." Yet all seven players Haskins used that night were black. He had white players, four of them, in fact, and a Hispanic. But they never got off the bench. The result was a striking historic contrast.

In a nation obsessed with race, at a time when the civil rights struggle was in overwhelming focus, that twenty-eighth NCAA championship game finally brought the issue into America's demographic meetinghouse—the sporting arena. On the edge of the Mason-Dixon Line, just a few miles from Washington, D.C., race met race on terms everyone could understand.

College basketball, in whose seventy-one-year history Rupp, Kentucky, and segregation rated considerable mention, confronted its future that night. For the first time in NCAA championship history, one of the starting teams was *entirely* black. And for the first and still the only time in major American sports, one team composed entirely of black starters and another that was all-white competed for a prominent national title. "What a piece of history," said Arkansas coach Nolan Richardson, who had played for Haskins' first Texas Western team. "If basketball ever took a turn, that was it."

While the influx of blacks into a sport they eventually came to dominate—in numbers and style—already had begun, Texas Western's victory soon came to be regarded as the exact moment everything changed. "The Emancipation Proclamation of 1966," Pat Riley would later call it.

■ ■ ■

For much of mainstream America then, the notion that a team playing only blacks might be able to defeat a well-coached, talented white squad—a team like Kentucky—was preposterous.

Recent NCAA champions (Cincinnati in 1961 and 1962, Loyola of Chicago in 1963) started three, even four blacks, but no major college team had broken that invisible barrier by starting five. University of San Francisco coach Phil Woolpert, whose Bill

Russell–dominated clubs won back-to-back national titles in the mid-1950s, once played five blacks simultaneously during an NCAA tournament game, but an alumni outcry prevented him from ever doing so again.

The 1965–66 Boston Celtics would be the first NBA team to regularly start five blacks and they would win another championship that year. But fans and sportswriters liked to point out that white sixth man John Havlicek was the Celtics' second-leading scorer and was always on the floor in the closing minutes of the game. And white reserves like Don Nelson and Larry Siegfried played and scored more than some of the starters.

Blacks weren't disciplined enough. They weren't mentally tough. They didn't have heart. If they fell behind, they'd quit. Their abilities were God-given and needed harnessing. At least one white was required, the thinking went, to provide stability and discipline— the quarterback in football, the shortstop or catcher in baseball, the point guard in basketball.

"There was a certain style of play whites expected from blacks. 'Nigger ball' they used to call it," said Perry Wallace, who made history of his own a month after the 1966 championship game, when he became the first black basketball player signed by a Southeastern Conference school, Vanderbilt. "Whites then thought that if you put five blacks on the court at the same time they would somehow revert to their native impulses. They thought they'd celebrate wildly after every basket and run around out of control. [They believed] you needed a white kid or two to settle them down."

Texas Western's victory challenged that racist logic. Haskins' players performed with poise and control, just the opposite from what most whites expected.

In time, blacks and liberal whites would attach tremendous symbolic significance to the game, and its importance would be magnified because the loser was Kentucky. The white Wildcats were disparaged in black communities as the "Bluegrass Bigots" and Rupp, a Bull Connor look-alike, was an apt stand-in for Jim Crow.

"It broke down all the myths," said sociologist Roberts. "The myth that African-Americans couldn't compete. The myth that they needed some white leadership on the floor. In fact, it might be the point where another myth began—the myth of the invincibility of the black basketball player."

One coach at a major Texas college had warned Haskins earlier that season: "They don't have the capability to think when the pressure is on." Haskins ignored the advice and went on to win the national championship.

■ ■ ■

The Miners' upset promised a new era and soon delivered one. Black basketball players suddenly believed something fair and positive was possible for them at a white college. "Young black players told me years later that it gave them confidence and courage," said Harry Flournoy, a Texas Western starter that night. "Some of them, before that game, had been afraid to go to the white schools."

In the next four years, a 1972 study would note, the most substantial increase in integration in the history of college sports took place. The percentage of blacks on college basketball teams jumped from 10 percent in 1962 to 34 percent by 1975. And between 1966 and 1985, the average number of blacks on college teams increased from 2.9 to 5.7. Suddenly, schools North and South had a license, an urge in many cases, to seek out black athletes.

Unwritten rules at Northern schools about how many blacks could play at one time gradually disappeared. Athletes who had been directed to small black colleges now were hunted down by big universities that once considered only the most elite—"the whitest," some would argue—black high-schoolers.

But the game's impact was most dramatic in the South. There it signaled the official end of athletic segregation. "It was quite clear after March 1966 that Southern basketball teams would have to change or become increasingly noncompetitive nationally," said historian Charles Martin.

The next season, for the first time, there would be black freshman basketball players in every Southern conference, two even in the last holdout, the notoriously segregated Southeastern Conference—though none at Rupp's Kentucky. (Rupp's first—and only—black recruit, Tom Payne, did not play until the 1970–71 season and he lasted just one year. In Rupp's final game, when even Auburn had four blacks and Mississippi two, Kentucky was again all-white.)

The black rush to predominantly white colleges became so great so quickly, that a year after that game an *Ebony* magazine writer compared it to "the thundering hooves of a cattle stampede." Even Alabama football coach Bear Bryant, a man whose racial leanings were more akin to Rupp's than to the changing tenor of the time, could see the future by then. "We're looking at some young negroes in the state," he told *Ebony* in 1967. "The time is coming when in this entire area you won't see too many of these boys going away."

Bryant couldn't have known how right he was. By 1983, forty-two of the fifty starters on SEC basketball teams were black. And the four Southern schools that made up that year's Final Four in Albuquerque—Houston, Louisville, Georgia, and North Carolina State—filled their twenty starting spots with twenty blacks.

"Texas Western broke open the old safe rules that teams had always worked under, these self-imposed restrictions about how many blacks you could have on a team," said Perry Wallace. "Before, even those schools that recruited blacks limited themselves. They would have maybe one big rebounding type and one little fast ball handler who could create some things. After that game, we all knew something big had happened. It was clearly a watershed. But while we were all so very excited, we were still a little unsure of what it meant. What was going to happen next? Would they let it continue?"

They were questions that dogged every step forward in the civil rights movement. And like that wider struggle, Texas Western's shining moment soon would be smeared by the social spasms of the late 1960s.

A polarizing combination of white backlash and black militancy was beginning to forge a harder-edged view of America's racial dilemma in 1966. The Black Panthers were founded that year, and Alabama governor George Wallace, pandering to white fears and prejudices, prepared for a run at the White House. James Meredith was shot on a march from Memphis to Jackson, Mississippi, in June, and that same month, in a speech at Greenwood, Mississippi, Stokely Carmichael first used the term "Black Power."

In this charged atmosphere, everything was reexamined through a racial lens—even sports. "Until that time, conventional wisdom held that sport treated blacks fairly and that it contributed mightily to good race relations," wrote historian Adolph Grundman. "[But by the late 1960s] intercollegiate sports stood as one more example of the limitations of equality of opportunity."

The new stridency produced black voices like that of sociologist Harry Edwards, who pointed out the obvious: white colleges were exploiting these youngsters. "The black athlete on the white-dominated college campus . . . [is] abused, dehumanized, and cast aside in much the same manner as a worn basketball," wrote Edwards. Since perhaps 80 percent then were not graduating, and most lived isolated lives on white campuses, it was difficult to argue with Edwards' conclusion.

Perry Wallace himself had witnessed the phenomenon on recruiting visits to Big Ten schools, and it left him with mixed reactions.

"I'd see black kids playing basketball for Illinois or Michigan and it all looked glamorous on TV. But when I visited those places I saw that the black athletes really didn't do that well," he said. "They lived in their own little subculture. They were given rinky-dink courses where they really didn't tend to pursue excellence in education. Some were inarticulate and illiterate. But I also felt that just exposing these people to that environment helped in the next generation. Bill Russell might not have gone to college without basketball, but his daughter was admitted to Harvard."

Questions about the relationships between blacks and college athletics bobbed to the turbulent surface. Academics and those few journalists curious about the trend sought a petri dish where it could be observed. "And where else," asked Haskins, "were you going to find a white college then with a lot of black athletes but Texas Western?"

In his groundbreaking 1968 series on black athletes, *Sports Illustrated* writer Jack Olsen vilified the college, by then the University of Texas at El Paso, describing it as a "status-conscious university seeking fame by importing negro athletes."

Olsen's "Black Athletes: A Shameful Story" trod boldly where few other sportswriters had dared. The school, with its relative abundance of black athletes, was a natural focus for the writer. He noted that those athletes, including some of the basketball players, often complained of a double standard. He examined some of the heartbreaking realities they encountered on predominantly white campuses. Olsen also questioned the university's motives in recruiting these youngsters.

The series' real focus was world-class long-jumper Bob Beamon and his equally bitter UTEP track teammates. Not long after Martin Luther King's assassination on April 4, 1968, they had boycotted a meet with Brigham Young University to protest the Mormons' racial doctrines. The college's president, Dr. Joseph Ray, responded by suspending them from school.

But the basketball players were quoted extensively too. For African-Americans, 1968 was light-years removed from 1966.

David Lattin, Willie Cager, and Willie Worsley—key members of the 1966 team—complained about their social isolation, their courses, the way they were treated in contrast to white students, and even athletic director George McCarty's use of the word "nigger." (The AD always insisted he was saying "negro," but with his drawl, he pronounced it "nigra.")

Haskins and McCarty had been interviewed by Olsen simultaneously and the coach recalled the AD using the word "nigger" only once, and that was as the point of a story. Haskins, who prided himself on being able to size up a man's motives, felt the writer was setting them up for a hit. He said some of his players had telephoned him before he met with the writer to warn him about Olsen and the questions he had been asking them.

"I sat there strumming my fingers," Haskins said. "I wasn't buying his act. That [series] hurt us bad. And it was so untrue. They said George kept saying, 'Our nigger athletes.' I was in the room and George did not say that. What he did was tell a story of driving in a car in the 1950s to Abilene with Charlie Brown [one of Texas Western's first black players] sitting in the back seat. George said he started to tell a 'nigger' joke and then he caught himself and apologized to Charlie. And Charlie told him, 'Go on, tell the damn story.'"

Lattin, in an interview with Olsen, told him that Haskins had once reprimanded him for holding hands with a white girl. Haskins admitted to Olsen that he had cautioned his black players about interracial dating, but explained that while it didn't offend him, there were "downtown people" upset by it.

"I would talk to our players when they came here and the only thing I said was that in that day and time, I didn't think things were right for them to be dating," Haskins said. "Most of the black kids in that time, whether they wanted to go with a white girl or not, didn't. They kind of kept their place."

In the wake of these widely read stories in the nation's premier sports publication, some blacks began to view the school in a more critical light. Haskins began to meet recruits who turned away from him specifically because of the *Sports Illustrated* series.

Lou Henson, a longtime coach who was at New Mexico State at the time of the magazine articles, benefited—along with other coaches—from the aftershock. "I know for a fact it hurt Haskins [and his recruiting]. Everyone I talked to had read the Olsen article. . . . The black athletes all knew [about] it."

The Texas Western players now contend that, for the most part, they were misquoted, misinterpreted, or simply misunderstood by Olsen. Things were far from perfect in El Paso, they say, but they were young in 1968 and there were people—black and white—who tried to fit Olsen's findings to their own agendas.

"Remember this was 1968 and it was a couple years after our championship," Willie Worsley said. "There were some people on the team who felt a little jealous, a little angry at being forgotten. Because at that time when teams would win the national championship, you'd see them on TV all the time. We never got on TV. They still treated us like second-class citizens. The town treated us like King Tut, but no one else. And there were some black militants and people on both sides that wanted to make a big deal out of things [in the *Sports Illustrated* piece]. The writer talked to other people about us and a lot of the things they said weren't so."

According to Louis Baudoin, if his black teammates came off as sounding angry in the articles, it was understandable.

"They *were* angry—as angry as Beamon was," he said. "That was such an angry time nationally. Some of them handled it better than others. Some just bit their tongues. But that whole thing is something that's healed with time."

Haskins and others at UTEP still dispute much of Olsen's series, while the writer just as vigorously defends his work. Most of Olsen's criticisms seem justified, but the series did help contribute to certain misconceptions about the 1966 champions that soon became accepted truth.

Very quickly afterward, many wrongly believed that Texas Western's surprise title had been accomplished extralegally, with a team of urban hired guns. "Here comes this team out of El Paso with these black kids and everybody says, 'Well, there's a bunch of renegades,'" said Moe Iba, Haskins' assistant at the time. "They didn't know the kids individually so it was easy for them to say."

Rupp welcomed the targeting of Texas Western. He would call its players "a bunch of crooks," and erroneously claim the school had been placed on probation soon after its championship. He even said one of the Miners had been recruited from prison. "I don't think Duke [another all-white Final Four team in 1966] and Kentucky had to apologize to anybody for the way we played without 'em [blacks]," Rupp said.

When ten years later, in his book *Sports in America*, popular author James Michener—relying on many of these same mistaken notions—characterized the 1966 champions as "loose-jointed ragamuffins. Hopelessly outclassed," their historical fate seemed sealed.

"The El Paso story is one of the most wretched in the history of American sports," Michener wrote. "I have often thought how much luckier the white players were under Coach Adolph Rupp. He looked after his players; they had a shot at a real education; and they were secure within the traditions of their university, their community and their state."

Even Dr. John W. Oswald, Kentucky's president at the time, a spectator at the game, and someone who fought Rupp over integration, bought into this mythology. "I'd like to have been able to state it as well as Jim [Michener] did in his book," Oswald said in a 1989 interview. "I think what happened to that Texas Western team was really pretty outrageous. None of those players, as I understand, ever went on for another semester, much less graduated."

The real story of Texas Western's championship team is far different from the myth that has grown around it.

Instead of playing like the uncontrollable playground thugs they were alleged to have been, the Miners walked the ball upcourt, employed an intricate passing game, and were ferocious on defense.

"If you want to get down to facts," said Willie Worsley, "we were more white-oriented than any of the other teams [in the Final Four]. We played the most intelligent, the most boring, the most disciplined game of them all."

And instead of forgoing an education, they used theirs to gain entry to the middle class. "Almost all of them got their degrees and they've done something with their lives," said Iba.

Now they are salesmen, detectives, teachers. Nine of the twelve Miners, four of the seven blacks, eventually got their degrees. The remaining three left within a semester of theirs and did not suffer because of it. David Lattin, six credits shy, is a public relations executive with a Houston-based liquor distributor; Orsten Artis, a semester shy, is a detective sergeant in Gary, Indiana; and Bobby Joe Hill, also a semester short, recently accepted a buyout after several decades as a senior buyer with El Paso Natural Gas Co. His daughter finished law school that same year.

"We've all got good jobs," said Nevil Shed, who is now the director of intramurals at the University of Texas at San Antonio. "It's altogether different from what they said, and it really, really hurt me. . . . If I see one of those sportswriters who said that stuff, I always say, 'Hey, I'm here. I'm one of those old black misfits. The ones you said didn't graduate.'"

What no one mentioned at the time was that until the mid-1970s, four of Kentucky's five starters, including All-Americas Riley and Louie Dampier, had not yet earned their college diplomas.

"That's just the way the thinking was back then," said Lattin. "It was 1966. And 1966 was a crazy time in this country."

■ ■ ■

Imagine America as an enormous table on which 190 years of customs and traditions had been set down carefully like dinnerware for a great feast. Imagine also that, quite suddenly, something began to tilt that table. At first, the tilt was nearly imperceptible, just some minor tottering here and there. But as the pitch grew steeper, the crystal began to rattle. Soon the china and silverware were crashing to the floor.

That was the 1960s, and by the third week of March 1966, most Americans were beginning to realize that their table was listing badly.

The signs of social change, and resistance to it, were everywhere that week: after a summer in which there had been civil disturbances in forty-three black neighborhoods, Los Angeles's Watts exploded in riots for a second time; New York City police barricaded the nightclub district of Greenwich Village that Saturday to "keep out undesirables"; the New York State Commission of Education, responding to a teenage girl's lawsuit, ruled public schools could no longer compel students to wear a particular style of clothing.

Even television was slipping into the abyss. Raised on the moral certainties and familiar themes of detective and cowboy stories, many Americans were baffled by that season's hot new show, *Batman*. What the hell is this, they asked, with the "Pows" and the "Bangs" and the sarcasm? It wasn't literal. It wasn't familiar. And the kids loved it.

The sporting world was also experiencing unprecedented turmoil. In early 1966, Muhammad Ali, boxing's heavyweight champion and a Muslim, challenged his draft status, beginning a process that eventually would cost him his crown; the Dodgers' Sandy Koufax and Don Drysdale, two of baseball's best pitchers, held out in tandem for a combined $500,000; and, for the first time that Saturday, in Houston's Astrodome, a big-league baseball game was played on a surface other than grass.

Nowhere, however, was the status quo vibrating more noticeably than on the nation's college campuses. Students, increasingly politicized by the military draft and the civil rights movement, demanded more freedoms, challenged curriculum, dabbled with drugs, and questioned the incomprehensible conflict in Vietnam.

At the University of Maryland, March 19, 1966, was a sunny and unusually warm Saturday. Located along Route 1 in College Park, just north of Washington, the big campus on that last day of winter was teeming with the kinds of contrasts that were peculiar to the 1960s. Side by side in its student newspaper, *The Diamondback,* were notices for meetings of the bridge club and Students for a Democratic Society; campus discussions on the Vietnam War were set for the following week, as were interviews with recruiters from tobacco companies and defense contractors, and that afternoon, at several segregated apartment complexes adjoining the campus, black and white picketers from ACCESS (Action Coordinating Committee to End Segregation in Suburbs) clutched signs demanding "Equal Access to Suburbs."

Meanwhile outside Cole Field House, a green-roofed arena that resembled a World War II–era Quonset hut, some early-arriving fans for that night's NCAA championship basketball game carried Confederate flags. "It was such a chaotic time," said Kentucky forward Larry Conley. "Things were changing all over the place."

Later that night, on the floor of that arena, Conley and four of his white Kentucky teammates shook hands with Texas Western's black starters.

■ ■ ■

In this racial drama, a perfect morality play for the decade's heightened social consciousness, Rupp and Haskins were cast perfectly. Rupp, the snarling epitome of an unyielding establishment, made a compelling villain. Haskins, the laconic loner who rode in from the West, was an appealingly American hero.

These antagonists had been born in small Midwestern towns

within 150 miles of each other—Rupp in Halstead, Kansas, Haskins in Enid, Oklahoma. Each was the disciple of a legend, Rupp having played for Phog Allen at Kansas and Haskins for Hank Iba at Oklahoma A&M.

Yet it would have been difficult to envision two more distinct personalities.

The Kentucky coach was stiff, formal, and predictable. He liked Lawrence Welk and dark Cadillacs and, even if he had not been bald, never would have let his hair down. He was notoriously thrifty and loved to discuss his many accomplishments. "[Rupp] was the biggest egotist that I've ever known," said Kentucky's president John Oswald. His suits were always brown, his pajamas always red, and his teams, with only two exceptions in forty-two years, always white.

Haskins hunted, fished, gambled, and could drink most men under the table. He fussed and fidgeted so badly that friends had difficulty imagining him asleep. "Tarzan with his loincloth on fire," is how Eddie Mullens, then Texas Western's sports information director, described him. He tipped well, drove pickup trucks, and had no detectable ego or fashion sense. "What you see is what you get," said friend Jimmy Rogers. "He is the most unpretentious person you'll ever meet."

Both men could be harsh and intimidating, and their practices were grueling, humorless sessions. But Haskins' players, unlike most of Rupp's, seemed to understand that their coach's gruffness masked a warm heart.

Curiously, according to documents in the archives of the two schools, that night's absolute racial contrast would not have been possible if both Rupp and Haskins had not resisted their universities' presidents.

At Kentucky, the northernmost member of the SEC, Rupp's reluctance to integrate had troubled president Oswald long before that game. Under 1964's Civil Rights Act, colleges that discriminated jeopardized their federal funding. Oswald had opened most of the university to blacks without much difficulty, but he found the already legendary basketball coach a formidable hurdle. "Rupp, in his very first discussion with me," said Oswald, "sounded like a bigot."

Still, Oswald pushed. "He drove Adolph crazy telling him to recruit blacks," recalled Rupp's assistant coach Harry Lancaster. And Rupp—a power in the conference, the state, and the sport—pushed back. "[Athletic director Bernie] Shively came in and told me that Dr. Oswald was very interested [in recruiting blacks]," Rupp recalled later. "I said, 'I can get them, but can you get 'em in [school]?'"

Meanwhile at Texas Western, where alone among white schools in the southern half of the nation black athletes had been competing for a decade, Haskins faced the opposite problem. His college president, Dr. Joseph Ray, was concerned that the coach was playing too many.

Haskins' pragmatic attitudes coupled with the school's Mexican border location and lax admission policies made the recruitment of blacks relatively easy. But when the 1965–66 season began, he was doing more than finding and playing them. He was starting five blacks, a radical concept anywhere then, particularly at a state-supported school in conservative Texas. "It was going to reflect on me," Ray recalled, "if we played all black boys."

So Ray told his athletic director to inform Haskins that "we couldn't play more than three black boys." The coach objected. Haskins now says he doesn't remember the incident, but Ray recalled that Haskins came to his office and convinced the president to change his mind.

Haskins recruited black after black to El Paso not because he was a social crusader but because he understood they helped him win. "He didn't do it to make a statement and he didn't do it to step on anybody's toes," said Paul Cunningham, a UTEP forward in the 1980s and now a broadcaster for Miners games.

Seizing an opportunity in a region where no other coach recruited them, Haskins sought blacks even more diligently. With the aid of one of his first Texas Western players, Willie Brown, and a New York City Parks Department worker named Hilton White, he established a pipeline to that city that would bring him three key players on the 1966 team. And because blacks had been playing at the El Paso school since 1956 (five years before Haskins ever came to the school), he gained contacts in many other black communities. White coaches who saw black players they liked but could not recruit, often tipped Haskins to them.

Rupp, meanwhile, kept his team all-white out of a combination of pride, prejudice, and practical concerns. He always had done things his way and been wildly successful. His way did not include blacks. "I think the feeling among a lot of people at the university was that Adolph was a racist who was never going to bring blacks onto the team. That's just how they felt about him," said Robert L. Johnson, a former vice president and head of athletics at Kentucky.

At best, Rupp possessed the patronizing attitude toward race that was common among Southerners of his generation. There were some things blacks simply weren't equipped for, men like Rupp believed. Meeting a real university's academic standards and beating talented all-white basketball teams were two.

Anyone who recruited a lot of blacks, Rupp felt, must be cheating. In later years, he and others would accuse Texas Western of that and more. "I hate to see those boys from Texas Western win it," he said. "Not because of race or anything like that but because of the type of recruiting it represents. We won't go raid some schoolyard. Hell, don't you think I could put together a championship team if I went out and got every kid who could jam a ball through the hoop?"

So when that groundbreaking 1966 game was over and a defeated Rupp departed the floor, a resentment nearly as thick as smoke engulfed him. "TWC," he allegedly sniffed, back in his locker room. "What's that stand for? Two white coaches?"

■ ■ ■

For all the significance that later would be attached to the game, the subject of race barely was mentioned in contemporary accounts. In fact, reporters seemed to go out of their way to avoid it.

"It was nothing but ethical that the coaches at their press conferences here would not comment on the ethnic backgrounds of the teams," wrote *El Paso Herald-Post* sportswriter Bill Ingram that weekend. "It is a matter that requires some delicacy of handling."

But while the 150 sportswriters at College Park that weekend— virtually all of them middle-aged white men—made little of the two teams' racial differences in print, such discussions were widespread on press row and among fans. "There are overtones of race," wrote Bill Conlin of the *Philadelphia Daily News,* one of the few to raise the topic, "and you need earmuffs to avoid the black vs. white theme of tonight's title game."

Some, while dodging the serious implications of the racial subtext, could not resist backhanded references to it. "Rod Hundley, the former West Virginia and Lakers star, had the funny quote of the tournament when he was talking about Texas Western," wrote John W. Stewart in the *Baltimore Sun.* "'They can do everything with the basketball but autograph it.'"

That same day, Stewart's *Sun* colleague, James H. Jackson, presented this entirely inaccurate scouting report on Texas Western: "The Miners, who don't worry much about defense but try to pour the ball through the hoop as fast as possible, will present quite a challenge to Kentucky. . . . The running, gunning Texas quintet can do more things with a basketball than a monkey on a 50-foot jungle wire."

In reality, Texas Western's stingy defense yielded only 62 points a game—8 points fewer than Kentucky allowed—and their offense slowly walked the ball up the court. It was the kind of thoughtless, offensive stereotyping this game would help erode.

The participants themselves contend that their desire to win and play well obscured any sense of a larger importance. "If I would have come into that game talking about, 'Okay, whitey, man, your ass is mine,' or he said, 'Okay, nigger,' the game probably would not have been played as good as it was," said Texas Western's Nevil Shed. "I don't think we ever made a gesture of, you know, 'Yeah, us blacks we got a Black Power kind of thing and we're gonna beat those whities.'"

"There's no way we went into that game thinking this would be great for blacks," said Worsley, now the dean of boys at Harlem's Boys Choir High School. "Why should we? Who knows when they're going to make history? At that time, we didn't know it. We all had our own little set of priorities. Me personally, I knew nothing about Rupp. I didn't know who the hell was coaching for Kentucky. And you can ask me now and I still can't tell you who coached Duke. We knew they were segregated. We weren't as stupid as people thought. But Rupp didn't wear a uniform. He wasn't the one who was going to run by me."

In his role as a prominent college basketball commentator, Kentucky's Larry Conley is asked often about the game and its implications.

"I've had a lot of chances to consider this over the last thirty years," said Conley, a senior on that Kentucky team, "and it's something that really never entered our minds. We were playing another basketball team. That they started five blacks was inconsequential. All the racial overtones developed much later. We were kids, nineteen, twenty, twenty-one, trying to play a game. I've had several black writers ask me about that since then and I always say, 'Let me tell you something, I wanted to kick their ass all the way back to El Paso.'"

Haskins, who had never even seen a black basketball player until he was a junior at Oklahoma A&M, still says racial considerations were the furthest thing from his mind that season. "I started my five best players," he said. "That they were all black and that it was the first time five black players had started in an NCAA championship game meant nothing to me."

"He's not lying," said Earl Estep, a former college teammate of Haskins' and still a close friend. "I don't think he recognized what he did. I don't think he even understood it. The black-white thing was nothing, absolutely nothing to him."

But it was something to the spectators who paid $14 apiece for tickets when they went on sale in August—some scalpers outside Cole Field House got as much as $115 that weekend. You didn't have to be among them long to hear some sort of chanted racial insult. Ethnic jokes and stereotyping still were socially acceptable then, and that kind of taunting by sporting crowds was common, North and South.

Only a month earlier, at a Georgetown-NYU basketball game in New York City, a Georgetown student dressed in Nazi-like attire led Hoyas fans in "Sieg Heil" chants. When a student at predominantly Jewish NYU later complained, a Georgetown official defended the action as a parody. "We have friends who are Jewish people," the Reverend Anthony Zeits told the *New York Times*. The unusual, unofficial mascot, he said, would be permitted to continue—except when Georgetown played NYU.

Now, waiting for the championship game to start, boisterous Kentucky fans hoisted Confederate flags and the school's pep band played "Dixie." Two years earlier, the band had gotten itself in trouble with Oswald when, just as a black Iowa center had fouled out, they struck up "Dixie." Oswald had assured concerned minority leaders that it would never happen again, but "Dixie" remained a part of the Wildcats' basketball atmosphere.

"They would get on their feet and play that song and wave the

Confederate flags," recalled Oswald's son, John, who attended the 1966 championship game as a ten-year-old. "I remember at that game I asked my older sister why they were doing that and she said that was their sort of subtle way of noting that an all-white team was playing an all-black team."

There were other incidents of race-taunting at that Final Four. "The crowds were more than interesting," reported *The Diamond-back* on the consolation game between all-white Duke and inte-grated Utah that preceded Texas Western–Kentucky. "Southern hospitality was plentiful except when Utah's Jerry Chambers [a black from nearby Washington] began to seriously threaten Duke's lead. . . . Disparaging remarks were shouted from Duke's trainer's bench whenever Chambers was within hearing range and the refer-ees were not."

■ ■ ■

As Rupp and Haskins gathered their teams around them for final in-structions, Cole Field House stirred to life with typical pregame ac-tivity. The cheerleaders solicited noise from clusters of fans seated near the floor. Referees tested the game ball's bounce as they moved toward midcourt. Reporters rustled their notepaper. But if anyone sensed they were about to witness history, they kept it to themselves.

College basketball had been lurching toward this moment since February 9, 1895, when the Minnesota State School of Agriculture defeated Hamline, 9–3, at St. Paul, in the first recorded intercolle-giate game. Almost since then, the forces for and against the integra-tion of university athletics had been rumbling, mostly unobserved, like shifting subterranean plates.

Now as referee Steve Honzo tossed the basketball into the air for this most unusual championship game's opening jump, the earth was about to shake.

2.

The Rules of Integration

"There is no more difference in compromising the integrity of race on the playing field than in doing so in the classroom.... One break in the dike and the relentless sea will rush in and destroy us."
—Georgia governor Marvin Griffin, 1956

Whenever Rupp was pressed about integrating his team, he would always point, with considerable justification, to the perils of taking a black youngster to Mississippi. It was easy for him, and others in the border South, to deflect civil rights criticism by pointing at that turbulent race-heated state. "What do you think they would do if I brought a Negro there?" Rupp asked reporters rhetorically in 1961. The answer was apparent.

Even civil rights activists avoided the state. "We were all Southerners and we knew the depth of the depravity of Southern racism," recalled Andrew Young, then a Martin Luther King aide. "We knew better than to take on Mississippi."

The trouble that awaited Rupp's all-white teams at Mississippi and Mississippi State was, of course, tame compared to what King and his followers encountered there. Mississippi State fans liked to pummel Kentucky players when they fell into the stands chasing loose balls, once plucking hair from the blond head of All-America Cotton Nash. They jeered the Wildcats, raised nasty banners, and took great delight in insulting the pompous Rupp.

But that was all good-natured sparring. The prospect that whites and blacks might play and sweat together on a basketball court was something else entirely. That was inflammatory.

The Supreme Court's 1954 *Brown v. Board of Education* decision (which overturned *Plessy v. Ferguson's* "separate but equal" doctrine) shook the South like nothing since the Civil War. Racial fears and hatreds intensified and sports were not immune from the reaction. Many segregationists saw the playing fields, where American mythology insisted brotherhood and sportsmanship prevailed, as particularly vulnerable to "race-mixing." Television was then beginning to make intersectional sporting events—games pairing nationally known schools from different regions of the country—more attractive. And intersectional games might, they feared, mean interracial games.

Several Deep South states, including Mississippi, responded to the possibility with laws prohibiting, or aimed at prohibiting, interracial athletic competition. "When Negroes and whites meet on the athletic fields on a basis of complete equality, it is only natural that this sense of equality carries into the daily living of these people," warned Georgia State Senator Leon Butts in 1957 after submitting a bill to ban such activities.

Throughout the first half of the century, segregation was an unquestioned reality in college sports, as it was in every other facet of Southern life. When, after *Brown*, the first cracks in that wall became visible, the response was typically harsh. "Name one field of endeavor that has been taken over by Negroes and succeeded. Name one!" challenged a 1961 *Jackson* (Mississippi) *Daily News* editorial on the subject. "The same group that killed boxing and is dooming baseball will soon take over professional football, and it too will perish."

Southern colleges with national aspirations in sports scheduled very carefully. They made sure any intersectional games came against schools willing to accommodate this athletic apartheid. Those contests that crossed the Mason-Dixon Line were governed by an unwritten "gentlemen's agreement" that required teams traveling South to withhold black players. Some Northern schools did so even when they met Southern opponents at home. In 1945, for example, when Tennessee played at Long Island University, LIU coach Clair Bee did not dress two black players.

This Northern acquiescence lingered in the years immediately following *Brown*. But in 1956, Harvard's basketball team, which did not have a single black player at the time, provided an indication of what was to come. Harvard canceled a four-game Southern trip to protest athletic segregation. That same year several large Midwestern schools announced they would not compete in the South if their black athletes could not play. The pool of racially pure opponents was shrinking.

By the early 1960s some Southern schools dared to play integrated opponents away from home—some, like Kentucky, even played those games in their own arenas. "Although Rupp was at best a paternalist in race relations, he and the university viewed the scheduling of an occasional interracial game as the price of success," wrote historian Charles Martin.

Rupp never publicly aligned himself with the Deep South schools' segregationist posture. He had little respect for Southern basketball, always looking North and East when he sought a challenge. When Kentucky began to play integrated opponents, it was one more thing he could lord over his SEC rivals. "We play teams from the Big Ten and the Missouri Valley Conference who have Negro boys who can jump a mile," Rupp said, "and we hold our own." It was the perfect situation for Rupp. He could use black athletes to build up his own program without having to recruit them.

The Deep South schools continued to resist any concession on race. One of the low points in the futile struggle came in December 1956 when Mississippi's two largest universities (Mississippi and Mississippi State), within twenty-four hours of each other, withdrew their basketball teams from the finals of Christmas tournaments after learning they were integrated.

The University of Mississippi forfeited the championship game in an Owensboro, Kentucky, tournament because a black played for its next opponent, Iona. The previous day, Mississippi State administrators had pulled their team from an Indiana tournament when newspapers revealed it had beaten an integrated squad, the University of Denver, in the opening round and would be playing another, Evansville, for the championship.

A year later, Mississippi's college board barred all-black Jackson State from the NCAA small-college tournament because it would have faced teams with white players. Just in case Jackson State didn't get the message, a legislator introduced a measure to suspend state funding for *any* institution that played in an integrated game.

■ ■ ■

The star of that 1956–57 Mississippi State team was sophomore Bailey Howell, a 6-7, crew-cut Tennessean and a future NBA All-Star. Two seasons later, in 1959, Howell, a bruising inside player with a sweet shot from the outside, averaged more than 27 points and 15 rebounds a game. That year he led the Bulldogs to their first SEC championship. They went 13-1 in the league, beat Kentucky, and were 24-1 overall. Ranked number three in the country when the NCAA tournament began, Howell and his teammates could only watch it on TV. State laws kept them from competing in the integrated event.

"Things were different in those days," said Howell, retired now in Starkville, "you didn't question authority. But what's disappointing is we didn't get to see how good we really were."

Kentucky's overwhelming success in SEC basketball—the Wildcats won either the conference's regular-season or tournament championship in fifteen of the NCAA tournament's first twenty years—had prevented race from becoming an issue in postseason basketball. The SEC's Deep South schools, who would have objected to integrated NCAA or NIT games, generally weren't good enough to confront that possibility. But when, as in 1959, one did, in-state politicians kept them at home. The Mississippi State Bulldogs were forced to reject another NCAA bid in 1961. And another in 1962. (In two of those years, Rupp's Kentucky took the spot for the SEC.)

Such rigid attitudes increasingly isolated Mississippi State, Mississippi, Alabama, and Louisiana State. Except for the SEC, the Atlantic Coast, and Southwest Conferences, all major-college leagues were integrated by the early 1960s. Even some Mississippians began to ponder the practicality of their traditions. How realistic was it, some in-state critics asked, to play big-time college sports if a team ultimately was prevented from competing for a championship?

So, in 1963, when the Bulldogs captured another SEC title, their fourth in five seasons, Mississippi State coach Babe McCarthy felt bold enough, or frustrated enough, to concoct a daring plan that would take his players out of state and into the NCAA tournament held in East Lansing, Michigan.

On March 2, Mississippi State president Dean Colvard, a North Carolinian, announced that this time the Bulldogs would play in the national tournament unless "vetoed by a competent authority." His peremptory statement precipitated a statewide debate and a flurry of legislative and judicial activity among concerned segregationists.

The reactionary *Jackson Daily News* preached against Colvard in a typically obtuse editorial that illustrated the odds the administrator and McCarthy were bucking: "Harping over a crack at a mythical national championship isn't worth subjecting young Mississippians to the switch-blade society that integration spawns," it warned.

Mississippi State had been given a first-round NCAA bye and was scheduled to play the winner of the Loyola of Chicago–Tennessee Tech game. The fact that favored Loyola started four blacks only escalated the segregationists' efforts. (Loyola would demolish Tech by an NCAA tournament-record 69 points, 111–42.) On March 13, two Mississippi legislators were granted an injunction that in effect prevented school administrators from taking the Bulldogs out of state.

McCarthy, anticipating such last-minute maneuvering, outwitted them. The coach, Colvard, athletic director Wade Walker, and assistant AD Ralph Brown had flown to Nashville earlier in the day. Later, the team, accompanied by the school's sports information director and trainer, left the campus for the airport in Starkville, located in northeast Mississippi, two and a half hours from the nearest big city, Jackson.

The reserves boarded their flight without problems. Just before the plane's departure, their teammates emerged from hiding and took their seats. During a stopover in Nashville, McCarthy, Walker, and Brown joined them. All made it safely to Michigan.

Questions of the law and race aside, McCarthy believed his club's slow-down style could trouble third-ranked Loyola, which had averaged an amazing 91.8 points a game that season. Their style certainly always bothered Rupp, who hated Mississippi State's stalling tactics as much as he disliked its flamboyant coach.

But while McCarthy's gamble was successful, his Bulldogs were not. In a matchup of the nation's best defensive and offensive teams, one that began with an explosion of flashbulbs as the black and white players shook hands at midcourt, Mississippi State's deliberate play only briefly frustrated Loyola. Eventually, Loyola's superior talent prevailed, 61–51.

Mississippi State would not return to the NCAA tournament for another twenty-eight years. When it did, in 1991, there were no injunctions. And ten of its thirteen players were black.

Loyola went on to win that national championship and with its four black starters—Jerry Harkness, Les Hunter, Vic Rouse, and Ronnie Miller—became the immediate historical antecedent to Texas Western. Yet in 1963 the Ramblers' success, in the minds of many, only confirmed racist stereotypes. They played the up-tempo, up-and-down pace whites expected from blacks. And, critics never failed to note, their point guard, John Egan, was white.

"A lot of people felt that way," said Harkness, who operates an athletic footwear store in Indianapolis. "They'd say, 'Well, they can play well at center but nowhere else.' Then there would be a great black forward and they'd say, 'Well, they can play well at forward and center but nowhere else.' Then they'd say the same thing about other positions when blacks proved they could play them too. The last one was point guard. A lot of whites had to have something to hold on to.

"But I think Egan knew better," said Harkness. "He was concerned about his job. I didn't realize it until later but he was really nervous about [being perceived as a token white]. Pablo Robinson, who was black, could have played there. Egan did bring a certain type of leadership that was necessary, but there could have been black guys that could have played that same role."

Now a Chicago attorney, Egan admitted his situation led to some uneasiness. "I always felt I deserved to start," he said. "But even then things could become so polarized. I had this feeling the others might think I was starting because I was white, because of tokenism. The thought bothered me."

Loyola played several games in the South in those years and its experiences were typically sobering. "We went to Marshall in West Virginia and there was a lot of profanity directed at us," said Harkness. "Then we went to Houston and it was awful, really awful. They threw things at us and just called us all kinds of names. When we had to go through the tunnels, they just spit down on us."

Coach George Ireland spoke out for his players when they were denied access to hotels in Houston and New Orleans, and suffered because of it. "I used to get phone calls in the middle of the night from bigots all across the country telling me we'd better not show up at this place or that," he said. "It was terrible."

It was the price schools paid for breaking ground.

"There was an unwritten rule that you didn't take more than one or two blacks on your team," said Harkness. "George Ireland broke that rule. And it wasn't easy for him because that's the way things had been since black guys started playing basketball."

■ ■ ■

Few blacks played the game in the years immediately after James Naismith—like some latter-day Luther—nailed his thirteen rules of basketball to the Springfield, Massachusetts, YMCA's wall in the winter of 1891. Black coaches familiar with the new sport were scarce and few institutions with courts were open to them. In Pittsburgh, for example, blacks were permitted to use the Washington Fieldhouse, one of the city's few public basketball facilities, only twice a week, and then for only two hours at a time.

"The newly minted sport of basketball would have little impact on them for most of the decade after its invention," wrote Nelson George in *Elevating the Game: Black Men and Basketball.* "Basketball was the by-product of a very rational, very rigid, very white world of values and institutions far removed [from black culture]."

That world grew more rigid in 1896, its lines of separation given official sanction when in *Plessy v. Ferguson* the Supreme Court confirmed the logic and legality of segregation. The South responded by ridding itself of the last shackles of Reconstruction, while the North was mostly silent. At the turn of the century, the troublesome problem of race was sublimated to the progressive optimism then sweeping America.

In Northern cities, where their customs and culture often mirrored those of white society, middle-class blacks staged debutante balls, stratified along class lines, and dedicated themselves to principles of Christian progress as fiercely as Fifth Avenue Episcopalians. They too saw basketball, athletics in general, as a morally uplifting activity.

At the social clubs they were busy establishing (like genteel white Americans) in New York, Philadelphia, Chicago, Pittsburgh, and elsewhere, the game eventually took hold. Soon such black teams as Brooklyn's Smart Set Athletic Club and Pittsburgh's Loendi Club were taking on all comers and beating most.

Edward Henderson, a black Washingtonian who was a student at Harvard when the twentieth century began, had watched the Crimson basketball team while studying there. He wasn't impressed. The indoor game, Henderson said, reminded him of tennis. "A sissy sport," he termed it. But after graduation, when he returned to his hometown as a public school teacher, he needed activities to occupy his students. He taught them basketball. Within two decades, throughout the segregated nation's capital, the sport was being played in black elementary and secondary schools as well as in its social clubs.

It was an easy progression from there to the black colleges, which then catered to what author Wells Twombly termed, "a rare and privileged class." By 1910, Washington's Howard University had the first varsity team at an all-black college. The Colored Intercollegiate Athletic Association—including Howard, Shaw, Lincoln, Virginia Union, and Hampton Institute (which had the conference's only indoor court) was formed in 1912.

Gradually a few black players began appearing at predominantly white colleges in the East and Midwest, though only a few dozen are known to have performed in the first two decades of the 1900s. Most were not only the team's lone black but also its best player, beginning a pattern of tokenism that was to continue for more than a half-century. (Even as late as the period between 1958 and 1970, nearly three of every four blacks on integrated college basketball teams were starters.)

"Why . . . should a college that was overwhelmingly white display a mediocre or ordinary black athlete?" wrote Ocania Chalk in *Black College Sport*. "If the play was to be less than outstanding, it was just as well that it should be wrapped in white skin."

The gifted Paul Robeson, whose muscular, 6-4 physique made him one of the first great black big men, played at Rutgers in 1918–19. Among the other pioneers in the early decades of the twentieth century were Wilbur Wood at Nebraska, Cumberland Posey at Penn State (who later went on to play Negro League baseball), William Kindle at Springfield College, Charles Drew (the inventor of plasma) at Amherst, and John H. Johnson and George Gregory at Columbia. (When Gregory became the first black All-America basketball player in 1930–31, he was joined on Walter Camp's team by a guard from Purdue, John Wooden.)

Socially stranded on white campuses, these men often found college life difficult. On the court, they were frequently abused physically and verbally by fans and opponents. Off it, they were prevented from joining fraternities and clubs, and were excluded from much of normal college life. It was a pattern that persisted for many years.

"Black athletes at predominantly white universities had been both segregated and despised, yet cheered at games," wrote sociologist Donald Spivey. "This dual existence for black athletes in collegiate sports—simultaneously scorned and loved—was a microcosm of the contradictions of a segregated society. Martin Luther King, Jr., would later speak of the dual nature of an American society 'that both loves the Negro but is repelled by him.'"

Beyond those few schools, segregation still held, even in the nation's best-known conference, the Big Ten. In 1934, Michigan coach F.C. Cappon violated an unwritten rule by permitting Franklin Lett on the freshman team. Pressure from other schools forced him to dismiss Lett, informing him in a letter that "there has never been a colored boy to play [varsity] basketball in the Big 10. It has been a mutual agreement between the coaches not to use a colored boy."

As a result, blacks' initial impact on the game at the major-college level was minimal. Between 1939 and 1949, the first eleven years of the NCAA tournament, not a single black appeared on the rosters of any of its champions.

■ ■ ■

Blacks had been migrating North for decades, but the pace quickened in the years during World War II. Since the armed forces needed bodies and the Northern defense plants workers, the war inadvertently acted as an impetus for desegregation. Afterward, with black veterans increasingly demanding full civil rights, the issue of collegiate integration was raised to a national level. A presidential commission, established by Harry Truman in 1946, called for an end to discrimination in higher education.

The postwar prosperity also increased America's appetite for sports. Baseball boomed as never before. Professional basketball teams popped up everywhere from New York to Sheboygan. And in big-city arenas that had been built for boxing, college basketball doubleheaders became exceedingly popular attractions.

Colleges that previously had not emphasized athletics recognized the potential benefits of relatively inexpensive basketball programs and quickly grew more ambitious. Several small, urban Catholic universities (DePaul, Manhattan, La Salle, Georgetown) dropped costly football teams and concentrated on the indoor sport. They expanded their recruiting, increased the number of scholarships, and, with a mixture of altruism and pragmatism, found spots for a black player or two.

"The galloping professionalization of collegiate sports after World War II, particularly football and basketball, made the recruitment of black athletes especially enticing," wrote historian Grundman. "Many athletic programs saw this untapped source of talent as a shortcut to national recognition. Consequently, universities outside the South were in the enviable position where they could build their athletic programs and claim that they were advancing the cause of race relations in America."

These city schools didn't have far to look. Urban blacks found basketball well suited to their environment. "Equipment requirements were minimal," noted tennis legend and civil rights advocate Arthur Ashe in *A Hard Road to Glory*, "and public courts were usually within walking distance."

The cities traditionally had been home to basketball's best players, and after the war a tremendous urban fan base also had developed. College doubleheaders routinely outdrew games of the various professional leagues in the large cities of the East and Midwest.

The big-city basketball craze had been born in the early 1930s when New York sportswriters organized a tremendously successful tripleheader for charity at Madison Square Garden. By 1934, one of those sportswriters, Ned Irish, was promoting basketball on his own at the Garden and elsewhere.

Rupp's Kentucky teams were invited to New York regularly, and the Wildcats' 1934 Garden game with NYU is credited with pushing college basketball into the national consciousness. Rupp's first-class program was unique in the South, where basketball traditionally existed deep in the enormous shadows of football. Few schools there, black or white, played it seriously in the game's early years. It wasn't until the national Amateur Athletic Union championships were held in Atlanta in 1920 that the sport began to take root there. A year later, the first Southern Intercollegiate Championships took place in the Georgia capital. Rupp's Kentucky team finished second in that event his first two seasons before the formation of the SEC in 1932 took most of the big schools and effectively killed the tournament.

Inspired by New York's success—Garden doubleheaders attracted more than a half-million spectators in 1950—the Boston Garden, Chicago Stadium, and Philadelphia's Convention Hall soon were booking their own college games. The urban Catholic universities were geographically positioned to take advantage of the trend.

Though college basketball integrated more rapidly than most public institutions (10 percent of major college teams included a black in 1948, 28 percent six years later, 42 percent in 1962), it generally took place without great fanfare—except when these schools faced Southern opponents.

On December 23, 1946, Tennessee traveled to Pittsburgh to play Duquesne, whose star was black center Chuck Cooper. Tennessee coach John Mauer, the man Rupp had replaced at Kentucky, was stunned to see a black opponent, having assumed Cooper was white. He pulled his team off the floor and threatened to leave unless Duquesne agreed not to play Cooper.

Duquesne wouldn't relent, though coach Chick Davies did offer to withhold Cooper unless the game was close in the final minutes. Despite a crowd of 2,600, the game was forfeited and Duquesne awarded a 2–0 victory. Ironically the previous week, in Duquesne's game with Morehead State at Louisville, Kentucky, Cooper had played in the Southern arena without incident. Four years later, he would become the first black drafted into the NBA.

"[But] once Southern schools adjusted to the fact that Northern teams might include African-Americans, they sought to dodge such encounters through careful scheduling," wrote historian Martin. "This technique usually proved successful but at the cost of avoiding intersectional play."

The issue of blacks in college basketball finally surfaced among a wider public in 1950. City College of New York, coached by Nat Holman, an ex–Original Celtic, started three blacks—Floyd Layne, Joe Galiber, and Ed Warner. They helped CCNY win not only the NCAA title that year but the NIT as well. (CCNY also demolished Kentucky, 89–50, in New York that season. It was Rupp's worst loss ever and prompted the Kentucky legislature to fly its flag at half-mast.)

Those colleges that might have been motivated by CCNY's success to recruit blacks were moved to reconsider by events the following year. Several CCNY regulars, including some of the blacks, were accused of shaving points in the same far-reaching scandal that eventually would tarnish Rupp and Kentucky.

A subsequent investigation into Holman's program revealed that academic records had been falsified to admit some of the players. Within three years CCNY had virtually abandoned basketball. To many, CCNY's story was a parable: go out of your way to recruit blacks, it seemed to say, and you reap trouble. Point-shaving scandals, then and again in 1961, appeared to confirm that.

Nineteen of the twenty-nine teams implicated in the major college sports scandals during the '50s and '60s included blacks. On those teams, 74 percent of the blacks were involved as opposed to only 11 percent of the whites. Sociologist Spivey, in a 1983 study, cited reasons for those lopsided statistics: "The vast majority of blacks in big-time intercollegiate sports are from lower-class backgrounds and, hence, most desperately in need of financial assistance. . . . Second [they] are blue-chip players."

Whatever their origins, the incidents raised doubts about the viability of recruiting blacks, doubts that would surface in subsequent years when issues of academic qualifications and eligibility dogged them. But given the growing pool of black talent and the burgeoning power—financially and culturally—of sports, most major colleges outside the South continued to recruit blacks, though still a carefully restricted number, throughout the 1950s.

■ ■ ■

Eastern Jews had dominated the collegiate game for decades because, explained the *New York Daily News* with the kind of racial stereotyping that then passed for fact, "the Jew is a natural gambler and will take chances." Similarly harebrained reasons eventually would be used to justify black prowess in the game, but such racist rationales were first used to explain their success in other sports. "The Negro excels in the [track and field] events he does because he is closer to the primitive than the white man," said Dean Cromwell, Jesse Owen's coach at the 1936 Olympics. "It was not that long ago that his ability to spring and jump was a life and death matter to him." (That reasoning, ironically, was echoed three decades later by Rupp when in a radio interview he explained the quickness of blacks this way: "[In Africa] the lions and tigers caught all the slow ones.")

At first, these black players' approach to the game was indistinguishable from that of their white counterparts. Basketball was a mostly slow, patterned, and physical game as yet devoid of any great flair. It wasn't that black players weren't capable of a more athletic and improvised style, it was just that most were reluctant to call attention to themselves in what was still an alien world.

"In the 1950s, [blacks had] one game for the white coaches and another for the playgrounds," said Chet Walker, a star at Bradley and later in the NBA. "No black high school player . . . wanted to be labeled a [Harlem Globe] Trotter. [But in the playgrounds] we were . . . free to strut."

By the 1950s some black basketball teams had been playing

white teams for decades, but generally only in barnstorming professional games that carried no official sanction. That way, when the white teams lost—and they lost at least as often as they won—fans and the mainstream press could shrug it off as an insignificant exhibition. In those interracial contests that were advertised as championships and were won by blacks, the white press usually referred to the victors as "colored world champions." "To the white man," Eldridge Cleaver would later write in *Soul on Ice*, "prefixing anything with 'Negro' automatically consigned it to an inferior category."

Throughout the 1920s and 1930s, the all-black Harlem Renaissance was one of the nation's finest professional teams. Founded in 1923, and assuming the name of the Harlem ballroom where they played, the Rens' first game came on November 3, 1923. They played the white Collegiate All-Stars that night and won, 28–22. In their twenty-six-year existence, against competition black and white, professional and amateur, the Rens compiled a 2,318-381 record and became a great attraction for fans of all races.

"As blacks they were not welcomed into the organized white leagues but league teams were glad to play host to the Rens because their appearance assured a good gate and there were no organized black leagues for basketball as there were for baseball," wrote Robert W. Peterson in *Cages to Jump Shots: Pro Basketball's Early Years*.

These professional pioneers developed a rivalry with the era's other great basketball barnstormers, the white Original Celtics, the teams trading victories in small towns and cities everywhere but the Deep South. The Rens' success did little to erase stereotypes about black teams—stereotypes that would persist until Texas Western's title. "They have a great bunch of players," the Celtics' Dutch Renhert told reporters before one game with the Rens, "but we generally succeed in outsmarting them one way or another and they are inclined to let down when you get ahead of them."

Both teams participated in an unofficial world championship

tournament begun in 1939 by a Chicago newspaper. The Rens won the first event, defeating the Oshkosh All-Stars—the National Basketball League champions who were led by ex-Kentucky star LeRoy Edwards—in the finals.

In the late 1940s and early 1950s, the Harlem Globetrotters, whose barnstorming games were evolving into clownish spectacles, met the NBA-champion Minneapolis Lakers a number of times. The Globetrotters won the first few games and the Lakers, with George Mikan, triumphed in the final few. But despite the racially charged interest these matches generated, they were never anything more than glorified exhibitions, usually officiated by referees hired and influenced by the home team.

The NBA's decision to integrate in 1950, three years after Jackie Robinson's entrance into baseball doomed the Globetrotters-Lakers rivalry. Three blacks joined the struggling pro league that year. Two, Chuck Cooper and West Virginia State's Earl Lloyd, were drafted. The other, Nat "Sweetwater" Clifton, was signed off the Globetrotters' roster.

The NBA's predecessor, the Basketball Association of America, had pondered some official racial barrier when it was formed in 1946. "An inquiry was made as to whether or not there was any rule which might be regarded as discriminatory with reference to the engagement of players," read the carefully worded minutes from the BAA's first meeting, "and the ruling from the chair was there was no such rule."

Privately, however, owners in the new league were reluctant to burden themselves with another potential problem, particularly one that might affect attendance. Because crowds already were small, owners had come to rely on those one or two nights a season when they could book the popular Globetrotters into their arenas. And many feared that by signing blacks, they might jeopardize their relationship with powerful Globetrotters owner Abe Saperstein.

When on April 25, 1950, Celtics owner Walter Brown picked

Cooper in the second round, other owners questioned Brown's sanity. According to a *New York Times* account, the room fell silent. Finally another owner asked Brown: "Walter, don't you know he's a colored boy?" "I don't give a damn if he's striped, plaid, or polka-dot," said Brown. "Boston takes Chuck Cooper of Duquesne."

Afterward, Saperstein, who believed black basketball players were his exclusive domain, boycotted Brown's Boston Garden for many years. "Saperstein . . . liked to portray himself as the benefactor of all Negroes in sport," said the Celtics' Bill Russell, who was no fan of the man and had turned down a lucrative offer to play with the Globetrotters. "He also believed he had earned a monopoly on the services of every black athlete in the country. . . . [He] worked against the aspirations of an entire race just to keep his little franchise."

By 1955, Russell, the first of the mobile, shot-blocking big men who, literally and figuratively, would raise the level of basketball, previewed the game's future.

La Salle, the defending national champion led by three-time All-America Tom Gola, advanced to the NCAA championship game that year against the undefeated University of San Francisco. In the midst of its then-record sixty-game unbeaten streak, San Francisco started three blacks, Russell, K.C. Jones, and Hal Perry. Remarkably for that era, the San Francisco Dons had six blacks on their team. Just four years earlier, when K.C. Jones arrived, the team had only one in its history, Carl Lawson. The Dons' unusual racial makeup, rarely mentioned in the press, did not go unnoticed by opposing fans. During practice in Oklahoma City for their 1955 NCAA game with Wichita State, fans yelled "Globetrotters" at them and threw pennies on the floor.

Against La Salle, Russell collected 23 points and 25 rebounds. Jones outscored Gola, 24–16, holding the La Salle star without a basket for a twenty-one-minute stretch, and San Francisco won the first of two straight national titles, 77–63.

Russell not only dominated college basketball but later transformed the Boston Celtics into the NBA's greatest dynasty. A month after Texas Western's championship, Russell became the first black head coach in professional sports with the Celtics. Just as significantly, his independence and intelligence helped to alter the way black athletes were treated and perceived. A native of Louisiana who moved to Oakland when he was nine, Russell chafed at any hint of discrimination or prejudice. He rejected a lucrative offer from the Globetrotters after college and, as a member of the 1956 U.S. Olympic team, made an issue of its segregated training facilities.

In addition to Russell, the 1950s saw the arrival of blacks who still rank among the greatest collegiate, and later professional, players ever—Elgin Baylor at Seattle, Oscar Robertson at Cincinnati, and Wilt Chamberlain at Kansas. The 1958 All-America teams of both the Associated Press and United Press contained four blacks—Chamberlain, Baylor, Robertson, and Temple's Guy Rodgers. Those same four, plus Kansas State's Bob Boozer, were named to the National Basketball Coaches Association team. That first all-black All-America team proved, if nothing else, that many coaches who would not yet recruit black players were color-blind when it came to recognizing superior talent.

But all of these players were at schools in the East, Midwest, and West. The first breach in the South's Cotton Curtain did not come until 1956. That year, Charlie Brown, an Air Force veteran, and his nephew, Cecil Brown, played for a college in the remotest corner of the old confederacy, in El Paso, at some place called Texas Western College.

■ ■ ■

The Browns' El Paso experience was relatively painless and, having noticed that, several black athletes followed them there. For the rest of that decade and much of the next, Texas Western would remain the only integrated team in the region.

It wasn't until North Texas State in 1961 that another Southern school suited up a black basketball player. Three years later, emboldened by Loyola of Chicago's success and the gradual weakening of Jim Crow's grip, and aware that Rupp was ignoring a vast talent pool, two Kentucky teams, Louisville and Western Kentucky, recruited blacks for their teams.

"When I was being recruited, I visited [black stars] Wes Unseld and Butch Beard at Louisville," recalled Vanderbilt's Perry Wallace. "Whatever Louisville had been about in the past, it enthusiastically recruited those guys. All of a sudden they went from saying, 'We don't want you here' to 'We want to recruit you and we want to show you an enthusiastic face.' From a threshold matter, they were saying, 'We want you to come here and we want you to do well.'"

As much as anything or anyone, Rupp was the impetus for the change of heart at Louisville and Western Kentucky. He had always looked down his nose at those schools, refusing to play or even acknowledge the potential in-state rivals. Once they opened their doors to blacks and the contrast with Rupp's white teams grew more stark, Kentucky's chances of landing minority players diminished enormously.

Blacks in the commonwealth later would watch with glee when Western Kentucky (in the first meeting between the schools, in the 1971 Mideast Regional), with a Kentucky-born, all-black starting five, scored a 107–83 win over a Kentucky team that had a lone black player.

Rupp was upset before that game in Athens, Georgia, when Western Kentucky star Jim McDaniels suggested the NCAA pairings favored Kentucky. "I doubt that he has the intelligence to comprehend how the NCAA brackets are made," Rupp said of McDaniels. "You can quote me on that."

When McDaniels, who had 35 points against Kentucky, fouled

out, he looked over at the Kentucky coach and raised his hands high over his head in a sign of triumph.

The dominoes were starting to tumble. In 1965, Maryland's Billy Jones became the first black to play varsity basketball in any of the three major Southern conferences (SEC, ACC, and SWC). Elvin Hayes and Don Chaney debuted at Houston that same year. Before Kentucky and Texas Western met in 1966, TCU, Florida State, Memphis State, Loyola of New Orleans, and Duke had received commitments from black high-schoolers. The five NCAA champions from 1961 to 1965–Cincinnati twice, Loyola of Chicago, UCLA twice—each had anywhere from two to four black starters.

Still, by the time of Texas Western's championship, only 58 percent of the 235 major-college teams pictured in the Converse Yearbook included a black player. The Miners, with seven, were an aberration. The average number of blacks on those integrated teams was only 2.8. There was still not a single black player in the SEC in 1966.

Later, as their numbers grew at formerly segregated colleges, some more conservative white fans and alumni displayed an uneasiness toward the trend. At Alabama, no one questioned Bear Bryant when the racial makeup of his football team began to turn. But basketball was a different story.

"As Coach Bryant would say to me, his players are all covered up with helmets and shoulder pads. It's hard to tell who's what," said C.M. Newton, the Kentucky athletic director who was Alabama's basketball coach in the school's early years of integration. "[In basketball] everybody in the stands was counting, '1 . . . 2 . . . 3 . . . 4.'"

When one of Newton's heavily integrated Alabama teams beat Kentucky at Lexington, he received a letter accusing him of "polluting the South." The writer said he hoped the coach's daughter married a black and produced Mongoloid grandchildren. He signed it "A Southern Gentleman."

It was a difficult transition toward integration because it was being led by men like Bryant, men raised in the comfortable traditions of segregation. But in a way, just as it diminished Rupp's reputation, the challenge to adapt would enhance the Alabama coach's.

"Coach Bryant was a product of his time," said Newton. "He heard the stereotypes. He believed them. He asked me one day, 'How do you coach them? How do you treat them?' I said . . . 'Like anyone else.'"

Soon blacks were a familiar presence on Bryant's teams.

■ ■ ■

By the mid-1960s, blacks were an increasingly familiar presence in college basketball. Yet even then, few in the sport could have imagined that the day was coming when five of them would start at a predominantly white college, especially one in Texas. Someone—the alumni, the administration, perhaps the coach himself—would surely object to that.

What no one knew back in 1966 was that Don Haskins was about to unleash a revolution. Haskins wouldn't open the door to black success in basketball. What he would do in the 1965–66 season was prove that blacks all around the country were capable of opening it all by themselves.

3.

Enid to El Paso on the Lone Wolf Express

"All of us who were young saw that '66 game and felt like there was hope for us. . . . The man gave black people a chance."
—Chuck Foreman, former Minnesota Viking

Enid High School's junior-senior prom for 1947 was as unpretentious as the residents of that northern Oklahoma town. Students hung a curtain from the center of the convention hall. On one side, chairs, tables, and flowers were arranged neatly but unimaginatively. The girls wore dresses, frilly but plain, and the boys baggy suits, some of them over cowboy boots.

On the night of the event, big-band recordings droned over the giggles and conversations of the teenagers. Had these prom-goers listened carefully, however, they would have heard a rhythm of a different sort—the hollow tap, tap, tap of a basketball on a hardwood floor.

On the other side of that curtain, alone, Don Haskins was practicing. He didn't care that his classmates were dancing, laughing, and kissing just a few feet away. The seventeen-year-old was shooting baskets.

"I thought everybody on the other side of the curtain was nuts," Haskins recalled. "I was perfectly content. I had no desire whatsoever to be on the other side."

Through more than thirty-five years of coaching college basketball, Haskins has been happy to stay on his side of the curtain. As the sport grew and prospered in bigger cities and at better-known institutions, he remained at a mountainside school a long way from anywhere. "There's not anybody ever that could have done the job he's done there," said Moe Iba. "I mean El Paso is out there in a world all its own. And year after year after year he comes up with teams."

His coaching contemporaries switched jobs frequently—some moving to the pros, some to higher-profile colleges, still others into different occupations. He had his chances to leave, especially after Texas Western won that title in 1966, but Haskins stayed behind. There were wide-open spaces in El Paso. He could hunt there, hide there, coach there, and no one would ever really care if he dripped hot sauce on his shirt.

"He comes and goes as he pleases," said Eddie Mullens, a longtime friend. "He doesn't have to punch a clock."

He has stayed long enough to see his name on both the school's basketball arena and an entrée at his favorite restaurant, Rubio's. (The "Don Haskins Extra-Large Enchilada" comes with a fried egg on top.) "You couldn't blow him out of El Paso," said Iba. "The people in El Paso accept him the way he is."

As Italian suits, BMWs, and nouvelle cuisine became the accoutrements of successful coaches, Haskins stuck with his clip-on ties, pickup trucks, and extra-large enchiladas. Though he became the border city's best-known citizen, he has only a small group of close friends. They play golf and poker with him, drink beer with him, eat Mexican food with him. And even in El Paso, it's difficult to keep up with him.

"Until he had his heart attack [in 1996], Don lived a pretty fast life," said Earl Estep, a friend since Haskins' days at Oklahoma A&M. "When he and I talk, we always talk about 6:15 in the morning. Then he'll go to the office, and if it's not basketball season he'll be out of there by 11:00. He's gone. He'll get himself a case of beer and a fifth of whiskey. . . . He goes all day long. He's a goer. Then about midnight or one or two o'clock, he'll go home. He'll just crash. Then at 5:30 or six o'clock he's up again. 'Course that lifestyle is why he had the heart attack, I guess."

Once, briefly, he peeked at the other side of the curtain. In April of 1969, Haskins decided to leave Texas Western and replace Bob Calihan at the University of Detroit. He accepted the job, went North, visited with school officials, and was introduced to the Detroit media. The next morning he was on a plane heading back to Texas. On a layover at Dallas's Love Field, he called George McCarty, Texas Western's athletic director, and pleaded for his old job.

"I got up there and they showed me around this huge office," Haskins said, sounding like a twentieth-century Huck Finn. "[It] even had a wet bar. It was going to be mine. They took me down and introduced me to the former coach, the guy they got rid of. His office was about the size of a closet. I got to thinking that if I didn't win, I would be the guy in that closet next time. The next morning I hopped on a plane back to El Paso."

They weren't going to "sivilize" Don Haskins.

■ ■ ■

Enid, Oklahoma, is a nondescript plains town about 100 miles northwest of Oklahoma City. Its only notable physical characteristic is the vast sky that encloses the city like an arched-glass lid.

"It's an endless sky," said Bill Humphrey, a classmate of Haskins' at both Enid High and Oklahoma A&M, "the kind of sky you miss in a big city. I have a friend, an attorney in Washington, D.C., who comes out here twice a year just to see the sunsets."

Compared to the great empty spaces that surround it, Enid is a remarkably small town. Pickup trucks still park perpendicular to the stores on Grand Street, and the post office, library, and Garfield County Courthouse are clustered around a grassy square near Grand and Independence Streets. Oil derricks, wheat silos, and grain elevators reveal its business base even before you arrive. And like most flatland towns, tornadoes and booming electrical storms are as common as a rain shower in April.

Located in Cherokee country, Enid had been the site of a trading post and water stop along the Chisholm Trail between Texas and Abilene, Kansas. "There were springs here that the Indians found and [cowboys] would rest their cattle here overnight, water them up, and then get on the next day," said Humphrey. Later the town became one of the nation's leading wheat-storage centers, and in 1893, Enid incorporated.

When Don Haskins was born on March 14, 1930, 35,000 people lived in the town (98 percent of whom, bragged the city directory, were native-born). There were a few black families, but they attended their own segregated schools and had little interaction with whites. In fact, the blacks were largely invisible to the larger white population. If there were any racial problems in the 1930s and 1940s, Enid's white residents can't recall them now.

"There were a lot of black people here but we were segregated and didn't see them," said Shirley Haskins, the future coach's cousin. "I remember in '55 I was working at Sanford's Drug Store. It was kind of a hangout for Cokes and stuff. The Harlem Globetrotters came in one day and it was shocking for me to see them come in because none of them ever did it. None of the blacks ever came to Sanford's. They had their own place, I guess. I remember being surprised by it. Not offended but surprised."

The town's blacks tell a slightly different story. "There were problems here like there were anywhere else," said one black clergyman, who did not want to be identified. "I don't mean to say Enid blacks were being lynched, but there were places back then where we were not welcome, people who were hostile to us. It was like two different worlds back then, and in many ways, I'm sorry to say, it still is. Just last year, one of our churches was burned down."

Haskins never even faced a black basketball player until he was a junior at Oklahoma A&M. And it was there in Stillwater, just sixty miles away, that he witnessed two events that shaped his attitude on race.

A&M was a member of the Missouri Valley Conference. The Big Six (later the Big Eight) and the MVC were then the last segregated conferences with members outside the South, largely because of the passionate insistence of its southernmost member, Oklahoma A&M. The schools had secretly agreed to keep the MVC all-white, but two years after the end of World War II, the conference voted to end racial discrimination by the start of the 1950 football season.

One of the conference's first black stars was Drake tailback Johnny Bright. Bright—the conference's best player—was the nation's leading ground-gainer when his team traveled to Stillwater for a game with Oklahoma A&M on October 20, 1951. That day, he became the first black to perform at A&M's Lewis Field.

Most of A&M's players were, like Haskins, from small homogeneous Oklahoma towns. Most of what they knew about blacks they had learned from jokes. Whether it was at the urging of their coach, J.B. Whitworth, or not, they made up their minds to go after Bright that day.

On Drake's first play from scrimmage, Bright took the snap, handed off, and then rolled away from the flow of play. A&M defensive end Wilburton Smith, without ever looking toward the ballcarrier, ran at Bright and hit him with a forearm to the face. There were no face masks on helmets yet and the blow broke Bright's jaw. In great pain, he returned to the game and on the next play, Bright, without the ball but still being shadowed by Smith, was hit in the face again. "No matter what I did, somebody hit me," said Bright. He left the game a short while later and his jaw was wired shut before the team returned to Des Moines.

After A&M's 27–14 victory, Smith and Whitworth denied targeting the black opponent. Drake coach Warren Gaer predicted Whitworth would no longer defend his players once he saw photos of the incidents. "I just can't believe a coach would tell a boy to play that way," said Gaer. "He [Smith] must have done it on his own." Photographers caught the plays in detail and when newspapers and *Life* magazine ran the pictures, Whitworth apologized, though continuing to call Smith a "good kid."

"He hit Johnny with his forearm two times," said Whitworth. "Smith is not the dirty type of player. He just lost his head for a few minutes." The incident created such bitter feelings that not long afterward Drake withdrew from the conference. The incident also soured Bright for life. When it came time for him to turn professional, he spurned offers from the National Football League and chose to play in Canada.

Haskins was sitting in the Lewis Field bleachers that day. He knew Smith well. But he also knew what he had seen. "Wilburton Smith was a nice, quiet kid. He played the piano and all that stuff," said Haskins. "I don't know what happened but there's no question they were out to get Bright. It was really bad. A thing like that, it made you think about the way things were in the world."

In view of what was to occur fifteen years in the future, Haskins might have had an even greater epiphany during a basketball game that same year. When A&M met conference opponent Wichita, he found himself playing against a black opponent for the first time.

Wichita had been expected to finish near the bottom of the

MVC that season. But because this was during the Korean War, the NCAA permitted freshmen to play and one of Wichita's stars that night was a black freshman named Cleo Littleton.

"Littleton was one of the first black players in the Missouri Valley Conference and he was good right off the bat," said Bill Connors, an A&M classmate of Haskins' and later a sportswriter in Tulsa. "He immediately went into the Wichita lineup and began making waves. And instead of being a second-division team, Wichita was a first-division team. It wasn't long before some of the other schools in the conference began recruiting black basketball players."

Haskins, always seeking an edge, noticed the trend. As a coach, he has had few problems dealing with black kids. They were considered outsiders and that's how Haskins always saw himself.

"He's like John Wayne in that way," said Estep. "The outsider riding into town alone, leaving alone. Don can communicate with anybody, especially with blacks that had a hard time growing up and are street-wise. You know, Don might have grown up in a small town but he's street-wise. And he doesn't feel like he belongs in high society either.

"These kids he gets, he knows they're black but he also knows they can play and he can get it out of them," said Estep. "He was kind of a poor boy growing up and he can talk to kids that are underprivileged. Don doesn't know anything about racism."

■ ■ ■

Paul and Opal, Haskins' parents, would move from one modest home in Enid to another in the years to come, but when their first child was born they lived in a little bungalow on Ash Street.

The Rock Island and St. Louis & San Francisco Railroads both passed through Enid and their tracks crisscrossed the town at several junctures. The Haskinses' home was, as residents liked to say, "east of the tracks," on the poorer side of town. "There was definitely a social difference," said John Hronopulos, a boyhood friend of Haskins' and his teammate on Enid High's basketball teams. "West of the tracks was the snobbier side of town. Don and I were East Siders but we always thought we were better than the West Siders in things like sports."

Paul Haskins drove a truck for several local firms and his family—a wife and two sons—always had their most basic needs met. He was a quiet man and a fine athlete (having played semipro baseball in his native Arkansas). Opal Haskins, who lived on the East Side until her death in 1996, was a strong and opinionated woman. "Uncle Paul was more lenient than Aunt Opal," said Shirley Haskins. "We all had kind of a strict upbringing. Not an unloving one, but strict."

From his mother, Haskins inherited his rugged independence. "She was a character," said Eddie Mullens. "She told you how to count the cabbage in a hurry. That's where he gets it. There's no pussyfooting around with Don. He'll tell you. You might not want to hear what he'll tell you, but he's damn well going to tell you."

As a toddler, Haskins' left leg was seriously burned when a hot iron fell on him, leaving him with a long scar and a limp that lingered until he was a teenager. He credited bike rides and long walks with his dad, while the two were hunting in the surrounding woods, for strengthening the leg to the point where he could play basketball. Every Enid boy had a bike then and Haskins often took long rides alone. He also loved horses and sometimes he and his younger brother, Jerry, rode them at the ranches and farms just outside of town.

There were few public basketball courts in Enid, but Haskins and his pals found private ones they could use. Phillips University, on the East Side, often left its gym unlocked and, on summer mornings, so did Emerson and Longfellow Junior Highs. "And there was a family named Bolene that was pretty wealthy and they had a clay tennis court that was also a basketball court," said Hronopulos.

"They used to let us kids play on there all the time. Seemed like Don was a natural right from the beginning." Even so, he was cut from his junior high team in seventh and eighth grades. Finally, when he was a ninth-grader, Coach Herb Steen selected him.

Enid High School burned down in the early 1940s. By the time Haskins and Hronopulos entered tenth grade, their class of 272 had to use the Longfellow building while they waited for the new brick high school on Wabash Avenue to be completed. "It was during the war and they were unable to get materials to rebuild it," said Hronopulos. "I think finally, about the last month or two of our senior year, we went to the new school."

By the time he was a junior, the skinny 6-3 Haskins, who had unruly blond hair and a troublemaker's grin, was the star of the Plainsmen basketball team. An extremely accurate shooter, he was selected to the Mid-State and All-State teams as a senior. "Oh, I could shoot," he said. "I had this funny shot where I'd be flying all over the place on my follow-through, but I was very accurate. I believe I was one of the first players to try a jump shot and I was pretty good with it. It's funny but after I got to college and Mr. Iba showed me the right way to shoot, I was never quite as good."

Basketball was his first passion, and in his senior high school yearbook, it was the only activity listed next to his photo. "Don wasn't a straight A student but he was never in danger of flunking out or anything like that," said classmate Humphrey. "I don't know how he felt about classwork but he was a wonderful artist, really gifted. He could draw horses and dogs and they would be perfectly proportioned."

On the court, he was one of those players with terrific natural gifts but an inability to take anything too seriously. Enid coach Dale Holt taught him a lot of basketball, but could never quite harness his head. "I was a smart-aleck," Haskins said, "and I was until I got to Oklahoma A&M and Coach Iba got ahold of me." Not surprisingly for a man who would spend his adult life in El Paso, Haskins kept more and more to himself as he got older. "Don was a pleasant person," said Humphrey. "He knew everybody but he was sort of a lone wolf. He didn't run with any one group."

He worked and hung out at Harold's Snooker Parlor, played basketball and baseball, but was never a threat to be named either Most Popular or Most Likely to Succeed. "Don was his own man," said Hronopulos. "He definitely was not a socializer. He still has not been back to a single one of our high school reunions."

Despite his attitude and mediocre grades, Haskins attracted the attention of dozens of colleges. "Don was a terrific high school player," said A&M classmate Connors. "That was right at the time the first jump shooters were coming out and Don was one of the first outstanding ones in Oklahoma. He was considered an exceptional prospect and had a chance to go to a lot of places." But there really wasn't much of a decision to be made for a basketball fan from Enid, so he chose A&M.

Located in Stillwater, Oklahoma A&M was less than an hour away. Local youngsters grew up following Hank Iba's renowned basketball teams, which won back-to-back national championships while Haskins was in high school. They all listened to John Henry's radio broadcasts of A&M games on KVOO and occasionally, said Humphrey, several of them would drive to A&M's campus and watch Iba conduct practices.

For someone who would adopt Iba's system in detail and who later became one of the old coach's closest friends, Haskins quickly realized he was out of place at Oklahoma A&M. He was a substitute for most of his career and in 1950–51, the season A&M advanced to the Final Four before losing to Kansas State, Haskins was academically ineligible. "I loved to play," he said, "but I didn't like to go to school."

And he didn't care much for anything but shooting. "He was a poor defensive player," said Connors. "I don't think it was so much a lack of speed, I just think he didn't want to do it. He wasn't really sold on it. He thought he could start and play whether he played defense or not. But if you ever knew Mr. Iba, you knew he'd run you off if you didn't work on defense. I don't know if Don ever started a game there. But if they went against somebody that had a good zone defense and they were having trouble, he would play and play a lot. He had some good games.

"Don has told me many times that he left [A&M] very frustrated and unhappy. He didn't like that kind of basketball. And when he started playing AAU [Amateur Athletic Union] ball he thought, 'Boy this is great. I'm finally getting to do what I want to do. I can shoot all the time and I don't have to play defense a lick.' But they were going 5-15, 6-20 and getting beat all the time. And after a while, he said, 'You know, maybe Mr. Iba knew more than I thought he did.' So when he got ready to coach, he decided he'd go back and coach the Iba way. And later he became as close to Mr. Iba as any of his protégés."

With 7-footer Bob Kurland, the Aggies had been the NCAA champions in 1945 and 1946. Iba's teams were, even by the standards of that era, extremely patient on offense and aggressive on defense. (Haskins' UTEP teams still play the Iba defense and so do teams coached by former Haskins assistants like Iowa State's Tim Floyd. "I've been doing this a long time and I've never found a better way," said Haskins in 1997. "We played Iowa State and I watched Tim's practices and drills. On defense they were doing the same drills I learned in college.")

Like many coaches in that era, including Rupp and Kansas's Phog Allen, Iba demanded a rigid adherence. Inevitably, that created conflicts with the then-laid-back Haskins. "The whole time I played there I got chewed out by him," Haskins said. "I needed it because I was the kind of guy who bitched and bitched about every little thing. And he was a taskmaster. It was a damn nightmare playing for him. I consider Mr. Iba one of the greatest people in the world now. But I hated him then."

Once after a win, Iba was unhappy with the Aggies' defense. He took his team to the chalkboard for a late-night lecture. Haskins, a sophomore, fell asleep. "Next thing I knew, this big old eraser clipped me right between the eyes," he said. That same year, Haskins made the All-Tournament team at the All-College Tournament in Oklahoma City, one of the nation's premier Christmas events. Iba, knowing the award left his player feeling cocky, responded by benching him for the next three games.

The coach liked his teams to work the ball around the perimeter and get it inside to his bigger people. But Haskins couldn't resist the outside shot. "I remember watching Iba practices and he would yell at everybody," said Humphrey, "but he'd yell at Don like crazy. 'Cut that out!' Or 'You can't do that!'"

Iba refused to let his players sit or drink water during practices and insisted they eat cereal after games as well as two dips of ice cream. He believed that kind of nourishment replenished the body. "I didn't eat cereal for ten years after I got out," said Haskins.

■ ■ ■

Haskins' first job had been racking balls at Harold's basement pool hall. A natural athlete with a gunslinger's competitiveness, he took to pool and snooker right away and the skill earned him money during and after college. "Haskins was so talented at anything he did," recalled college friend Estep. "Everything was easy for him. He was on a basketball scholarship and he wasn't supposed to get any money but he'd go pitch [semipro] baseball and they'd pay him cash. He was one of the best baseball pitchers you ever saw. Don could do anything."

When he was in college, there was no money from home, so whenever Haskins needed it, he'd just find a pool hall and a sucker.

"When we used to hustle pool, he didn't go in and act like he couldn't shoot and let a guy win $1 or $2 and then take him for

$300," said Estep. "He'd walk in and say, 'I don't think anybody in town can beat me. Probably nobody living can. So go get your best guy and bet all your money on one game and we'll take his action.' And I never saw anybody come close to beating him. Willie Mosconi came to A&M one time representing Brunswick Billiard Co. and we had a big pool hall and snooker hall there. Everybody was trying to get Don to play Mosconi and they played straight pool and Mosconi beat him something like 125 to 50. These guys [pros like Mosconi] were always looking for local guys they could hustle, so the two of them played a little nine-ball. Well to make a long story short, they played seventeen games and Don Haskins ran the table seventeen times straight."

That competitiveness has been a constant throughout Haskins' life. He wants to win at everything: basketball, pool, golf, poker, elementary school football. "In grade school, at recess, Don and [childhood friend] Bob Barnes and myself would challenge the rest of the class to a football game," recalled Hronopulos. "And we would always beat their ass."

Friends point to Haskins' competitiveness as the reason he recruited so many black players when he got to Texas Western. If Martians had landed and displayed some basketball ability, Haskins would have been the first to recruit them—in large numbers, too.

"He is one of the most competitive humans you will ever meet," said Gene Iba, a nephew of Haskins' college coach and, like his cousin Moe, a onetime Texas Western assistant. "When you get across the table from him, you better work harder than you ever worked or you're going to lose."

Though Hank Iba rode Haskins hard throughout the player's college career, the pupil somehow absorbed the basketball lessons. For his first dozen years at Texas Western, Haskins ran Iba-like practices, rarely giving his players a water break, running them up and down arena stairs. Shouting. Berating.

"His workouts were the worst things you were ever going to experience while you were alive," said Nolan Richardson. Nevil Shed, a forward on the '66 team, remembered that Haskins met him at the airport when Shed arrived for school, joked with him, shot baskets with him. "I thought, 'Yeah, I'm going to like this guy.'" Then practices began. "I tell you I thought this is the worst man on two legs with a potbelly."

Like Iba, Haskins became one of those coaches who downplayed his team's chances, no matter how bad the opponent, and never took any credit for its successes. "Victories belong to the boys," Iba used to say. "The defeats are mine." The pupil followed the example. "To hear Don talk you wouldn't ever think he was going to win a game," said friend Jimmy Rogers.

Haskins met Mary Gorman of Bartlesville, Oklahoma, at A&M and the two were married in 1951. By the time he left in 1953 to play AAU basketball, their first of four sons, Mark, had been born. Haskins was still twelve credits shy of a degree but felt he couldn't afford to stay in school any longer. (He eventually finished his degree work at West Texas State.) Playing both baseball and basketball for the Artesia (New Mexico) Travelers—a semipro organization sponsored by the electric company that employed him—Haskins earned $350 a month. Soon, however, he hurt his elbow and abandoned pitching—but not before he had made the contact that would lead him to Texas Western.

After an Artesia game at the El Paso college, Haskins met the Miners' basketball coach, George McCarty, who had come to some of Iba's A&M clinics and recognized the former Aggie player. "After the game he took me over to a little room and talked to me," recalled Haskins. "He said, 'Why don't you get into coaching?'"

■ ■ ■

The tiny town of Benjamin, Texas, about 130 miles southeast of Lubbock, needed a coach for its high school's boys and girls basketball teams and its six-man football team. Haskins took the job in 1955 for $2,800 a year plus another $400 for driving the school bus. Employing many of Iba's techniques, he quickly won games and earned a reputation in the town of about 300 people. "You get some effort from the kids and it's fun," he said about his first taste of coaching. But in getting that effort, he resorted to some unusual tactics.

Once, after both the boys' and girls' teams lost by a point in games in some distant Texas town, Haskins pulled the bus up to Benjamin's gymnasium at about 11:30 P.M. He marched the players from both teams inside and conducted a practice that ran until 5:00 A.M. Parents were furious. "I was wrong," he said, "in a lot of those things I did early on."

"He sure did bring a sense of excitement to the town," said Benjamin resident Johnny Hudson. "If you were at the town square or over at Red Kilgore's—he had a hamburger stand on the main street—that's all people would talk about. Basketball. He could just flat-out coach. I think the football team went 7-3 that year, and that was the first winning season in about twenty or thirty years. He was a genuine human being and that came across from the start."

The same genuineness that later would make him an El Paso legend, the ability to convince anyone that he was no better than them, endeared Haskins to Benjamin.

"He would visit the players at their homes," said Jim Bateman, a former player there. "He'd go out dove and quail hunting with your parents. That was the kind of person he was. He was welcome everywhere he went. The whole attitude of the school changed. It had never been the kind of place where there was a whole lot of pride, especially in athletics, because we just weren't very good. But after Coach Haskins arrived, you could say, 'I'm from Benjamin High School' and be proud of it."

In 1956, larger Hedley [Texas] High School hired him away for a $500 increase in pay. And that was just for coaching; he didn't have to drive the school bus at Hedley. His boys basketball team went 114-24 in four years there and in 1960 he left for an even bigger Texas high school, Dumas. His first and only season there, Dumas won the regional championship and finished 25-7.

McCarty, by then the dean of men and football coach at Texas Western, telephoned Haskins in the summer of 1961 and told him the college's basketball coach, Harold Davis, had quit. Davis' last two teams had gone a combined 18-31. In twenty-six seasons, the Miners had never won more than fifteen games.

McCarty thought the school, despite its location, could do better. No other college east of there in the Southern half of the United States was recruiting blacks. Texas Western had been doing so since 1956 when Charlie and Cecil Brown arrived, and the Miners were able to look for the best of them all over the country. The black kids seemed to feel comfortable in El Paso. Soon, McCarty realized, the rest of the nation was going to catch on and Texas Western's edge would be gone.

Haskins drove to El Paso for an interview with athletic director Ben Collins and president Joseph Ray. Ray asked the coach if he could control a men's dormitory. Assuring him he could, Haskins was hired on the spot. Ray said he had been impressed with Haskins' quiet confidence. "[It said] I'm a ding-dong dandy from Dumas and you ought to see me do my [stuff]," Ray recalled of the interview.

Haskins' $6,500 salary was $2,500 less than what he had been earning at Dumas but Haskins and his family could live and eat their meals in the dormitory, Miners Hall. The coach hooked a U-Haul trailer to his Dodge station wagon and drove from Dumas to El Paso, collecting a $45 speeding ticket on the way. Arriving at the dormitory, then junior Nolan Richardson was waiting to help his new coach unload. An El Paso high school star, Richardson had averaged 21 points a game on Davis' last team. "I hear you think you're a scorer," Richardson said Haskins told him at that first encounter. "I also hear you can't guard a telephone pole."

In his first game as a college coach, December 2, 1961, Haskins' club defeated Iowa State at Ames, 66–59. Willie Brown, a black New Yorker who had been recruited by Davis, scored 21 and Richardson 12. That 1961–62 team went 18-6. Richardson averaged 10 points a game.

The following season a phone call from an old friend of Haskins' began the process that would put Texas Western on the college basketball map. Gerald Stockton, who had played with Haskins at A&M, was coaching Cameron Junior College in Oklahoma and he had a 6-8 center, Jim "Bad News" Barnes, who was averaging nearly 30 points a game there.

Stockton insisted the Miner coach come up and take a look at his star center. Haskins and Moe Iba eventually made so many trips there that they exhausted most of Texas Western's $5,000 recruiting budget. What happened on their last visit is probably part apocryphal, but remains one of those stories Haskins and his friends love to tell and one that accurately illustrates Haskins' confidence and competitiveness.

Sensing that Barnes was close to making a decision but having exhausted all of the normal arguments, Haskins finally challenged him to a foul-shooting contest. He had sized Barnes up and knew he would respond. It was one more hustle.

"I told him we'd shoot 25 and if I made more than him, he'd sign with us," said Haskins. Haskins went first and made all 25. "I don't know how true that story is but I don't doubt for a minute that Don could have made 25 in a row. He could really shoot," said Hronopulos. When Barnes missed his second attempt, the papers were signed on Cameron's foul line.

Barnes, said Mullens, "was big and graceful like the athletes today," and in his two years at the school he led Texas Western to its first two NCAA tournament appearances. The Miners went 19-7 in 1962–63, as Barnes averaged 19 points and 16 rebounds in his first season. In the first round of the NCAA tournament, Texas Western was beaten by Texas, 65–47.

The following season, Haskins began to believe that maybe his team could win a national championship. "That was a good team," he said, "a very good team." Barnes' numbers jumped to 29 points and 19 rebounds a game and the Miners improved to 25-3. They beat Texas A&M, 68–62, in the Midwest Regional in Dallas, the school's first NCAA victory, but then lost in the next round to Kansas State, 64–60, a defeat that gnaws at Haskins to this day.

He felt the officiating was far too severe. "They called it like a damn girls game," he said. Barnes picked up four quick fouls and was never a major factor. "I watched films of that game afterward and am still bothered by them [the foul calls]," said Haskins. "That was a team that could have gone all the way."

And at that point in his young college career, Haskins had no way of knowing he'd get another chance just a few years later.

4.

"The Best Damned Basketball Coach in the United States"

"Twenty years from now Rupp's win-loss record will be in the record book, but do you think his name will be indelibly inscribed on anyone's heart?"
> —Martin Pedigo of Lousiville in a February 15, 1967, letter to University of Kentucky president John W. Oswald

"People forced him into some of his traits by their unreasonable demands. He sealed himself off and became gruff because of the pressure for tickets and interviews and all that. That was the only way he could protect himself."
> —Joe B. Hall, Former Kentucky head coach and Rupp assistant

His father's death shook Adolph Rupp's world when he was eight years old. All the disruption that followed in his remaining sixty-eight years—the game-fixing scandal, the few big losses, the whispered accusations—didn't get any easier for him to accept.

Rupp hated change and fought it so fiercely that he is remembered as much for that resistance as his remarkable coaching record. The more he aged, it seemed, the more discipline and order became his talismans against uncertainty. Increasingly he demanded more of both, in his profession and his life, until finally any assessment of his brilliant career had to weigh his reputation as a tyrant, a misanthrope, a racist.

He never apologized for his aloof, boot camp tactics and he knew the 1951 gambling disaster that fingered several of his star players tarnished him, but it's doubtful Rupp ever regarded his civil rights ignorance as a significant flaw.

Yet history has demonized him for that and the legacy would have surprised Rupp as much as it does his family, friends, and many former players.

"I'm sick and tired of people characterizing Coach Rupp as a very wicked person," said Tommy Kron, one of the players on his 1966 team. "I'm not excusing anybody from being a bigot or racist, and I'm not suggesting he was, but society was rife with those kinds of people back then. Even my own father had a view of black America that was inaccurate."

Unlike most of his contemporaries, though, Rupp possessed the means and opportunity to alter the world he ruled. Instead, because he so stubbornly adhered to antiquated notions and kept his team all-white into the 1970s, Rupp is recalled as a villain in a sport now dominated by a race he excluded. "Rupp was, to many blacks, the basketball version of Birmingham police chief Bull Connor," wrote Nelson George, "and the embodiment of segregation's lingering hold on the South."

At 6-1 and 225 pounds, with a massive head and no-nonsense eyes, Rupp could be a severe and imposing figure, particularly to the teenagers he coached. "I was afraid of him as a player," admitted Joe B. Hall, the ex-Kentucky player and assistant who succeeded Rupp in 1972. "You were afraid to fail him."

While most of his players later pronounced a reluctant respect for him, few felt that way in their college years. C.M. Newton, a former Kentucky player and now its athletic director, told broadcaster

Curt Gowdy that Rupp was "a complete dictator. He could go in any direction—he could charm you, scare you, threaten you—but you stayed scared of him."

In his final years, after the 1960s cultural revolution had altered attitudes and coaching styles but not Rupp, he often found himself defending this behavior. "If discipline means meanness," Rupp said, "then I guess I'm a mean man." Few of his players would have argued. "With us there was no joking, no laughing, no whistling, no singing, no nothing. Just basketball," said Alex Groza, a star on Rupp's national champions of 1948 and 1949. "When we traveled he often communicated with us through a team manager." The Associated Press, in its obituary on Rupp, noted that "some people accused him of taking the fun out of the game. But he retorted that 'My boys get their fun playing for national championships.'"

Rupp believed that life and basketball games ought to proceed as he plotted them. That was why he worked so hard, prepared obsessively, and drove his boys like a martinet. Wearing a uniform that seldom changed—matching khaki trousers and shirt and white sneakers—Rupp conducted somber closed practices during which his screams and whistles were the only permissible sounds. "He *demanded* perfection," Harry Lancaster, his longtime assistant, wrote in his memoir. "He could ream a player out until his asshole just hit the floor with a dull thud."

Then, if somehow fate still crossed him, as in the loss to Texas Western, for example, or the college basketball scandal fifteen years earlier, he could be sure it wasn't his fault. And at those moments, he would search for something or someone to blame. Not surprisingly, the culprit was never Adolph Rupp himself.

The winningest coach in college basketball history at the time of his death lost, on average, fewer than five games a season in his forty-two years at Kentucky. All, he believed, were caused by his players' mistakes, incompetent officials, or bad luck. "He just needed to feel he hadn't been beaten fairly or it wasn't his fault," wrote sportswriter Dave Kindred in 1991. "Adolph Rupp won [876] games and lost none. It was his players who lost those 190."

As a solemn young Freeport (Illinois) High School coach, when his team lost a game they should have won, Rupp blamed the blue suit he wore. From then on, through the remainder of his high school career and the more than 1,000 games he coached at Kentucky, Rupp wore a brown suit on the bench.

Rupp's faith in himself and his system was enormous. Through a half-century of nearly unbroken success, he rarely altered his practice habits, his basketball philosophy, his wardrobe, or his menu.

■ ■ ■

Whenever the issue of his team's racial makeup was raised, Rupp faulted the more stridently segregationist Deep South members of the Southeastern Conference instead of his own personal leanings. Mississippi State in Starkville was a place where Rupp and his teams traditionally received rude welcomes. "If they treat me and my boys like that now," Rupp said, "what do you think they would do if I brought a Negro there?"

Rupp was unquestionably the commonwealth's favorite son for more than three decades. He was a rumored candidate for lieutenant governor in 1952. Happy Chandler, the honey-tongued ex-Kentucky governor and former baseball commissioner, was a close friend, and the state's leading politicians and richest men often came to Rupp's modest brick home at 175 Eastover Avenue for conversation and favors. "He could have been governor of Kentucky," said Lou Carnesecca, the retired St. John's coach. "He could have been a czar or a don."

Anyone who knew Rupp recognized that this was not someone to lead a revolution. He was a plump and comfortable middle-aged man when Jim Crow began to tumble, and for a while he seemed neither to notice nor care. When others felt the rumblings, they began to ask why his team remained all-white. Groping for satisfactory answers, he never found one.

As early as 1961, when many of the sport's superstars were black men like Bill Russell, Wilt Chamberlain, and Oscar Robertson, Rupp had hinted about recruiting a black player for his Wildcats. "The two finest high school basketball players in Kentucky, both Negroes, will enroll at the university," Rupp told the *Atlanta Journal* that year. Later, when called on that unfulfilled promise, he denied ever making the comment. For the next eight years, Rupp, who bragged about his prowess as a recruiter, occasionally claimed he had tried unsuccessfully to sign a few blacks. No one remembers him trying very hard.

Oddly, Rupp's toughest, and ultimately most revealing, racial dispute occurred away from the public gaze in his own backyard. It began in 1963 when Dr. John W. Oswald, a liberal Northerner, became Kentucky's president and Rupp's nemesis. The late administrator's papers show that almost from the day he arrived he sought to integrate the school's basketball team. New sources of federal aid were at stake and Oswald knew Kentucky would have to comply with new civil rights guidelines to compete for the money as well as the flood of baby boomers then reaching college age.

As the 1960s rolled on with all their change and tumult, Kentucky remained a lily-white vestige of the past. It wasn't until the signing of 7-footer Tom Payne, who played a single season, 1970–71, that Rupp's team was integrated. By the time he coached his last game in 1972, only Kentucky and Mississippi State in the once rigidly segregated SEC remained all-white.

Family members and friends argue that while Rupp could have integrated earlier, he was no racist. Russell Rice, a former sports information director at the school, noted in the acknowledgments to his *Adolph Rupp: Kentucky's Basketball Baron* that while the coach was partially responsible for the delay, others were equally at fault. "Why doesn't someone blame those members of the black community who did not step forward to help him recruit those boys?" wrote Rice. "Why didn't they encourage those boys to challenge the system?"

It is a ridiculous notion. In the early 1960s, in Lexington, Kentucky, black leaders and high school students were in no position to squeeze a figure like Rupp. The Kentucky coach possessed the power to push for change and did not use it.

Rupp grew comfortable with his long-held authority, bitterly dismissing critics and anyone he saw as a potential threat. "Adolph," said Lancaster, who died in 1985, "[thought] that anyone who dared criticize him must be a damned fool." He frequently wrote biting replies to those who, in a letter or newspaper column, questioned his strategies. "I know I have plenty of enemies," Rupp admitted. "But I'd rather be the most hated winning coach in the country than the most popular losing one."

His ego was as large as his appetite for victory. In the late 1940s and early 1950s, Bear Bryant was Kentucky's football coach. Bryant was so successful that the basketball coach perceived a challenge to his campus superiority. Rupp and Bryant remained civil on the surface but the basketball man used his clout like a club. He flaunted his superior status at Bryant and frequently pointed out to reporters that football was the school's number two sport. "Rupp won a national title and got a Cadillac," Bryant said in 1966. "I won the Sugar Bowl and got a pen-and-pencil set." Hearing that, Rupp responded: "Bear forgets to tell people that he also got a cigarette lighter." Bryant, admittedly jealous, eventually left. "All Rupp wanted was to be number one and win everything," Bryant said years later. "Not just basketball games but everything. He was just like me."

Rupp could be ruthless and he admired that trait in his players. Early in his career, Lancaster sought his recruiting advice. "Harry," Rupp told him, "just read the papers and find out who's been making the most points. . . . Get to that town and buy the boy a big steak, three inches thick and a foot long. Then sit back and watch him eat. If he tears into it and gets it chewed up quick, sign him right there. But if he paws and pecks, pay for the steak but let somebody else get him. He's no good."

In a world so easily defined, Rupp never questioned his methods and had little use for those who did. "Any man that is successful will naturally be envied by those less successful," he wrote in his instructional book, *Championship Basketball.* He denied access to outsiders. Then, when attacked, he could reply that those people really didn't understand. Rupp normally would not allow players to speak with reporters unless he had cleared the meeting and its content. "A boy can make a very bad statement," he explained. "You are dealing with seventeen- and eighteen-year olds. They are not all twenty-two and twenty-three the way they are at some schools."

Some of this behavior was calculated, of course, an attempt— like the silent-practice technique he learned from his college coach, Phog Allen—to discipline and intimidate players. If his was the only voice they heard, it soon carried the weight of God's. "He liked people to think he was hard-hearted," said Jane Rollins, Rupp's secretary. It was a simple ruse for him. Unpleasantness came easy to Rupp.

And it wasn't only basketball players who shook in his presence. Waiters in the university cafeteria dreaded serving him. One claimed Rupp once sent back a three-minute egg more than a dozen times because it was not done to his liking. "Sure, I used to get into a lot of arguments. I was blunt," Rupp admitted to the *New York Times* in 1976, a year before his death. "But was I right? Time is the greatest proof."

Rupp apparently could abandon his martinet's role away from the basketball court. He loved a good joke and enjoyed the company of reporters and storytellers like Chandler. "He was a perfectionist," said Groza, "and that overshadows what a great sense of humor he had." In the bluster of fresh anger, he was often unintentionally hilarious. Losing to NYU in Madison Square Garden, Rupp gathered his players together at intermission and screamed: "Well, are you boys going to show them your clippings when we start the half or are you going to get your toes out of the wringer?" He could be just as caustic (yet comical) when the Wildcats were ahead. Routing Arkansas State, 47–3, at halftime, Rupp wanted to know how one opponent, No. 16, had managed to score all three points. "Who's on 16?" he growled. "I am," came the weak reply. "Then, dammit, get on him. He's running wild."

Kentucky player Phil Argento had this advice for freshman Dan Issel in the late 1960s: "Coach Rupp will say things that will crack you up, but if he's not laughing, you don't laugh. Then he'll say something that's not funny at all but he'll laugh. That's when you laugh."

Those closest to him recall a gentler Rupp. "He was a very gentle, very kind man," said his son. "[But] on the court his German heritage came through."

He was, they say, a fine family man, one who loved his wife, son, and grandchildren and devoted years of his time to Shriners' functions. He was tremendously loyal to the University of Kentucky even if, whenever he wanted a raise, he didn't hesitate to brand its officials cheapskates or plant a story that he might be leaving. Driven to succeed, he did. Yet on the day after his death, his hometown paper was compelled to point out in its obituary that many Kentucky players hated the man.

"I think his personality was shaped when he was a small boy growing up in Kansas," wrote Lancaster. "He grew up very hard."

■ ■ ■

Adolph Frederich Rupp was born in the living room of a little three-room farmhouse near Halstead, Kansas, on September 2, 1901, just ten years after James Naismith, seeking a winter's diversion for young men, had invented basketball. The fourth of six children, five boys and a girl, Rupp's childhood was marked by the same traits he demanded from his teams—hard work and discipline.

"We never got much news out there," said Rupp, who would subscribe to the *Halstead Independent* for the rest of his life. "The only thing we knew was that we chopped wood and piled it up high so we had enough to burn for heat. When the chores were done at night we had our evening meal and devotions. We went to bed at eight o'clock at night and got up in the morning in time to do our chores and go to school."

Rupp grew up on a 163-acre homesteader's farm seven miles north of Halstead, along Harvey County Road 801. Twenty-five miles northwest of Wichita and situated along the Little Arkansas River, Halstead was a tiny community of about 1,200 people, most of them Mennonite immigrants from southern Germany. Served by the Santa Fe Railroad, the town was all-white when Rupp lived there, a status it had ensured with a nineteenth-century ordinance that prohibited blacks from spending the night. Kansas had once been a haven for freed slaves, but at the turn of the century many of its schools and institutions were being segregated as fervently as in some Southern states.

Rupp's Mennonite parents were stern and hardworking. His father, Heinrich Rupp, emigrated to the U.S. in 1883, and claimed the farm in the federal land-grant program that populated the Great Plains. His mother, Anna Lichti, arrived in 1891. The two met in Kansas and married. Rupp always spoke kindly of his parents but his father apparently ran the household the way his son would run a basketball team.

Rupp's sister, Elizabeth, recalled that after dinner, Heinrich Rupp enjoyed reading his paper in the living room. Silence was expected from the children at most times, especially then. They tiptoed cautiously around him, realizing one slip might lead to a whipping. "His word was law," said Elizabeth Rupp. "And if you forgot it, he'd be there with a lash." Rupp never rebelled, but it's perhaps not surprising that he took quickly to a sport that got him out of the house.

By the time of Rupp's birth, Naismith had left New England. Basketball's inventor went first to Denver and then to the University of Kansas to become director of physical education. He brought his game, still played primarily in Eastern urban areas, with him. Kansans, their schools often too small to provide the numbers for football or baseball teams, embraced it. Farm communities across the state, looking to the university in Lawrence for guidance in most matters, erected baskets in the dirt yards of rural schoolhouses. Halstead's District 33 Elementary School eventually got two.

Rupp began playing basketball at the age of four. The older Rupp boys nailed a basket to a barn wall. Mrs. Rupp provided a makeshift ball and soon the farm was a gathering place for the brothers and neighboring boys. There is an old photograph of Rupp shooting baskets with a misshapen ball as a boy of fourteen. He is wearing a cap and so are the four other boys. In the background is the school, a simple white-frame building with three windows on one side.

"We had never heard of basketball way out there," Rupp recalled. "In those days the ball we had out on the farm was just a gunnysack stuffed with rags. Mother sewed it up and somehow made it round. You couldn't dribble it. Then in grade school we got a barrel and used that for a basket. The ball was a little bit better than the one we had on the farm but not much. We had an old ball and we'd have to blow it up every day and put a rubber band around it. We had to keep lacing it to keep it from falling apart."

He enjoyed playing. "Adolph liked the game right away," said his older brother Theodore. "He was always very concerned about wanting to play the game correctly and he was very serious about it for a youngster." Before Rupp was out of elementary school, Halstead had become such a basketball hotbed that its high school had won the state championship twice, even though the sport was still in its primitive stages and playing conditions were haphazard. "We were in the Little Arkansas Valley League," recalled neighbor Glenn Lehmann. "I remember at Sedgwick we had to run around a stove that was right in the middle of the floor."

The farm provided ample food for the family but little else and the children were expected not only to perform chores but to supplement the family income with outside jobs. Rupp had several, including a stint as a clerk and stockboy at Halstead's Williams Grocery Store. He was, by all accounts, a dogged student. Since his older brothers operated the farm in the wake of their father's death in 1909, Rupp was destined for college.

He graduated from high school in 1919 and soon afterward departed for the University of Kansas. Once there he took a job at a popular university restaurant, the Jayhawk Cafe. He began as a janitor and moved on to waiter and cashier. The cafe provided meals for the farm boy ("all I had to eat at first was two sandwiches a day") and it was there that he developed a lifelong passion for chili.

"I know he had a lot of ambition," said Theodore Rupp, five years older than his famous brother. "He worked all summer long to get enough to pay his $23 matriculation fee at the university."

Rupp arrived at Kansas during the era of muscular Christianity, when physical activity was seen as a pathway to spirituality. The "American Century" was young and educators believed that a growing obsession with sports helped ensure the superiority of America and the Anglo-Saxon race. Senator Henry Cabot Lodge of Massachusetts told Harvard's Class of 1906 that "the time given to athletic contests . . . [is] part of the price which the English-speaking race has paid for being world-conquerors."

Naismith, himself an ordained Presbyterian minister, viewed basketball more as a means of developing Christian gentlemen than producing career athletes. Extremely noncompetitive, Naismith had been an uninspired basketball coach, compiling a 54-60 record in eight seasons at Kansas. After the 1907 season he resigned from the position. By the time Rupp arrived, one of Naismith's former players, Forrest C. "Phog" Allen, was coaching the Jayhawks. "Why, Forrest," Naismith said when Allen told him he had taken the job, "basketball is just a game to play. You don't coach it." But Allen did. His practices were strictly run and he could be as dour as his most famous protégé. "You just do the playing," he told his teams. "I'll do the talking and fighting."

He did, however, occasionally invite players, including Rupp, to his home, where they would discuss basketball for hours. Rupp was never more than a substitute, but in his senior season Kansas went undefeated against collegiate competition. "If I said he was a great player I'd only be indulging in professional courtesy," Allen said years later, before adding with a smile, "The only reason Adolph went into coaching is because he was offered $10 more a month if he would. He really hates money. He hates for anybody else to have it."

Rupp graduated in 1923. Unable to find work, he returned to Lawrence and the Jayhawk Cafe. He enrolled in a few education courses and also became a teaching assistant in the Department of Home Economics, grading papers and tests. When that school year ended, Rupp accepted a coaching position at Burr Oak (Kansas) High School. Home in Halstead for Thanksgiving, he met the principal of Marshalltown (Iowa) High School. The educator, impressed with the ambitious Rupp, immediately hired him as a teacher-coach. A year later, he moved to Freeport High School in Illinois.

While he was in Illinois Rupp traveled to New York during the summer, to earn a master's degree in education from Columbia University. He was always planning ahead, worried what might happen if he lost a job. Surely coaching basketball would not be his life's work. "I always expected that I'd be teaching or in business someday," he said.

But enjoying great success year after year, Rupp stayed in basketball. And as conservative as he was about most things, he often was an innovator on the court.

Because the heavy laces on basketballs of that era made dribbling difficult, he favored an offense driven by screens and quick and precise passes. Dribbling was never mentioned in Naismith's original rules and Rupp felt the game often was marred by too much "damn bouncing the ball." The quick-passing style and aggressive man-to-man defense that his Kentucky teams would make their trademark brought him immediate success. He would use both, with very few alterations, until he retired in 1972.

In four years at Freeport, his reputation spread to Champaign, home of the University of Illinois. Following Freeport's 1930 season, the guest speaker at the school's banquet happened to be Illinois basketball coach Craig Ruby. Afterward, Ruby told Rupp that Johnny Mauer, Kentucky's basketball coach and a former Illinois teammate of Red Grange's, planned to leave. Mauer's teams had gone an impressive 40-14 in the last three years, and he wanted a three-year deal with annual increases.

Ruby informed Rupp that the Kentucky athletic department was filled with Illinois grads and he suggested the stout twenty-nine-year-old utilize those connections and apply. What followed was a process that foretold much about Rupp's ambition and persuasiveness—as well as his racial attitudes.

Upon arriving in Lexington for his interview, he was given a lunch of cold fish and cornbread and escorted to the school's athletic department. Its offices then were located on the fringe of the UK campus, close to the future site of Memorial Coliseum. In a 1974 interview, Rupp recalled being unimpressed by this first view of Kentucky: the office surrounded by "fifty-five little . . . nigger shacks"; the gymnasium, Alumni Hall, "a little old peanut holler, no better than Freeport's gymnasium." "I had a room at the YMCA that wasn't fit for a cat," Rupp recalled. "I said, 'Good God almighty, what kind of place is this Kentucky?'"

Theodore Rupp recalled a letter Rupp wrote him during his first days in Lexington. "He wrote back and said, 'This is nice country, I guess, but it's the dangdest hillbillyest country I ever saw.'"

If Rupp had doubts, Kentucky did not. There were seventy applicants for the job and it came down to Rupp and an Indiana coach who eventually eliminated himself by demanding $5,000 a year for three years.

It was somewhat unusual, even in that era, for a large university to hire a young man with only five years of high school experience. Surely his connections to Naismith, Ruby, and Allen helped. And since Rupp would have to assist with the football team, where head coach Harry Gammage and assistant Bernie Shively were also Illinois products, his Freeport background didn't hurt either. Still it was Rupp's naked self-confidence that probably won him the position. "He told us he was the best damned basketball coach in the United States," one Kentucky official remarked at the time, "and he convinced us he was."

It also didn't hurt that he was willing to agree to a two-year contract that paid him $2,800 the first year and $3,000 the next—less than he had been earning in Freeport. "I just wanted enough for Esther [whom he married in 1931] and myself to live on," he said. He returned to Illinois before notifying Kentucky athletic director S.A. Boles of his acceptance. On May 21, 1930, Rupp was revealed as Kentucky's new basketball coach.

■ ■ ■

College basketball was a long way from enjoying the popularity Rupp's teams would help create. Slow and plodding, with an emphasis on strength over grace and skill, it was as distant from the modern game as cricket is from baseball.

There were center jumps after each field goal and bruising, clumsy pileups beneath the basket. As recently as 1908, Harvard president Charles Eliot had sought to ban the sport because it was "even more brutal than football." There was no 10-second rule and teams often stalled in the backcourt when they had a lead. Shooting was scattershot, scoring was minimal—the game was an aesthetic nightmare. When, in 1936, Rupp recommended increasing a field goal's worth to three points, he based his argument on shooting statistics he had gathered. Collegians made 66 percent of their free throws, Rupp noted, but only 18 percent of field goal attempts.

The first of the 1,066 games he would coach at the school took place on December 12, 1930, a 67–19 victory over Georgetown (Kentucky). Ironically, Georgetown's leading scorer, with 10 points, was Harry Lancaster, his future assistant. Kentucky went 15-3 that year and never finished a season with a sub-.500 record while Rupp was there.

Right from the start, his teams were quicker and better-conditioned than his opponents'. Rupp was one of the first coaches to recognize the value of quickness and, throughout his long tenure, it was a trait he sought in recruits.

While Mauer had used the fast break occasionally, Rupp adopted it full-time, becoming its greatest advocate. Whenever they had the opportunity, the Wildcats ran. The faster-paced style appealed to students and Lexington's fans immediately. The *Lexington Herald* remarked that Rupp's first team won a game "romping like unhaltered colts in a pasture." Rupp refined the break and better implemented his patterned offense with a series of then unusual inside screens. Soon his Kentucky teams were scoring far above the era's modest average and gaining a regional reputation.

Rupp's first four Kentucky teams were a combined 66-9 and soon his ambition demanded a larger geography. He had a constant need to be the best, and to beat the best. In the 1930s, the best college basketball was not being played in the South, so he took his team to big arenas in major Eastern and Midwestern cities. When his Wildcats traveled to Madison Square Garden in the 1934–35 season to play NYU, an Eastern power, the New York newspapers gleefully promoted the game as a match between savvy urban sophisticates and hot-shooting hillbillies. NYU won, 23–22, and the entertaining and extremely physical game helped lift college basketball into the sporting public's consciousness. NYU scored the deciding point on a free throw after Kentucky was called for an illegal screen, a screen Rupp insisted was perfectly legal in the South and Midwest. The resulting furor, fanned by Rupp, helped create national standards for the game's rules.

It would be well into the next decade before Rupp and Kentucky really made a national statement. His 1948 and 1949 "Fab Five" team, featuring All-Americas Groza and Ralph Beard, won back-to-back national championships, and after the first, Rupp was named the coach of the U.S. Olympic team, which would win a gold medal in London that summer.

■ ■ ■

College basketball nearly perished in the years immediately after World War II. Gamblers, finding it easy to convince athletes to manipulate point spreads or, less frequently, throw games, operated brazenly. At Madison Square Garden, for example, bookmakers sat near the court, their shouts often audible to players on the floor. Things began to unravel for them, however, in 1945, when Brooklyn College expelled several players for accepting bribes.

That action was the result of a New York–based probe that eventually widened. Investigators would determine that between 1947 and 1950, when Kentucky was the country's dominant team, at least eighty-six games in thirty-three cities had been fixed. Rupp initially bragged that his program was spotless, telling New York writers that "they can't touch my boys with a ten-foot pole . . . [they are under] constant and absolutely complete supervision when on the road, especially in New York."

Yet among gamblers themselves, there was a widespread belief that Kentucky's players had been on the take consistently in their highly successful seasons after World War II. In the first four postwar years, Kentucky won 93 percent of its games, but "their percentage was not nearly so good against the spread," noted gambler Stanley Cohen. And when, as 10-point favorites against Loyola in the 1949 NIT, the Wildcats were beaten by 11, 67–56, even Rupp sounded suspicious. "Something's wrong with this team," he said.

Then in 1951, as Rupp coached the College All-Stars in an exhibition game against the NBA's Rochester Royals, federal agents entered Chicago Stadium. Groza and Beard, then playing with the NBA's Indianapolis Olympians, were attending the game and were arrested as it ended. Simultaneously in Louisville, Dale Barnstable, a reserve on those Fab Five teams, was taken into custody at his home. The three ex-Kentucky players were accused of accepting $1,500 apiece to lose to Loyola of Chicago in that NIT at Madison Square Garden.

When Lancaster heard the news, he immediately recalled his uneasiness after the upset loss two years earlier. Rupp's thoughts, typically, turned to blame. "Here are the New York papers printing odds. . . . If newspapers are allowed to print odds for the benefit of guttersnipes who infest the fringes of the sport, maybe we should check up on some newspapers too. Why take it out on the kids if the point spreads are flaunted at them?"

A few days later, unable to resist chuckling at the irony, some New York writers, historically antagonistic to Rupp, sent an eleven-foot pole to the coach's office.

Groza and Beard eventually were barred from professional basketball and their banning led to the demise of the Indianapolis franchise. Rupp's sympathy toward them ended when some of their testimony was revealed by New York Judge Saul Streit, who had suspended the players' sentences. Streit's sixty-three-page report, eighteen pages of which were devoted to the coach's role, was a blistering indictment of Kentucky basketball and of Rupp.

Streit called Kentucky's program the "acme of commercialism and overemphasis." He accused Rupp of consorting with gamblers, of speaking to players about point spreads, and openly subsidizing his team with the help of Lexington businessmen. Barnstable told investigators that players not only received monthly stipends but often were given $50 or $100 after a significant victory. Rupp interrupted one team meeting, Streit noted, to call Cincinnati gambler Ed Curd for the betting line on Kentucky's game with Xavier that night. Rupp and Curd, said the report, ate dinner together on a few occasions at New York's Copacabana Club and Rupp once visited Curd at his home.

Rupp, not surprisingly, denied any wrongdoing and was never accused or convicted of any offense. He termed Curd a casual acquaintance and explained that he had gone to the man's home to solicit a Shriners donation. But the door was open now and a subsequent NCAA investigation resulted in one of the harshest penalties in collegiate history. Kentucky had to cancel its 1952–53 season. "I'll not retire," said an angry Rupp at the time, "until the man who said Kentucky can't play . . . hands me the national championship trophy."

Soon after Streit's report, Rupp ordered that all pictures and memorabilia relating to Groza, Beard, and Barnstable be removed from Memorial Coliseum. In 1967, an interviewer asked the sixty-six-year-old coach if, in the intervening years, he had reconciled with the three. "Go on to your next question," Rupp instructed him.

■ ■ ■

Unlike many Southern schools, Kentucky did not play in a racial vacuum. The Wildcats scheduled several Eastern and Midwestern teams, many of whom, after World War II's leavening effect on segregation, signed black players. There is evidence Rupp took some pride in that. If nothing else, he could use it to belittle opponents further. "We've never played Southeastern Louisiana or McNeese State like so many Southern teams do," said Rupp in a 1966 interview, noting that Kentucky, virtually alone in the South, played against talented black athletes. In fact, Rupp's worst defeat ever, an embarrassing 89–50 thrashing at Madison Square Garden in the 1950 NIT, came against a CCNY team that started three blacks.

Rupp liked to say he had tried to recruit Wilt Chamberlain in the mid-1950s, when the 7-foot Philadelphia phenom was the talk of basketball. "But could I take him to Atlanta, New Orleans, or Starkville?" Rupp asked rhetorically. It was a moot point. Chamberlain, eventually landed by Allen at Kansas, said he never considered Kentucky.

Even had he been so inclined, and there is no indication he was, Rupp surely would have met great barriers had he tried to integrate that early. For all his clout, he answered to the school's athletic board and alumni and among that collection of well-off, mostly conservative Kentuckians there was no consensus for change.

"Frankly I do not feel that we have quite reached the point where we should take this step." Kentucky president Frank Dickey wrote to a Kentucky Athletic Association board member in 1962, when the issue of integration was raised, "but I should welcome the opportunity to discuss the matter with the entire board." A year later, when it was raised again, W.H. Grady, a Kentucky alumnus and ex-trustee, wrote to Dickey that he was "unalterably opposed to this repulsive thing."

In fact, a national magazine article on Oscar Robertson sparked criticism of Rupp in Lexington when it mentioned that the coach had considered recruiting the black star. The coach felt obligated to deny the report publicly. "How absurd can you get," he sniffed.

Yet even if outside factors really did prevent Rupp from integrating, he missed numerous chances to seize some moral authority on the issue. "Any opportunity for leadership within the conference should not be lost," an athletic association member pointed out at a 1963 meeting on the matter. That session concluded, however, with a milquetoast statement, urging integration at "the earliest possible time" but also urging that Kentucky's SEC membership be preserved.

In 1963, John Oswald, a forty-seven-year-old Minnesotan, arrived at Lexington from the University of California to become Kentucky's president. He was determined to integrate the university. Oswald's background was in science, and he approached this task rationally. He'd identify the problem, create a solution, and watch things change smoothly. That methodology remained intact until Oswald had his first meeting with Rupp. The new president was in for a surprise.

5.

A Long Way from Anywhere

"El Paso is truly a bi-cultural community and the courtesy and charm of Spanish America combines with the informality and friendliness of the American West. . . . [Students] develop the breadth and tolerance which can come only from close contact between men of different races, creeds and ways of life."
    —Texas Western's 1966 student handbook

"The way our boys line up now, my six best boys are black. If I leave two or three of them out because they're black, they'll know it. [And] the white boys will know it."
    —Don Haskins to Texas Western president
    Joseph Ray early in the 1965–66 season

On a warm evening in July 1964, Willie Worsley said goodbye to friends in his South Bronx neighborhood. Standing under the Third Avenue El, some of them were drinking cheap wine from bottles still encased in brown bags. Others he saw that night were high on heroin. A few, he just never found. "Maybe they're in jail," he thought. It wouldn't have shocked him.

Worsley, an only child who had led DeWitt Clinton High to the city basketball championship the previous season, would miss his mother and his friends, but he wasn't entirely unhappy about abandoning these streets—even if it did mean going to remote El Paso, a journey of more than 2,000 miles, far from the action of the city.

"I had a couple of buddies from the Bronx, Willie Cager and Nevil Shed, who were down there at Texas Western," said Worsley. "Willie Brown, another friend of mine from New York, had just gone there. They all told the coach about me. . . . I was a high school All-America. I had a few other offers. They said they were small but looking to bring some good people in. 'Black' never came into it at all. I was eighteen and I knew with Shed and Cager I was not going to be totally alone down there."

Cager could not have said the same thing when he arrived in El Paso back in 1963. He had dropped out of Morris High School in the Bronx a few years earlier to support his mother and his siblings. He continued to play in New York recreation leagues until someone told him about Texas Western and its good history with black athletes. Cager traveled there on his own. He took a job at a service station—sleeping in the back while he earned his diploma from El Paso Technical High School—and enrolled in college.

"There was no shenanigans at all," said Louis Baudoin, a teammate. "Willie did it all on his own."

Those first New Yorkers had been directed to El Paso by Hilton White, a recreation director for the New York's Department of Parks who coached various amateur playground teams. "Hilton was our coach in rec ball," said Worsley. "He was kind of like what an AAU coach is now. He knew the talent and he knew the colleges." While in the Army, White had been stationed at El Paso's Fort Bliss and he realized Texas Western was a place where blacks could live and play college basketball without great difficulty.

Regardless, moving to distant El Paso was a formidable journey for these inner-city black kids—as it was for any other student from outside the region. When Bum Phillips coached Texas Western football in 1962, he was recruiting a quarterback from some faraway East Texas town. The youngster decided to drive there for a visit. After a full day in the car, he pulled into a gas station near Abilene and asked the attendant how far it was to El Paso. "Oh, 'bout 400 miles," he said. The recruit turned the car around and drove home.

"El Paso," said Moe Iba, "is a long way from anywhere."

Worsley had met Iba while the coach was on a recruiting visit, but had spoken with Haskins only by phone. He had never been that far from home and he knew that once he got there, he wouldn't be seeing New York again until the summer.

"The thing about El Paso was that very few of them got home very often," said Iba. "When they came to school they were at school from the end of one summer to the beginning of the next. It was hard but, hey, these kids knew hard. For a lot of them this was the best they ever had. They got to go to school. They had a good place to sleep, three meals a day, an opportunity to get an education. They were very glad to be there."

Worsley knew none of that when, the morning after his farewells, he arrived at La Guardia Airport for his first airplane trip, on an American Airlines jet bound for El Paso.

"I was scared as all get-up. I'm eighteen years old. I'm from the South Bronx where you've got gang wars going on. I ain't scared of nobody. But put me on a plane and I'm about this big," he said, pinching his thumb and forefinger together. "Being from a low-income background, when I traveled, I traveled by Greyhound. Going to an airport and checking luggage was totally Greek to me. When they told me to fly down, I said, 'Can't I catch a bus?' They told me it would take about two and a half days on a bus."

So Worsley said goodbye to his mother, boarded the plane, and, trying to look brave and self-assured, found his aisle seat. A middle-aged white woman stepped over him and sat by the window. Normally, when white women saw him approach, they clutched their handbags. But this woman, apparently sensing his anxiety, spoke to him. Worsley told her where he was headed.

"She said, 'Oh, I live near the college. I'm going to help you,'" he recalled. "She gave me her seat next to the window so I could look outside. She fixed my seat belt because I didn't know how; cars didn't even have them then. My ears got clogged and she gave me some gum. This was quite strange during the '60s for a white person to be so friendly to a young black kid. This person was treating me like her son. She didn't try to put her purse away. I thought, 'If the people in El Paso are half as nice as this lady, I'll be comfortable.' And when I got there, they were."

■ ■ ■

From his office window on a clear morning in December of 1965, the president of Texas Western College could observe miles of barren landscape to the south and west. El Paso in winter, Joseph Ray always thought, looked like the moon. Everything was parched and colorless—the jagged, arroyo-veined peaks of the Franklin Mountains, the cactus-stubbled hillsides, the dull flatlands.

The border city occupied an area that sixteenth-century Spaniards seeking gold had crossed on their way to Santa Fe, 325 miles to the north. El Paso del Norte, they called the arid valley. Even the Rio Grande flowed feebly here, a mere muddy ribbon separating Texas's western elbow from Mexico. For Ray, sixty-two, born in Kentucky's lush Bluegrass country, this dusty vastness, with its Hispanic-spiced culture, was alien terrain.

Southwest, toward Ciudad Juárez, Ray could see the crude shacks that littered the Mexican slopes of these Rocky Mountain foothills like broken shells. They made Texas Western's buildings seem shamefully opulent.

The campus buildings had surprised Ray when he became president more than five years earlier. He had expected architecture reminiscent of Spanish missions. Instead, he discovered structures that, with their expansive, gently pitched roofs and colorful banding, replicated ancient Himalayan forts. They only added to El Paso's otherworldliness.

Now Ray looked across his desk at Haskins. A blond Oklahoman with the wide, leathery face of a cowboy and restless blue eyes, Haskins and his teams had brought the school some small recognition in recent years.

When Ray came to El Paso, the college had been, in his words, "a cut well below the university level." Anyone with a Texas high school diploma could get in. Few out-of-state students applied. Its Engineering Department was not accredited. Not many faculty members had Ph.D.'s and those who did rarely stayed more than a few years. "The controlling assumption [was] that we were a community college," Ray said. Technically a part of the University of Texas system, the connection was so insignificant that even many of Texas Western's administrators weren't aware of it.

"We had long been the stepchild of the U of T system," said Dr. Mimi Gladstein, who has taught English at the school for more than three decades. "One of the reasons they gave for why they were not giving us more advanced-level degrees was that we didn't have the community that justified it. What they were saying is that Mexicans don't need Ph.D.'s."

When Ray had hired Haskins out of a Texas high school in 1961, it was not solely for his coaching abilities but because the president believed the big man could maintain order in a men's dormitory. Since then Texas Western had run off five consecutive winning seasons and made its first appearances in both the NCAA and NIT tournaments.

This season Texas Western was unbeaten. Even Ray, no ardent sports fan, had started attending games in tiny Memorial Gymnasium. Memorial was only four years old that season but suddenly the Miners had outgrown it. He loved the way these players seemed to relax early, fall behind, and then, with a quick burst of confidence, rally to win. El Paso residents, at least a full day's drive from any big-league sports franchise, were developing a similar passion for their hometown Miners.

The fact that all five starters, and seven of the twelve, were black didn't seem to matter.

"We were used to them," said Ray of the local reaction to the team's racial makeup. The city of 350,000 and the college then were only about 2 percent black, the remaining population of each split almost equally between whites and Hispanics. Texas Western, virtually alone in the South, had been recruiting black athletes for a decade. While much of America was enduring civil rights spasms, El Paso, isolated from the rest of Texas by geography and the area's bicultural attitudes, had been by comparison an oasis of understanding.

But playing seven blacks, and more significantly starting five, was something else. Even at Northern colleges, where black athletes had been appearing with increasing regularity since World War II, rosters rarely contained more than one or two. Haskins insisted the racial makeup of his team was simply coincidence. "I used to hear other coaches say, 'What is your quota?'" recalled Haskins. "I didn't know what they were talking about. I was just looking for kids who could play."

He had inherited several blacks on his first Miner team (one was Nolan Richardson, an El Paso native who went on to coach Arkansas to a national championship). And to the shock of his colleagues, he kept increasing their number, finding the quick, tough players he favored in Northern cities and junior colleges.

Just as Haskins had been cautioned, Ray had heard from another university president who assured him he would "rue the day" he allowed five blacks to start. Though Ray, who died in 1991, saw himself as a liberal—and for a Kentuckian of his generation he probably was—his views on race hardly qualified him as enlightened.

"I don't think I have got that kind of prejudice," he said in 1981, "but I myself think that there's a difference between blacks and whites. I think it makes a difference. For example, I heard a raunchy old story one time. I'll tell it to you right now. It's a conundrum. The question is what do they call a black man in Plano, Texas. They just call him plain, ol' nigger. Now that to me is excruciatingly amusing. But that doesn't mean that I disparage black people."

While Ray contended he felt no external pressure, the racial implications of the basketball team's starting unit concerned him enough at the beginning of the 1965–66 season to discuss the matter with George McCarty, by then the athletic director of the school.

"It was going to reflect on me," Ray said, "no question about it, if we played all black boys." He told McCarty to inform Haskins that "we couldn't play more than three black boys."

Haskins objected and now, squirming uncomfortably in the president's office, he tried to explain why.

"[He] said, 'Dr. Ray, George told me what you said,'" Ray recalled sixteen years later. "'The way our boys line up now, my six best boys are black. If I leave two or three of them out because they're black, they'll know it. They'll know it. The white boys will know it. They all know who the best basketball players are, just as I do.'

"I said, 'Well, Don, you let me think about this overnight.'"

The next morning Ray telephoned the coach. "Don, you coach the basketball [team]," he said. "I'll try to do the rest of the job myself."

■ ■ ■

Texas Western did not suddenly begin recruiting black athletes when Haskins arrived in 1961. In 1956, it had been the first school in the Southern half of the U.S. to integrate its athletic teams. (The Southwest Conference, which dominated sports in Texas, would remain

segregated for another decade. The University of Texas didn't suit up
its first black basketball player until 1970.)

Though riots in 1956 had kept blacks from enrolling at Tex-
arkana Junior College in East Texas, no one paid much attention
when Air Force veteran Charlie Brown and his nephew, Cecil
Brown, transferred from Amarillo Junior College in 1956 and joined
Texas Western's varsity basketball team.

"It's the character of this town," said Professor Gladstein. "We
are in Texas but we are not like the rest of Texas. Our school has
been in the forefront of civil rights all along. I think we graduate
more Hispanic engineers than any other university in the country
and have for years."

Though the University of Texas Board of Regents then had a
policy against athletic integration, Texas Western, a remote school
the board usually ignored anyway, was granted a dispensation. Ray
said that when a member of the board visited the campus in the
mid-1960s, he was shocked to learn the school was a part of the
statewide system.

"There is evidence all over the place of how this particular community has been shortchanged [by politicians in Austin]," said Gladstein. "It's because we're different. We never vote the same as the
rest of Texas. More than 60 percent of our students are Hispanic."

El Paso's school system had been integrated in 1955 and that
same year the college, threatened with a lawsuit, became the first
four-year college in the state to integrate. Twelve blacks were admitted into a student body of 3,900 without incident. And since the
Miner athletic teams tended to schedule integrated schools to the
west and north, and not the segregated colleges from East Texas or
the Deep South, black faces were nothing new to Texas Western's
fans or opponents.

"Charlie Brown lives in San Francisco now and he told me that
one night he and Harry Edwards, the Cal-Berkeley sociologist who
writes a lot about black athletes, were having a drink," said Glad-

stein. "Charlie told him that he had played for Texas Western in the 1950s and that he made All-Border Conference. And Harry told him, 'No you didn't. They didn't let black players play in those days.' He couldn't believe that was so. But it was."

Brown, who grew up in Longview, Texas, had gone into the Air Force after high school and then enrolled at Amarillo. Three years of military life had toughened him as it had Jackie Robinson. After the twelve blacks entered Texas Western in 1955, McCarty, then the basketball coach, had permission to integrate his team. He had read and heard about Brown, a junior college star, and by telephone recruited the then twenty-six-year-old and his nephew Cecil.

Despite its relative openness, Texas Western did not yet permit blacks to live in campus dorms, and Brown, assisted by white teammate Alvis Glidewell, found an apartment downtown. On game days, McCarty had set aside an empty room in the athletic dormitory, Miners Hall, in which Brown could dress.

"I wasn't allowed in the movies downtown and things like that," recalled Brown, "and there were a few minor [racial] incidents with professors. But there were absolutely no problems with anyone in athletics there. . . . I always said Texas Western was going through integration, I wasn't."

While conditions for blacks were better in El Paso than almost anywhere else then, they were hardly perfect. A study by the city's Department of Planning and Research revealed that in the 1960s very few blacks held positions dealing with the public. The report noted that the better jobs went, in order, to whites, Hispanics, and then blacks.

Cecil Brown never played much but Charlie was the Border Conference MVP that season, averaging a team-high 21 points and 7.5 rebounds a game for the 10-9 Miners. Brown would lead Texas Western in scoring and rebounding all three of his seasons there and would make All-Conference in each.

Games in Arizona and New Mexico usually presented no difficulties, he recalled, but there were some minor problems in East Texas and Missouri. Eventually, Brown moved into a dormitory. When El Paso schools would not permit him to student-teach, the college made arrangements for him to fulfill his student-training requirement on campus. "I think if I'd have gone to any other place in Texas, say Texas Tech or the University of Texas or SMU, I never would have gotten beyond the first semester," said Brown, "because in those environments things *were* black or white."

El Paso high school star Nolan Richardson, Bobby Joe Hill, Willie Brown, Andy Stoglin, and other black players soon followed.

■ ■ ■

The Texas legislature created the State School of Mines and Metallurgy at El Paso in April 1913, the city's setting in the Franklin Mountains making it a perfect laboratory for geology. The border city was growing rapidly then, primarily because Fort Bliss, the largest U.S. cavalry base, had experienced a boom in the years during and after the Mexican Revolution.

Because of the city's proximity to Mexico and its relaxed racial attitudes, the government found it practical to station black soldiers in El Paso. The United States began sending black troops there in the aftermath of the Civil War. The famed Buffalo Soldiers cavalry division ended up at Fort Bliss. But despite being in uniform, these pioneers often complained of discrimination when they ventured into the Texas city and its public accommodations.

The mining college's first students rode the streetcar to Fort Bliss, then commanded by General John "Black Jack" Pershing. They walked through the camp to the school, located on an eighteen-acre site at its eastern edge. Construction of a new campus on the opposite side of the Franklin Mountains began in 1917. By 1918, five buildings had been completed there, though their unusual design left conservative El Paso residents shaking their heads.

The architecture was the inspiration of Kathleen Worrell. The wife of dean Stephen H. Worrell, she had seen, in the April 1914 issue of *National Geographic,* a pictorial spread on the remote Himalayan country of Bhutan entitled "Castles in the Air." An isolated country in the heart of the mountains, with India to its south and Tibet to its north, Bhutan's terrain in certain areas resembled El Paso's—jagged, sparsely vegetated hillsides with the "overpowering heat of the valleys." Bhutanese forts and monasteries, tucked into the nooks and slopes of the Himalayas, were painted a dull gray, with bright red bands near their tops. Gilded shingles covered softly angled roofs. Worrell convinced her husband that mimicking the architecture of those buildings would give the newer school an immediate identity.

Aside from its architecture, however, Texas Western was for the next half-century an undistinguished institution, academically and athletically. By 1924, 506 students were enrolled but the school still had no gymnasium and its basketball teams often were forced to play outdoors.

Texas Western's 1941 basketball team, under the leadership of coach Marshall Pennington, won the Border Conference championship but created little excitement. Between that 14-11 season and 1955, the Miners had one winning team. But under McCarty, who arrived in 1953, they posted winning records for five straight years beginning in 1955. When McCarty became dean of men in 1959, Harold Davis took over and two losing seasons followed.

Ray arrived in 1960 and his ambitions spread quickly. He wanted more students and better programs. He doubled the school's enrollment in eight years and pushed it further away from its mining roots. Having grown up in the shadow of Rupp's Kentucky, Ray also recognized the value of athletics in building a university. "Athletics is the common denominator that unites and integrates all or at least most of those with whom a favorable image is essential," he would write in 1968.

That optimism infected McCarty. He realized that Texas Western, able to attract black athletes, had enormous potential in sports. Seeking a replacement for Davis, he and AD Ben Collins sought someone who could tap it. He remembered reading about the success Haskins' Dumas teams were having. McCarty telephoned him to make sure he had finished his college degree work. Haskins told him he had gotten a degree from West Texas State and McCarty invited him to El Paso for an interview.

"We knew his basic philosophy," said McCarty, "and thought he would be good for us."

■ ■ ■

Like the sheriff in many Westerns, Haskins was no idealist. Recruiting blacks was never a moral issue for him. He was paid to win and he'd do whatever was necessary. But those who later would accuse him of winning by recruiting suspect students failed to consider that virtually anyone could then get into Texas Western. And once there, it was extremely difficult to flunk out.

"It was a fairly simple little school," said Baudoin. "There were not many graduate programs in existence then. You really had to struggle if you wanted to get a master's degree there. I really envied the kids who were at sound, well-developed academic programs. A place like Vanderbilt would have been paradise for me."

Though Ray eventually would try to stiffen them, admission requirements in the early 1960s were a diploma and, for students in the top half of their class, a combined 700 SAT score (800 for lower-half applicants). Even students unable to meet those bare-bones standards could still gain admission.

"Anybody who graduated from a Texas high school or from any accredited high school could go to summer school, take two courses, make Bs, and be admitted in September," said Ray.

When the college sought to become a university in 1965, a visiting committee from the University of Texas system refused the request until "such status is merited." That committee pointed out that while the school's handbook indicated students needed to maintain a 1.5 GPA for twenty credits—a 2.0 after that—the policy had been suspended. "It was observed that the retention policy was most liberal," the report noted. "Out of 7,422 students, 1,400 are on probation, 450 on academic suspension."

None of the basketball players were Rhodes scholars. Most of the blacks, in fact, tended to be seen as problem players by everyone outside of El Paso. Nevil Shed, David Lattin, and Bobby Joe Hill had enrolled only after they had dropped out of their previous schools, and Willie Cager had to earn a high school diploma in El Paso before he could attend. But school records reveal that they maintained passing grades in a wide range of courses. The fact that some left without a degree when their athletic eligibility expired was hardly shocking in that era.

"There were many black athletes, at many major universities, who weren't graduating then," said Lou Henson, the longtime collegiate coach.

Haskins pulled it off, pulled these kids together, because they respected his toughness and the discipline he imposed, and because the school's academic standards were flexible enough—often downright lax—to make GPAs a relatively minor concern.

"Nolan Richardson and I will occasionally lapse into conversation about Don Haskins," said Larry Conley. "What he did in '66 was just amazing. He took a bunch of kids, a lot of them problem kids, brought them in, disciplined them, and made them into a working, cohesive unit that won a national championship."

If the measuring stick of any basketball program is the lives of its participants after college, then Texas Western obviously did something right. Each of the players on that 1966 team, even the three blacks who stopped just short of their degrees, has been successful since.

But at the time, because this team looked and, in interviews, sounded like no other basketball team in NCAA history, the widely accepted view was not that different from Rupp's: basketball was the only reason they were in college.

"We weren't the smartest kids and we weren't the dumbest kids," said Worsley. "Sometimes people would talk to us and say we sounded like we weren't too bright. Well, if we had had a typical family situation, sitting around the dining room table and using big vocabulary words, I'm pretty sure our vocabulary would be up to that level. But it's all what you're exposed to. Let me take you down someplace where it's another culture and you may seem slow in that culture. It was all new to us and once we got a chance to learn, we all did."

One distraction all Texas Western students faced was its proximity to Juárez, a wide-open city located just over the border in Mexico. Ray understood the school's geography would be a selling point in a more international future, but in the 1960s most of the college's dealings with Mexico involved extricating students from trouble.

"There was no open drinking in El Paso back then," said Haskins of 1966. "There were bars in [nearby] New Mexico, but to get a drink in this town [El Paso] you had to go and sign a card [to join a private club or association] and pay $5 or something. If you were out at night and you wanted to get a drink, you had to go over there [to Juárez]. I was always afraid of a guy getting in trouble. Nowadays when a guy comes for a visit they can take him to a disco here in town. Back then there weren't any. It was Juárez or nothing."

Juárez's bars and brothels had been popular with Texas Western students and Fort Bliss soldiers for decades. When blacks began showing up in larger numbers at the college and the base, they found the Mexican city's unconditional freedom to be a godsend. Juárez had always had an attraction for El Paso's blacks. Back when many of the Texas city's movie theaters and restaurants were off-limits to them, black residents often traveled there to dine out or watch a movie.

■ ■ ■

Things started to hum shortly after Ray's arrival. Enrollment increased, new buildings rose, faculty were added, and, best of all in terms of national publicity, the school was chosen to train volunteers for President Kennedy's new Peace Corps. Idealistic young Americans traveled to El Paso in 1961 for a six-week course in road-building and surveying before embarking for Tanganyika (now Tanzania). The rugged terrain, said Corps officials, was similar to the African nation's.

The Southwest Conference was then an overwhelming athletic competitor for smaller Texas colleges. Schools like Texas, Texas A&M, and Texas Tech had million-dollar athletic budgets. But Texas Western, which spent about $400,000 on athletics in the mid-1960s, wisely had discerned the SWC's Achilles' heel—race.

SWC varsity sports would be segregated until 1966. And in the last few years before its integration, Haskins, track coach Wayne Vandenburg, and a series of Miner football coaches employed that trump card to great effect.

Not only would Haskins' black-dominated team win a national title in 1966 but black stars like legendary long-jumper Bob Beamon and future NFL linebacker Fred Carr would compete for the college in that era. "All of a sudden," said Cager, now a teacher in the El Paso school system, "we had these great black athletes all over the place. It gave us a real advantage until the other colleges' eyes got opened."

That led Ray and McCarty to seek bright young coaches who could relate to black athletes. In 1961 he hired Haskins and Bum

Phillips, an enthusiastic young football coach from Amarillo High School. But while Haskins could get by with just a few new recruits each year, Phillips needed far more. The school was so isolated that a lot of football prospects wouldn't consider it. Phillips needed to travel great distances, and that required a bigger recruiting budget. Frustrated, the future professional coach left after one season and a 4-5 record. The program stumbled along until, in 1965, Bobby Dobbs, a successful Canadian Football League coach, was hired.

The athletic department's financial situation began to improve in 1963. In September 1961, a month after Haskins' hiring, civic leaders promoted a bond issue to pay for a $30 million campus football stadium. Two years later the Sun Bowl was formally dedicated during halftime of a Texas Western–New Mexico State football game. The facility, cut into a rocky hillside on the northwest corner of the campus, immediately became the home and namesake for an annual postseason football game, which produced additional revenue for the school.

The football team, which had averaged 4,000–5,000 at old Kidd Field, was now attracting 20,000–30,000 to the Sun Bowl. Contributions to the athletic department, through the Miners' Scholarship and Development Fund, grew from $25,000 in 1960 to $130,000 in 1964.

Meanwhile, basketball was more than holding its own. After having played home games in tiny Halliday Hall, the Miners moved into 4,600-seat Memorial Gym in 1961. Very quickly, Haskins' teams got to the NCAA (1963) and NIT (1965) tournaments for the first time. Interest, among students and residents, increased.

Yet despite this expanding success, few people beyond the Southwest had ever heard of Texas Western when the Miners arrived in College Park, Maryland, for the Final Four.

"I think the funniest letter I got after the [1966] victory," said Ray, "was from an industrialist in Cincinnati, Ohio. He wrote on his firm's stationery, an engineering firm, 'I am pleased,' he said, 'with your victory in the NCAA finals. I have always been in favor of integration. I've always been opposed to segregation. And it satisfies me to see the national championship won by a small Negro college.'"

It was just one of the fallacies that arose about that championship game.

■ ■ ■

Andy Stoglin, now the basketball coach at Jackson State, graduated the year before Texas Western won its championship. Like most black graduates, he was ecstatic about his alma mater's accomplishment.

When it happened and the Miners' racial makeup was noted, Stoglin recalled an incident from his sophomore year, in the fall of 1962. Concerned that he was coming off the bench when he knew he was good enough to start, Stoglin had gone into Haskins' office to complain. Haskins stopped him, opened his desk drawer, and handed the player a fistful of letters.

"I started reading them," said Stoglin. "They were letters from whites saying, 'You're playing too many niggers' and that sort of thing."

"Read enough?" Haskins asked him.

Stoglin said he had.

"You know, Andy," said the coach, "one day I'm going to be able to play my best players."

6.

Basketball, Bluegrass, and Politics

"I would like to be assured that we are indeed recruiting Negro student athletes. I have already had several individuals make it a point to tell me that Coach Rupp will never have a Negro basketball player and the University is being hypocritical when it says that it is trying to recruit such men."
—March 29, 1966, memo from Robert L. Johnson, University
     of Kentucky athletic administrator,
     to athletic director Bernie Shively

The future blossomed on fallow land. The process that within a decade would transform Lexington, the University of Kentucky, and Rupp's image began in 1956 with the rumble of bulldozers across an old Newtown Pike farm. It was, Kentuckians liked to recall in the tumultuous years that followed, the exact moment one era yielded to another.

Sleepy Lexington, with 65,000 residents and no great ambitions, dissolved in the dust of those bulldozers. By 1966, the "self-satisfied little town" was a prosperous boomtown, the languid university an expanding research center, and Rupp a frowning symbol of a past the region was trying desperately to shed.

That farmland became the site of a huge IBM plant, the flourishing company's first facility outside New York. All of its electric typewriters—which were beginning to replace manual machines in offices around the globe—eventually would be manufactured in the Kentucky city. IBM awakened Lexington to the possibilities of progress. Soon after plans for the facility were announced, a bypass was constructed nearby to handle increased traffic and ease access for employees. Interviews began for thousands of jobs, with good salaries and benefits. New employees—educated, well paid, many of them from Northern cities—began relocating to Fayette County.

The company, said Clair F. Vough, the man who would become the plant's general manager, "had wanted a college town where people would want to live." That described Lexington in the 1950s. Home to the state's largest university, the city was also, in the words of one of its two daily newspapers, "an overgrown country town."

Named for the Revolutionary War battle that occurred six years before its 1782 incorporation, Lexington was one of the oldest cities west of the Allegheny Mountains. One of those rare communities not set on a body of water, it briefly served as the state's capital. Among its more prominent citizens were Henry Clay, Confederate general John Hunt Morgan, and a young Mary Todd.

By 1956 most of its residents—its white ones anyway—lived quietly in well-preserved homes on tree-shaded streets. Fraternal clubs, churches, and the university provided the social activity. Main Street, with its banks, shops, and movie theaters, was the community's hub. Churchgoing was nearly universal and routines inviolate. After Sunday services, people gathered at drugstores like Owen Williams', the ladies sipping soft drinks and whispering to each other while the men discussed the contents of the morning papers. Even television took hold more slowly in Lexington. On warm summer evenings, men and women still rocked and talked on their front porches, or drove out to Joyland for a ride on the amusement park's carousel.

"Oh, maybe on Saturday night you'd go to a show or a dance, but that was about it," Rupp would recall toward the end of his life. "There really wasn't much social life at all in those days."

There wasn't much modern industry either. Farming still dominated Lexington's business life, particularly the production of burley tobacco and the leggy thoroughbreds that ambled peaceably amid the Bluegrass hills. Those lush horse farms, neatly encased by white and black plank fences, were the community's pride, its commercial epicenter, and most popular tourist attraction. Set along Versailles Road and the Paris Pike on the outskirts of the city, they had changed very little in the last century.

Lexington's attitudes were almost as well preserved. Powerful class and race distinctions from the Old South endured. The region in the 1950s was, according to historian Ronald Oakley, "a land of Bible Belt religious fundamentalism, with a strong belief in an orderly and hierarchical society, with everything and everybody in its place."

Less than a century after slaves had been sold at the busy Cheapside auction, Lexington's blacks remained economically bound to wealthier whites. More than a third were employed in the finer homes, as nannies, cooks, gardeners, chauffeurs. Many lived in substandard housing, not terribly different from the ramshackle dwellings that Rupp on his first visit to the city had derided as "nigger shacks."

The horse farm owners were still Lexington's gentry. Merchants, professionals, and the staffs at UK and Transylvania College comprised its middle class. Those poorer whites not employed in agriculture labored for bad wages in aging tanneries, distilleries, and flour mills.

But such traditional jobs were vanishing as rapidly as iceboxes in the 1950s. Fayette County had 34,280 nonagricultural jobs in 1952, just 30,726 two years later. So when the burgeoning postwar economy began to redistribute industry to locations beyond America's largest cities, Lexington wanted desperately to attract some.

Civic leaders, whose relationship to Kentucky athletics often bedeviled Rupp—"the downtown faction," he called them—decided the past, as comfortable as it might have been, needed to be sacrificed. They formed the Lexington Industrial Foundation and went looking for companies that could offer stable, good-paying work. IBM, at the vanguard of contemporary technology, was the first to come.

"I think IBM opened the door and brought in people who had a different education, people who were from a different culture," said William D. Reed, a New Yorker who moved to Lexington with the company. "Lexington was a very delightful but typical Southern city."

"They brought a lot of upscale people," said banker Bob Showalter. "[People] who had different visions and different values and different mores."

The area's per capita income, $1,711 in 1956, jumped to $2,167 by 1960—an increase of 27 percent in a period when inflation was only 6 percent. More industry followed IBM: American Can Co., WABCO, Trane, FMC Corp, Square D. Co. The University of Kentucky's new medical school, approved by the legislature in 1954, was planning to open a major hospital center by 1960. Doctors, nurses, and professors were being interviewed and hired every day. That same year the university revealed plans for dental and nursing schools. Housing developments, apartments, and shopping centers soon would rise up along Tates Creek and Nicholasville Roads.

Lexington's new residents found much that pleased them. They liked the slower pace, the polite neighbors, the broader sense of community. Privately, their bosses appreciated the region's labor sensibilities—especially its anti-union sentiment. Accustomed to the

North's more subtle racism, however, transplanted Yankees were shocked by the grip of Jim Crow traditions.

Since stability was essential for good business, and since segregation threatened stability, segregation, this new elite decided, would have to go.

"When we first came to Lexington, I had never seen this before, but the old Good Samaritan Hospital had an obstetrics ward for black women in the basement and an obstetrics unit for white women upstairs," said Robert L. Johnson, a longtime administrator at UK who came from Boston in 1960 to help plan the school's medical center. "When we were building this new medical center, we made the decision that we were going to have an integrated facility. That was a given."

■ ■ ■

This was the changing city Dr. John Weiland Oswald discovered when in September of 1963 he became the University of Kentucky's sixth president.

Oswald's résumé read like John F. Kennedy's. At forty-seven, the educator was just a year older than the man who was then occupying the White House, and like the president he had played college football and served as a Navy PT officer during World War II.

A scientist by training—his Ph.D. was in plant pathology—Oswald was a meticulous, energetic Minnesotan who most recently had been a vice chancellor at the University of California at Berkeley. Graying at the temples but still trim, he had three children and an Alabama-born wife who was thrilled to be returning to the South.

Though Oswald had been a compromise choice of the Board of Trustees, he nonetheless had a mandate to raise the university's standards. UK wanted more students, better professors, and a bigger chunk of the millions in research grants that state and federal gov-

ernments were distributing to America's colleges in those flush years
before the costly escalation in Vietnam.

"Jack had come here as president to really make the University
of Kentucky," said Johnson. "Prior to his coming, in my judgment, it
was a regional, mediocre university. The medical center had proven
Kentucky could have a really first-rate institution. The Board of
Trustees, when President [Frank] Dickey was looking to leave,
wanted somebody who could move this whole university in the
same way as the medical center."

Kentucky always had measured its progress in education, race
relations, and other fields against the Deep South. "We're not Mississippi," newcomers heard repeatedly. The UK faculty could hold
its head high when the school was compared to LSU, Mississippi, or
Alabama. And its residents believed that Lexington, unlike Birmingham, Jackson, or even New Orleans, was a model of racial harmony.

"I don't think I saw a lot of overt racism in the sense that, 'This
is the way it ought to be. This is the way we're going to keep it,'"
said Johnson. "It was more the kind of cultural and institutional
racism that just never examined itself."

That kind of smugness was not unusual in the South. Even in
Bull Connor's Birmingham, business and civic leaders liked to brag
to outsiders about how happy and well-treated its "nigras" were. The
fact that many also assumed blacks shared that view was indicative
of the region's enormous understanding gap.

The races inhabited parallel universes. Until events forced
Southern whites to confront reality, blacks were confined to the
edges of their world. Their private lives—their churches, their music,
their interaction with each other—were insignificant, practically invisible, to white society.

"The tragic truth was that, as whites discovered a mythological
past for themselves . . . they practically lost all understanding of race
as a primary determinant in Southern culture and any real apprecia-
tion of the Negro. . . . the escape of black people from the white

mind was amazingly total," wrote Joel Williamson in *The Crucible of Race.* "Southern whites drifted into a racial dream world in which there really were no problems—that is if Yankees . . . and Communists would simply leave the blacks alone."

It was no different on some Southern campuses. Kentucky had been admitting blacks to its undergraduate schools for nine years when Oswald arrived and that, some presumed, ought to have ended the matter. The notion of actively soliciting qualified minorities, of increasing black enrollment to more than a tiny percentage of the student body, occurred to very few of these integrated schools.

"There was very little external pressure [to speed the integration of universities] in states like Kentucky and probably Tennessee because we were taking black students if they showed up," said Oswald. "'The schools are open to everyone. Let 'em come.' That would have been, I think, the kind of response I might have gotten from the faculty."

Oswald looked North. He saw Big Ten schools like Michigan and Illinois as the standard. Predictably, in making the necessary changes—destratifying the faculty, expanding curriculum, recruiting minorities, and closing University High, a UK-affiliated institution that was in effect a state-supported prep school for the city's elite—he irritated conservative Lexingtonians.

"There's no question his administration was a watershed, in that he helped bring the university into the modern era and provided leadership. But he didn't do it tactfully or amicably," said Thomas D. Clark, a UK professor and university historian. "He wasn't the best PR man there ever was."

Edward Breathitt, Kentucky's moderate Democratic governor, shared Oswald's vision and approved of his agenda, though he soon realized both could be political liabilities in the volatile '60s. "I had to put out a lot of fires on Oswald's behalf," said Breathitt. "Some I couldn't."

By 1963, fourteen years after Kentucky had become the first

major Southern university to integrate its student body, only a handful of its students were black. Rupp liked to boast that integration had occurred there without incident. It was another example of wishful thinking.

Eight years after *Plessy v. Ferguson,* the Kentucky legislature in 1904 passed the Day Act. Directed at Berea College's attempted integration, the law prohibited the teaching of whites and blacks in the same classroom. So when Charles L. Eubanks applied in 1941 to UK's civil engineering program—not offered at all-black Kentucky State in Frankfort—registrar Leo Chamberlain cited the law in refusing him. Eubanks took the college to court but, in 1945, his suit was dismissed.

In 1948, John Wesley Hatch applied to the law college. He was admitted instead to Kentucky State and, in what then passed for enlightened action, UK professors commuted to the state capital to teach him. That arrangement soon proved impractical and four Frankfort lawyers were hired to instruct Hatch, who withdrew after one semester.

Later that year Louisville teacher Lyman T. Johnson, who had a master's degree from the University of Michigan, applied to UK's graduate school. When he too was refused, he sued in federal court. This time the court ordered Kentucky to admit blacks to its graduate schools and its colleges of law, engineering, and pharmacy. UK president Herman Donovan asked the Board of Trustees to accept the decision without appeal and, after considerable debate, its members agreed by a 10–2 vote. In the summer of 1949, Johnson and twenty-nine other blacks registered.

(At least two crosses were burned after their admission, one on the front lawn of the administration building, the other at a university-owned farm. While both were attributed to the local Ku Klux Klan, such incidents were, of course, minor when compared to the Deep South's subsequent reaction to integration. Seven years later at Alabama, for instance, three days of rioting followed the attempted

The Baron of the Bluegrass, Adolph Rupp. *From top to bottom:* At home with his prized Hereford cattle in Lexington, Kentucky; in Huntington, West Virginia, in 1955, before the start of the National Biddy Tournament, smiling and holding the Confederate Flag; with longtime assistant Harry Lancaster, looking dismayed as he reads an AP report of the scandals that shocked his beloved program in 1951.

4

Two men who caused Adolph Rupp much consternation. *Top:* Kentucky president John Oswald who resolutely moved Rupp's program toward integration; *bottom:* Texas Western coach Don Haskins (with Miners stars Willie Cager, left, and David Lattin, right), who handed Rupp the toughest defeat of his legendary coaching career.

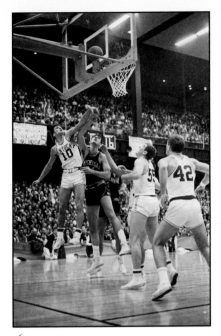

Louie Dampier (10) gets inside against Michigan's Jim Myers during the 1966 Mideast Regional Final—something the Wildcats weren't able to do against a stronger Texas Western team.

6

Rupp, in his typical brown suit, instructing Tommy Kron during a home game.

7

8

Rupp's Runts after defeating Michigan 84–77 in the regional final. *From left:* Larry Conley (with Rupp and trophy), Tommy Kron, Thad Jaracz, Pat Riley, and Louie Dampier.

The Miners were an unusually athletic team for 1966. Here, forward Willie Cager drops one in against Nevada on the way to a regular season Miners victory. Louis Baudoin (22) watches from the top of the key.

9

Three of the seven Miners who saw time in the championship game. *From left:* Nevil Shed, Bobby Joe Hill, and Harry Flournoy.

10

Speedy Texas Western guard Bobby Joe Hill drives past Tommy Kron early in the championship game.

11

12

Tommy Kron (30) and Orsten Artis (23) fight for a loose ball while Texas Western's Willie Cager and Kentucky's Pat Riley move in.

Kentucky's Cliff Berger (45) and Texas Western's Orsten Artis (23) and Willie Worsley (24) battle under the boards in the second half of the championship game.

13

Texas Western assistant coach Moe Iba (left) congratulates Miners head coach Don Haskins, as Nevil Shed (33) and the rest of the Miners celebrate their 72–65 NCAA championship victory.

14

15

Back home in Kentucky. *Above:* Coach Adolph Rupp (with Pat Riley, Tommy Kron, Larry Conley, Thad Jaracz, and Louie Dampier) addresses a crowd of fans at Blue Grass Field airport after the Texas Western loss; *below:* Louie Dampier signs an autograph inside Memorial Coliseum during a rally for the losing Kentucky team.

16

The 1966 Texas Western Miners, then and twenty years later. *Front row, left to right:* Bobby Joe Hill, Orsten Artis, Togo Railey, Willie Worsley, Fred Swacke (trainer, in the 1986 photo); *second row:* David Palacio, Dick Myers, Harry Flournoy, Louis Baudoin; *back row:* Nevil Shed, Jerry Armstrong, Willie Cager, David "Big Daddy" Lattin, Don Haskins.

admission of Autherine Lucy. The black student was expelled before enrolling. The reason? "Causing a disturbance.")

Segregation persisted in many Lexington institutions, but between 1949 and 1966, the city received some of its worst national publicity from racial incidents involving basketball.

In 1961, the NBA's Boston Celtics and St. Louis Hawks came to Memorial Coliseum for an exhibition featuring two great ex-Wildcats—the Hawks' Cliff Hagan and Boston's Frank Ramsey. The Celtics, with several black players, stayed at the Phoenix Hotel downtown. On the day of the game, Bill Russell and other black Celtics were refused service in the hotel's dining room. Those players immediately flew home. The game, much to the disappointment of the few black Lexingtonians who had managed to get tickets, was played without them.

Two years earlier Kentucky had met Temple, an integrated team from Philadelphia, at Memorial Coliseum. Courtside seats were valued possessions and before the game a young usher noticed that a pair of blacks were sitting there. Never having seen blacks in that area of the arena, he assumed they were interlopers and asked them to move. The men, principal Paul Guthrie of Lexington's Dunbar High and basketball coach S.T. Roach, displayed their tickets and the now-confused usher, a volunteer Boy Scout, summoned athletic director Bernie Shively. Shively told the men they'd have to change seats. Instead, they left the building, fearing a disturbance might jeopardize their publicly supported jobs.

When that incident was made public, Rupp invited Dunbar's team to practice at the Coliseum. "He did it out of the goodness of his heart," said Roach, whose teams went 512-142 from 1940 to 1965. "I'm sorry he didn't see fit to open the door to blacks. . . . With his stature he could have made all the difference in the world."

To his dying day, Rupp believed himself beloved in Lexington's black community. His son, Adolph Rupp, Jr., committed to removing the tarnish of racism from his father's reputation, recalled how the elder Rupp had helped a black high school player, Jim Tucker from nearby Paris, get a scholarship to Duquesne in 1950. He cited black referees his father had befriended, black coaches he had assisted, an occasion when the elder Rupp chastised a downtown restaurant for refusing to serve a visiting black player.

"He was an active Shriner all his life and every year he used to go into Prawltown (a poor black neighborhood) and hand out tickets to the Shrine Circus to the kids," said the younger Rupp. "Daddy was no racist."

Many blacks in the city, state, and nation, even twenty years after the coach's death, disagreed. They blamed Rupp for keeping Kentucky basketball all-white even after many Deep South teams had integrated. For them, his actions—and more significantly his inaction—painted an unmistakably dark picture of his racial attitudes.

"I went to coaches school every summer under Rupp," said Charles Livesay, a basketball coach at Douglass, another all-black Lexington high school. "It would slip out every now and then—he'd come up with 'nigger' talking to the rest of the coaches, talking about players."

For blacks like these, Rupp was, if not an outright racist, certainly a powerful symbol of racism. Even after he was long gone and Kentucky had won national titles with black-dominated teams, the wounds endured. When UK coach Rick Pitino lost a top recruit, Jason Osborne, in the early 1990s, it was because the player's parents refused to allow their son to play at the school where Rupp had coached.

"Most blacks in Kentucky hate this place," admitted William Parker, a black UK administrator, in 1988, "and you teach that to your kids."

■ ■ ■

Serious talk of integrating UK's athletic teams began about the same time IBM arrived. In the chaos that followed the Supreme Court's

Brown v. Board of Education decision, some Southern states transformed segregation's traditions into laws. One such measure in Louisiana, 1956's Legislative Act 579, banned all interracial athletic events in the state.

New Orleans then hosted the Sugar Bowl, a Christmas basketball tournament, and the participants for 1956 were scheduled to be Kentucky, Dayton, Notre Dame, and St. Louis. To protest the newly enacted state law, which the Supreme Court would declare unconstitutional in 1959, the three Catholic schools withdrew. This was an opportunity for Rupp, who always complained that he was powerless against segregation, to take a relatively painless stand against it by withdrawing his team too.

Assuming the tournament would be canceled, Kentucky governor Happy Chandler, a close friend of Rupp's, even made plans for a Blue Grass Classic in Louisville. It would have included Kentucky, Louisville, and two of the original Sugar Bowl participants, Dayton and St. Louis. Numerous alumni wrote to UK president Frank Dickey, pleading with him to withdraw the Wildcats from the Louisiana event. "Here is a situation where the University of Kentucky could courageously show that principle is more important to it than the 'sugar' in the Sugar Bowl," wrote Herschel Weil, a 1922 graduate.

But Dickey, as Rupp often did, pointed to contractual obligations. His response to Weil was a striking example of the region's prevailing logic, implying that an entire race of people was somehow less important than an agreement between a school and a basketball tournament:

"I agree with you that the problem of the religious and moral implications in this situation is a difficult one," he wrote. "However [I] feel that the moral values of integrity and honesty are also involved . . . a moral obligation and a commitment to abide by the contract."

Rupp rounded up segregated Alabama, Houston, and Virginia

Tech as substitutes and the Sugar Bowl went on. Not surprisingly, Kentucky won.

■ ■ ■

Rupp won his first of four national championships with the Fab Five in 1948. That same year he was selected to coach the Olympic team, which was made up of his players and several from the Phillips Oilers, the nation's best amateur squad. Among the Oilers was a black, Don Barksdale, a former college star at UCLA.

To raise money for the team's trip to the London Games, Kentucky played the Oilers in an outdoor exhibition game that drew 14,000 fans to Stoll Field, the university's football stadium. During a timeout, Barksdale drank from a water bottle and passed it to a white teammate, Shorty Carpenter. The white crowd in the bleachers—blacks were confined to standing room in the end zones—went silent. "You would have thought they all lost their voices," Barksdale, who died in 1990, recalled. "It got dead quiet. The rumbling that was going through that stadium was unbelievable. It was the scariest thing I ever got into. But it was all over once he took that drink. Thank God, Shorty Carpenter drank from that bottle."

Rupp played Barksdale regularly during the Olympic team's series of exhibitions and in London. If there were ever any problems between the ex-UCLA player and the coach, who had never had a black on his bench up to that point in his long collegiate career, neither man ever mentioned them and no one else noticed.

St. John's Solly Walker in 1951 became the first black to play against Kentucky at Memorial Coliseum. That game passed peaceably, some say because Rupp had phoned the local newspapers and urged them to appeal for calm. However, an Associated Press report later that year claimed Rupp also had contacted Frank McGuire, the St. John's coach, suggesting that he keep Walker home. If true, it wouldn't have been the only instance in that period when Rupp told an opposing coach he'd prefer not to play against blacks at home.

"I remember walking through the arena in Lexington with Adolph Rupp when we went there to play Kentucky," DePaul coach Ray Meyer wrote in his autobiography. "He put his arm around me and said, 'See Ray, there are no blacks in here. If you bring black players we can't play anymore.'"

One of the oddest incidents concerning Rupp and integration occurred early in 1961 when he told the *Atlanta Journal* that the two best black high school players in Kentucky would be joining his team the following year. The stunning comment shook the segregated SEC. Rupp, who once claimed he'd "say anything for a column," at first denied making it, then said he merely had been testing the waters. Shively was forced to issue a statement assuring his fellow conference ADs that Kentucky's policy of segregated athletics had not changed.

No documentary evidence ever has surfaced about an SEC agreement on segregation. Some, like Harry Lancaster, believed one never existed, though given the racism then extant in some SEC states, that seems unlikely. Clearly, there was at least a tacit accord among the schools. Rupp always alluded to one. "Until four or five years ago, the SEC had a rule prohibiting black players," Rupp said in 1970 after he finally recruited his only one.

Throughout the 1960s, questions about Kentucky's SEC membership persisted. More liberal alumni frequently encouraged the university to withdraw and form an integrated border states conference with, among other schools, Tulane, Vanderbilt, Tennessee, Georgia, and Florida. But the only change in conference membership occurred when Georgia Tech (in 1964) and Tulane (in 1966), citing ambitions to evolve into national universities, withdrew.

There is evidence that Oswald contemplated the same thing. In a 1964 letter to Bernie Moore, Kentucky's president seemed to be provoking the aging SEC commissioner. Kentucky's teams, he said, would be integrated in "the very near future." He also asked Moore to arrange a schedule that would allow his football team's "four basic conference games" to come against non–Deep South schools. Shively, however, counseled patience. He assured Oswald that if Kentucky just took its time, all its teams would be integrated by 1970. Besides, "if we eliminate Mississippi on our schedule, we will eliminate the best money game we have."

Kentucky remained firmly in the SEC. And seven years later still no black had played varsity basketball for the Wildcats.

Until Dickey was replaced by Oswald in 1963, graduates and Kentucky citizens petitioned him often about the subject. In responding to integration's supporters, the president typically praised the concept but politely explained why it was impractical. To those favoring the status quo, however, his replies suggested a more insidious attitude.

"There is a great difference between my saying that the situation is inevitable and that of openly pursuing or advocating such a movement," wrote Dickey to a Mississippian in 1962. "The former is the position which I have taken."

As the civil rights movement expanded, the topic continued to surface on an ever wider front in Lexington—in faculty petitions, at Kentucky Athletic Association meetings, and in the editorials of the city's two dailies, the *Herald* and the *Leader.* The surprisingly feisty student newspaper, the *Kentucky Kernel,* also pleaded regularly with school officials to pull out of the SEC, since that membership, supposedly, was all that was keeping UK's teams segregated.

When Shively told a reporter the university "would lose too much prestige if it withdrew," the *Kernel* disputed his reasoning in a March 24, 1963, editorial: "Across the nation, we believe, [its prestige] would rise almost immeasurably. . . . When a moral issue like this is at hand, shouldn't we take the step?"

Even Rupp, whose comments on the topic during this period frequently appeared contradictory, admitted Kentucky would survive. "In basketball," he said in January 1963, "the University of Kentucky would certainly remain as great whether in or out of the SEC."

Finally, the athletic association on May 29, 1963, announced that "immediately all of its intercollegiate athletic teams will be open to any student regardless of race." But there was an enormous caveat. It would do so only within the context of its membership in the SEC. In other words, Kentucky wasn't going to be a lone pioneer. Administrators had to have known the conference wasn't anywhere near opening its doors.

When more than two years passed without any change, black community groups began politely asking why. They now had an ally in Oswald, who, in addition to reassuring them, began taking an active part in some of their organizations. He raised funds for the Lexington-Fayette County Urban League, and for the first time invited local black leaders to university events, keeping them apprised of integration's progress.

"One of the things I did arrange was to bring the black community leaders that we could best identify—that's how little we knew of the black community—to the university," said Johnson. "We had a dinner and talked to them about the fact that this was a whole new ball game, that we wanted their help, that we weren't just talking. That's one of those evenings that stands out in my memory because one of our guests got up afterward and said, 'Some years ago I had a phone call from a Mr. Shively at the University of Kentucky and he wanted to know if we would be able to find a room for [black basketball player Don] Barksdale. Yes, we found him a room. But you know, I never had met Mr. Shively until this evening.' I don't think Bernie understood what this man was saying."

On December 14, 1965, the day Branch Rickey was buried in Portsmouth, Ohio, Governor Breathitt vowed an "immediate all-out effort [to integrate UK athletics] . . . the use of Negro athletes is seventeen years overdue in my book."

■ ■ ■

Since 1945 UK sports had been controlled by the Kentucky Athletic Association. Then president Herman Donovan had created the autonomous organization as a way to make athletics "the vanguard for building a great state university." He realized that successful football and basketball teams could unify a state like almost nothing else. Without them, a factionalized legislature could never be counted on for the kind of increased funding he envisioned would be required.

Sometime in 1946, Donovan contacted thirty-six Lexington businessmen and civic leaders who shared his philosophy. He raised $113,000, endowed the association, and soon after hired a young Paul "Bear" Bryant as Kentucky's football coach. "[This association] separates athletics from the university," Donovan explained.

Oswald viewed the group differently. To him, despite the presence of faculty and administrators on its board, it was potentially a maverick boosters club at a school with a history of athletic abuses. Following the infamous point-shaving scandal of 1951, a New York judge's report condemned the association's zeal, while also criticizing Rupp, boosters, the university, and its overemphasis on sports.

The new president moved immediately to return control of the association to the administration. He created a position with that power, vice president for student affairs, and gave the job to Robert Johnson.

"Athletics had always had this special relationship with its own athletic board," said Johnson. "It reported to the president but it didn't have any integrated relationship with the rest of the university. He said, 'I want to bring this back into the university.' That also meant I became the vice chairman for the athletics board. I became *the* functioning administrative person in the university that dealt with athletics."

That meant dealing with Rupp. For a native of upstate New York with no background in sports, it was a daunting mandate.

"Growing up male in this country I knew all about Adolph Rupp," said Johnson. "Then all of a sudden I was told I was going to be Adolph's boss. As somebody said to me, 'Adolph doesn't have a boss.'"

(Oswald heard the same thing when, on a flight to Washington, he found himself sitting with the son of former Supreme Court Chief Justice Fred Vinson. The younger Vinson was working for the Justice Department and Oswald inquired about the strained relationship between Attorney General Robert Kennedy and autocratic FBI director J. Edgar Hoover. "The best way I can explain it," said Vinson, "is that it's similar to the relationship between Adolph Rupp and the president of the university.")

Johnson's appointment annoyed Rupp ("He knew absolutely nothing about athletics," said the coach) and initiated a battle over integration between Oswald and Rupp that lasted, without a truce, until the day in 1968 when the controversial president departed Lexington.

"I'm not sure that the president of the university could ever have told Adolph Rupp what to do," said Perry Wallace, a black high school All-America from Tennessee who was recruited unsuccessfully in 1966 by Kentucky (but not by Rupp). "He was the Baron, a figure of power and legend."

These were two strong-willed men, arrogant, demanding, unyielding. Rupp, the nation's best-known basketball coach, was used to university presidents who bowed to his reputation. Oswald, an old Navy captain, was used to his orders being obeyed. "Dr. John W. Oswald . . . is a rare creature at the University of Kentucky," noted a

Louisville Times editorial. "He is not afraid of Rupp." The feeling was mutual.

They were destined to clash over something. The times demanded it be integration.

"Jack had a vision of bringing the University of Kentucky prominently into the world, in a scholarly sense but also in a contemporary sense," said Johnson. "One of the outstanding issues of the day, of course, was what the hell was going on in civil rights and integration and where we stood. He happened to have a group of people around him who were very much committed to this issue. He said we should integrate, the time has come, it's past time. We need to integrate the Southeastern Conference.

"He said, 'I know in my conversations that Florida will go along with this because they do not have the Old South patterns.' He said, 'Tennessee and Vanderbilt have indicated they'd really kind of go along with it. But Kentucky is the northernmost school. We ought to take the lead.' So we said, 'All right, we're going to do it.' And we went after it. . . . It was an issue that we were not going to let go of."

Neither, at the other end of the rope, was Rupp. And it was more than his stubbornness on the topic that infuriated Oswald in their long tug-of-war. Rupp, the president believed, placed his own interest before the university's. He frequently criticized the faculty (calling them overpaid at one meeting Oswald attended) and, to the president at least, appeared unconcerned about academics even though he had earned a master's degree in education from Columbia.

"I doubt if he knew UK had a library," said Oswald, "or if he did, where it was. . . . I just feel that [Rupp] was the biggest egotist that I've ever known. He is the only person, in my experience, who wanted to have a bigger office so that he'd have more wall space upon which to hang the plaques honoring himself. And I think I made Adolph angry when I asked him if he'd ever been to an art museum. And he said, 'What do you mean?' And I responded, 'In an art museum they have dividers that are on wheels and you can hang pictures on both sides. And you can walk around it and see the pictures on the other side. In your office you could have three of those dividers and you could triple the plaques you've got in here.' Oh, the less we saw of each other, the better we liked each other."

Oswald was just as unwelcome in Rupp's comfortable world. The coach, after all, had made Kentucky the nation's premier basketball program without university interference. His teams always made money even when the usually mediocre football team was draining cash. So why this sudden need for change? Why this push to find black players? It would all happen in due time. Who did this Northern liberal think he was?

"Locally here his image was negative," Rupp said in 1971, assessing Oswald (who had already left UK by then). "On the campus it was split. There were some that felt he was doing a great job from an academic standpoint. There were others, and a great majority of them, that absolutely despised him. I don't think that he particularly liked unusually successful people around him. I think what he wanted primarily was 'yes' men. I think he wanted to run the show. . . . He didn't want anyone on the campus that had a reputation that attracted the limelight away from him."

Whenever Oswald or Johnson confronted him, Rupp had his pat excuses ready: He couldn't take a black player to Mississippi. He couldn't find an academically qualified black (even though a Kentucky high school diploma was typically good enough for admission then). Or, if he did, none were good enough to play for Kentucky.

"Rupp wanted a superstar who would sort of bow down and thank him for bringing him to Kentucky," said Elizabeth Browne, Oswald's daughter. "And my father realized that just wasn't going to happen."

Kentucky had played integrated opponents for decades and whenever his racial attitudes were questioned, Rupp pointed that out, as well as the fact his first high school team at Freeport, Illinois, in 1927 included one black player.

"He was a very capable athlete," Rupp said of William G. Mosely. "All I ever thought we needed was someone who could participate and do it the way that would meet with the approval of everybody. This boy could do it, so naturally we played him.

"The university teams played against many Negroes," Rupp continued to defend himself. "Whenever we made trips to the North, we always encountered Negroes on those teams. Our boys understood that perfectly. But they did not play in the conference and I've had people tell me, 'You're a big man. I'm surprised at you. I'm disappointed in you. Why didn't you drop out of the conference?' Well now, Adolph Rupp does not drop out of a conference. Let's make that plain here so any dummy can understand. I don't determine the policies of the University of Kentucky and I never did."

■ ■ ■

The initial meeting between Oswald and Rupp took place in the president's office in the fall of 1963. For the new president, it was a distasteful and shocking introduction to a legend.

"Rupp, in his very first discussion with me, sounded like a bigot," said Oswald. "I guess primarily it was his language and expressions. He tended to refer to blacks in terms which are now considered derogatory.

"One of the first things I told Rupp was that I had heard so much about his success in basketball. But that it seemed to me that one of the things facing us as a border state public institution at that time was clearly the recruitment of some black athletes. And I added that in the area of basketball, they had already demonstrated that they're right at the top."

Following that meeting, Rupp, according to Lancaster, was angry and concerned about Oswald's intentions. "Harry," he told his longtime assistant, "that son of a bitch is ordering me to get some niggers in here. What am I going to do?"

It was a question Oswald probably asked himself. The president subsequently tried sweet talk, stern demands, memos, and face-to-face meetings. He used Johnson and Shively to pressure him. He informed Rupp that his reluctance to integrate might cost the university millions of dollars in funds. He hired Joe B. Hall, who had experience coaching blacks at Regis College and Central Missouri State, as a basketball assistant, specifically to help recruit black players. He sent Johnson and Shively on recruiting trips, and once even traveled to Louisville himself to try to convince high school star Wes Unseld to attend.

And still Rupp's teams remained all-white.

"Every other day it seemed Mr. Shively would come into my office and say 'Coach, I got a call from the president and he wants to know how you're getting along with these colored boys.' Well, maybe I hadn't even been out of town," said Rupp. "You just can't go out and find someone. If you could do that, I'd go out and get a 7-foot center every afternoon."

Part of the problem was that Shively, who had been on the same football staff Rupp joined when he arrived in Lexington in 1930, shared many of the coach's sensibilities.

"Bernie was a very lovely gentlemen and I never had any question about his integrity," said Johnson. "On the other hand, on the matter of integration, Bernie was, 'Well, we'll do it.' There wasn't any of the passion that the rest of us felt. . . . He didn't seem to grasp what was wrong. It had just been culturally built into the society and the institution."

But all around the university, more visible barriers were tumbling. The Civil Rights Act had been passed in 1964 and the Voting Rights act a year later. Like many Southerners, old and young, Rupp found something lamentable in the passing of an era, the end of a familiar order. For them, this new age was a depressing one. "There can be no doubt that the Southern white psyche in 1965 had reached a new low," wrote historian Joel Williamson.

Oswald was embarrassed by Rupp's inaction, so he could hardly relent, even after football coach Charlie Bradshaw signed two black high school football seniors, Nat Northington and Greg Page, late in 1965. Northington's signing came first and, indicative of the political capital the two men had expended on the issue, both Oswald and Governor Breathitt showed up for photographs at the player's Louisville home.

Though they were the first black athletes granted scholarships in the SEC, neither would play a varsity game at UK. Northington quit the team after his first year, and Page died tragically after suffering a paralyzing neck injury in practice before his freshman season.

The implications of Page's death could have been enormous. Kentucky finally had convinced two black athletes to attend, and one had died during practice drills. Oswald, who had played college football himself at DePauw, feared Page's injury might have occurred in some sort of punishment drill. An investigation promptly began and, much to the university's relief, concluded the cause of death had been a freak accident.

"It [Page's death] could have been terribly explosive," said Oswald. "And I think two years later, it could have been *the* issue on campus, you know, in a whole different environment."

Johnson continued to call on Rupp regularly, pushing and prodding the coach. On March 29, 1966, just ten days after Kentucky's loss to Texas Western, the administrator sent Shively a fairly stern memo. The heat was intensifying. Black students were publicly questioning the school's commitment to athletic integration. Rupp had assured Oswald he was recruiting two blacks, including Wallace, yet they were not among the recruits attending the postseason basketball banquet on March 24.

"It may very well be that these young men were unable to attend. . . . but I would like to be assured that we are indeed recruiting Negro student athletes," wrote an obviously exasperated Johnson in the memo. "I have already had several individuals make it a point to tell me that Coach Rupp will never have a Negro basketball player and the University is being hypocritical when it says that it is trying to recruit such men."

Rupp, through Shively, again told Johnson he had yet to find the right youngster.

"He would keep saying, 'The last thing we want to do is sign somebody who never gets off the bench. Then we'd be accused of tokenism,'" said Johnson. "Well, there was something to that. But there was also a double standard in that they'd picked a lot of white kids who were probably going to sit on the bench too."

Within a few weeks, Johnson reluctantly yielded again to Rupp and reality. "I don't see that we are in any position to push the basketball coaching staff in the recruitment of Negroes beyond what already has been done," he informed Oswald in an April memo.

But during this period, Kentucky actually did attempt to recruit several blacks, even though Rupp was normally a reluctant participant. For Rupp, a prodigious beef-eater, this was as if some young physician had demanded he become a vegetarian. There might be good reasons, he knew, but he still found the process distasteful. Consequently, his efforts, say the players themselves, were half-hearted and unconvincing.

"Harry Lancaster and Joe Hall came and both were very nice, but I was always concerned that Rupp never came," said Wallace, who, a month after the Texas Western win, signed with Vanderbilt. "It left you with concerns about the attitudes of the head man. Later when I had dealings with Rupp he was always very polite and nice to me. But of course I was a 'good boy.' I spoke well and was polite and always said 'Yes, sir. No, sir.'"

Butch Beard, an All-State player from Hardinsburg (Kentucky) High School in 1965, signed with already-integrated Louisville instead of Kentucky. Pat Riley, who one day would coach against him in the NBA, had escorted Beard around campus. Rupp had visited his home, but the coach spent much of his time there telling Beard's mother how much the rest of the SEC hated him. Neither Beard nor his mother were sold. "We decided that Rupp was under pressure to recruit a black player, but he really didn't want one," said Beard.

If Rupp ever did truly want a black player, it was Wes Unseld, who led Louisville's Seneca High to consecutive state titles in his junior and senior seasons of 1963 and 1964.

"Not only was Unseld the best high-school player in the nation, but he was also more brown than black—Rupp couldn't have asked for a better package," wrote Russell Rice in his biography of the coach.

When Rupp visited Unseld, the player introduced himself and his family and then very quickly excused himself. The coach felt snubbed, but Unseld insisted he had had a previous engagement.

"Somebody said I didn't have the courtesy to stay at the meeting," said Unseld, "but I was speaking that night at the La Grange Reformatory. . . . There was always some excuse [with Rupp]. Players didn't have the grades . . . the skills."

Unseld too eventually signed with Louisville and went on to become an All-America and a perennial NBA All-Star. Rupp, never able to accept any kind of defeat graciously, threatened to tell the story of how Louisville really convinced Unseld to attend, implying his in-state rival had cheated.

Yet who could blame Unseld for shying away from Kentucky? He received several death threats when word of his recruitment there leaked out. And even one of the more civil letters, signed by fifteen Lexington residents, urged him to play basketball out of state.

"There was a lot of pressure brought to bear from the black community to do it," said Unseld. "There was a lot of pressure brought from a lot of people that I'd better not do it."

When Rupp failed, Oswald, who thought the intelligent Louisville high-schooler was the perfect barrier-breaker, tried himself. Rupp apparently refused to join him so Oswald, accompanied by Lancaster, made an unprecedented visit to Unseld's home.

"The mother and father were very gracious to me and he was too," recalled Oswald. "He said, 'Thank you for coming but I've already decided to stay in Louisville.' He didn't say he wouldn't go to Kentucky. He had an opportunity to say some nasty things about Rupp or Kentucky, but he did not say them. I was halfway expecting him to say, 'I wouldn't play under Rupp.'"

Unseld's decision frustrated Oswald, who never again imposed himself so intimately in recruiting efforts.

"Dad felt Rupp had sort of undermined his efforts with Unseld," said Oswald's son, John. "I mean here was Dad in his [Unseld's] living room and Rupp wasn't with him. It was almost as if Rupp were sending a message by his absence. He [Oswald] had put his prestige and commitment on the line and Rupp sent an assistant."

(Two decades later, Unseld's niece enrolled at UK. "I thought, 'How could you?'" said Unseld, by then the coach of the NBA's Washington Bullets. "But I realized that had nothing to do with her. She wasn't even born.")

A wealth of black basketball talent was sitting right under Rupp's sizable nose. Lexington's all-black Dunbar High was a state powerhouse. Since its 1957 inclusion in the previously segregated Kentucky High School Athletic Association, Dunbar had, by 1965, compiled a 277-50 record. It's likely, though, that Rupp never gave much thought to Dunbar's outstanding record. Black high school basketball in the state prior to 1957 was like Negro League baseball had been in its heyday, obscure to the wider public. Newspapers for the most part ignored it and almost anything else concerning Lexington's black community, except crime.

"Blacks decided they were going to picket the Kentucky basketball games [in 1967], purely to bring attention to the fact that this was an all-white team," said Johnson. "I stood out there [at Memorial Coliseum] watching this. The photographer from the *Leader* was there and I asked him why he wasn't taking their photographs. He said, 'Why? They would never be published.'"

And in Kentucky's athletic offices, until Oswald's arrival, the subject of black basketball players rarely arose. Oswald instigated the 1965 hiring of Hall as a second basketball assistant, hoping the young coach could more easily attract minorities to Kentucky.

"The reason we got Joe Hall was we knew about Hall's experience and ability to recruit black athletes," said Johnson. "We were talking about going to recruit young black athletes whom Illinois and Ohio State and Indiana had been picking off for years. We were asking them to become the first people to integrate an all-white conference. Needless to say that was going to take an unusual youth and a great deal of personal involvement on the part of the people who were doing the recruiting.

"Let me assure you that even if you were white and 7 feet, 8 inches tall, and you came in to see Mr. Rupp, he would just sit there and look at you. You wouldn't get any feeling that, 'Boy, you're just terribly important to us.' And we were at a time when these young black athletes needed to be told, 'We want you more than anything else. Here's a sense of the kind of life you'll have on campus.' He just didn't have that."

By then, UK had its president, a vice president, two assistants, and, to some extent, the governor of the state, trying to recruit a black player, while the head coach followed his own separate agenda. Johnson recalled a 1966 recruiting trip that left him questioning these unusual circumstances.

"We were in Athens, Georgia, and Russell Rice asked me if I'd help recruit a young black athlete," said Johnson. "We had to charter a little plane to fly to Savannah and there I was sitting next to the pi-

lot with one propeller between me and the ground. I thought to myself, 'What the hell am I doing recruiting athletes?' That gives you
the idea of the commitment we had, even though we recognized that
the coaching staff was not going to show them the same kind of ex-
uberance and drive."

When the one black player successfully recruited by Rupp in his
forty-three years at the school signed a letter-of-intent as a high
school senior in 1969, a sportswriter who was a witness to the signing was struck by how awkwardly the scene played out.

"I was in Tom Payne's home on West Broadway [in Louisville]
as a guest of the Payne family when Rupp showed up," wrote Earl
Cox of the *Louisville Courier-Journal.* "Rupp simply wasn't at ease.
I think that made for an uncomfortable feeling for everyone present."

■ ■ ■

Oswald grew increasingly concerned about federal funding. The
American Civil Liberties Union—which filed a discrimination com-
plaint against the SEC in 1966—and the U.S. Office of Education
kept prodding Southern schools to reexamine segregation in their
athletic programs. The Office of Education distributed $1 billion an-
nually to universities that complied with Title VI of the Civil Rights
Act. But up to that point, only one college, Anderson in South Carolina, had lost funds for noncompliance.

At about that time, the president summoned Rupp for another
face-to-face meeting on the subject. Now Oswald was visibly angry
and the coach reacted in kind.

"We went up there and we really had it," said Rupp. "Mr.
Shively started laughing and said, 'I kind of enjoy this. I like to be in
a conference where two strongheaded fellows get together like you
two fellows do.' The president didn't like it too well. He said, 'Well,
I'm going to tell you what I'm going to do. I'm going to demand

that you get some colored boys. You're . . . probably jeopardizing us from getting all this federal help, which amounts to $11 million.' And he said, 'If we don't get this through, it's because basketball is the last segregated department that we have here in this university.'

"I said, 'Well, Doctor . . . suppose you help me go and recruit them.' It's just that simple. I made an effort. I said, 'I brought you the list that told you the times that we made an effort to go get these boys and we haven't been able to get 'em.'"

The university itself was split on the subject of Rupp. And as the turbulent '60s moved on, the division widened. Some worshipped him and welcomed the fame he had singlehandedly brought the college. They tended to see Rupp as others in the 1960s saw FBI director J. Edgar Hoover, a straight-arrow defender of an America under siege. To others, particularly younger faculty members, he was an unpleasant dinosaur.

"I think the feeling among a lot of people at the university was that Adolph was a racist who was never going to bring blacks onto the team. That's just how they felt about him," said Johnson. "My view of that is I do not subscribe to the group that thinks that Adolph was a racist. I believe that for two reasons. One, he wanted to win too much. And the other reason is Adolph had reached that point where he didn't recruit much of *anyone.* He was so used to potential All-Americas coming to him that he just didn't get off his duff to recruit."

According to Oswald, Rupp would have alienated himself from most of the faculty even if his team had been filled with black players.

"They loved his basketball teams, but there was about as much anti-feeling toward Rupp as there is pro-feeling toward Joe Paterno at Penn State," said Oswald, who went on to serve as Penn State's president from 1970 to 1983. "I mean they knew Rupp didn't tune into the academic area. . . . I don't really feel that he cared much at all, except possibly nostalgically and politically, about the University of Kentucky. He certainly didn't care about the quality of its faculty, the stature of its library, what was going on in research or any of that."

The *Kernel* reflected this on-campus sentiment against Rupp. In a 1967 editorial entitled "The Negro Dilemma," it questioned the coach's commitment to integration. "In regard to head basketball coach Adolph Rupp's perennial claims of unbiased recruitment attempts," it read, "we can only say that we will believe it when we see the evidence."

Oswald also had plenty of enemies in Lexington. As the 1960s ferment intensified, many, on campus and off, viewed this newcomer from Berkeley as a radical carpetbagger, someone trying to transform UK into the "University of California at Lexington."

"The feeling we got from people there was that my father was this Northern liberal come to integrate the university," said the educator's daughter Elizabeth, who went to high school in Lexington during her father's tenure. "A lot of people resented that. I remember in 1964, Martin Luther King was making marches to state capitals throughout the South and he came to Frankfort. I went and I remember when I got back to Lexington there was this really serious reaction. It was like, 'How could you do that? Are you a nigger lover?'"

Oswald had experienced the birth of the '60s protests at Berkeley. Arriving at Kentucky in 1963, a comatose campus by comparison, he determined he had at least a few years' grace period before the increasingly strident student movement reached Lexington. When it did, many of the conservative city's residents were appalled. They blamed the university president. An anti-Oswald faction developed on the Board of Trustees and bided its time. When the radical Students for a Democratic Society planned to conduct its annual meeting on UK's campus in 1968, his opponents seized the issue.

"We were asked [by community leaders] what we were going to

do," said Johnson. "And we said, 'Nothing. As long as they follow the rules.' There probably were more undercover law enforcement people at that conference than there were delegates. There wasn't anybody arrested by campus police, but the literature was obscene, in terrible taste. . . . There was one group from New York whose official name was the 'Up Against the Wall Motherfucker Chapter.' Every time they'd go to the mike they'd identify themselves that way. You can imagine how that went over in Lexington."

A Fayette County jury, with a fundamentalist Christian minister for a foreman, was convened to investigate the origins of the literature and the conduct of the SDS convention in general. Frustrated that it could uncover no criminal activity, the panel nonetheless issued a report highly critical of the university's administration.

That same year Breathitt was defeated in the governor's race by conservative Republican Louie B. Nunn. Nunn returned Chandler, the ex-governor and former baseball commissioner, to the university's Board of Trustees as chairman.

"Nunn was going to clean up the problems at UK," said the president's son, John. "The handwriting was on the wall for my dad."

But because Chandler, the state's dominant political force, had been commissioner when baseball was integrated twenty-one years earlier, he still had an excellent civil rights reputation. So while he opposed Oswald from the start, he never was able to speak out against him on that subject. "He didn't criticize any steps that I made in this direction," said Oswald, "which in a sense is a compliment because he was critical of most everything I did."

Shortly after Chandler's appointment, Oswald resigned. He had transformed a "country club for undergraduates" into a modern research university. But he never did budge Rupp.

When asked a few years later to summarize Oswald's tenure, Rupp came up with an obituary that in some ways could have served as his own.

"John Oswald," said Rupp. "Loved by some, admired by many, and just simply ignored and almost hated by a vast majority of people here in the commonwealth."

Near the end of his life, Oswald returned to Lexington to receive an honorary degree from the university. Rupp was long dead, Kentucky's basketball team was overwhelmingly black, and attitudes had changed.

"We were with him," said his daughter, Elizabeth, "and I'll never forget this. The faculty rose when he was introduced and gave him this great ovation. It was as if they recognized all his efforts and were saying that they had been justified."

7.

From Brooklyn or Yahoo, Texas

"We were like the strings of a guitar. Each one was different, but we sounded pretty good together."
—Willie Worsley

A fat October moon hung over Texas Western's deserted campus like a watchful eye. The commuters had gone home and the streets and walkways in the school's hilly northwest corner were empty. Behind a stone dormitory, the sporadic clamor of a basketball game echoed off its walls. Players laughed, whooped, and occasionally hit each other in mock anger. They threw passes behind their backs and dunked the ball. The quick little guards dribbled in and out of their legs.

El Paso was an isolated city, and on nights like this, when the winds moved through the canyons like whispering phantoms, the campus could seem as desolate as the nearby desert. Eighty percent of the college's students were commuters. Companionship, if those who lived on campus sought any, came from each other. These pickup basketball games helped.

The players that night were all members of Texas Western's basketball team. Practice for the 1965–66 season had begun, so the last place anyone would have expected to find them at 9:00 P.M. was on a basketball court. After all, only a few hours earlier they had concluded another grueling workout in a stifling gymnasium.

"We worked so stinking hard at practices," said Baudoin, a senior on that team. "But these games were completely different experiences. They were pickup and they were fun."

Someone, usually Baudoin or Nevil Shed, the team's most outgoing players, would grab a ball and start knocking on teammates' doors. They'd gather in a hallway, the coolest spots in Burges Hall, and walk to an illuminated half-court behind the girls' dormitory.

These nighttime sessions helped bond a group that appeared to have little in common. White, Hispanic, and mostly black, they came from big Eastern cities, Midwest farming communities, dusty Southwest towns.

"We had kids come from little tiny towns in the Texas panhandle, and then we'd get kids from great big cities," said Baudoin, from Albuquerque. "It was remarkable how similar those kids were brought up. We found it really wasn't that different to come from Brooklyn or Yahoo, Texas. We were like a bunch of brothers. We fought like brothers and we got along like brothers."

And they found freedom in those nights. The sun would set, the air would cool, and no one would be around to hound them. It was a break from days consumed by practice. In the gym at 2:00 P.M. for taping, they sometimes would not get back to the dorm until 6:30 or 7:00, often after the cafeteria had closed. They practiced seven days a week—with only Christmas and Easter off.

Classes had to be crammed into the mornings and homework was always a burden. Texas Western wasn't the Ivy League, but Haskins, a lackadaisical student himself at Oklahoma A&M, insisted his players attend classes and keep up their grades. "He wasn't going to put up with kids not going to school," said Moe Iba.

Once back at the dormitory, the players usually kept to themselves. They'd order chicken or pizza, play cards or basketball, sip cheap wine and talk. Sometimes they'd walk to the Student Union Building to shoot pool or get one of the famous foot-long chili dogs. Those hot dogs were lifesavers for the city kids. The area's Mexican cuisine—even dormitory cafeterias served tacos, tamales, and enchiladas—was as foreign as Haskins' drawl. "It took a long time before I could consume that stuff," said Shed, a New Yorker.

The relentless routine left all of them eager for Saturday nights. That's when they'd walk across the Rio Grande to Juárez. There they found bars, brothels, and hustlers.

"We used to laugh about it being a twenty-minute walk to Juárez and a three-hour walk back," said Baudoin. "If we partied, we partied hard and we paid for it. The hardest practices of the week were Sundays. They were endless because [Haskins] knew that we had been somewhere the night before."

Haskins always seemed to know. One day he found out that Bobby Joe Hill had been drinking in Juárez the night before. "He ran him until his lips turned purple," said teammate Orsten Artis.

The mix of young men and the anything-goes, alcohol-laden atmosphere of the Mexican border city was frequently volatile. Several of them had their eyes opened to tequila and prostitutes there. They joked that trainer Ross Moore used to dispense shots of penicillin as readily as aspirin.

With all that freedom combining with testosterone, brawls were inevitable. The athletes and the rest of Texas Western's students discovered natural enemies in the soldiers from Fort Bliss. During the Vietnam War's military buildup, new recruits inundated the old cavalry base. These soldiers tended to view the students as privileged kids, in college only to avoid the draft. Students, meanwhile, saw the soldiers as gung ho rockheads. "There used to be great running battles," said Baudoin.

The experiences bound the basketball players together. And the closeness showed up on and off the court.

With so many black players, the Miners occasionally had to endure racial taunts and discrimination on the road. "The further east we went in the South the worse it got because this was completely before black players," said Baudoin. "There were teams with quotas where they'd never put more than two black kids on the floor. I thought our kids handled it all really stoically, but there definitely was some garbage."

Following one victory at New Mexico State, Las Cruces, several players, white and black, borrowed a station wagon and went looking for a late-night meal. They never found one. "We sat in this one little place and nobody would take our order," said Baudoin. "That was embarrassing to me because New Mexico is my home state and I always had considered it a pretty liberal place."

Most of Texas Western's black players recall other incidents on road trips but few of the specifics. Occasionally they were ignored in restaurants or turned away from motels that looked to be empty ("Little places with linoleum floors," said Haskins). The fact that blacks made up a majority of the team helped. Had there been just one or two, as was the case at most integrated major colleges then, it all could have been unbearable.

"There was strength in numbers," said Cager.

Their teenage minds, they now say, did not focus exclusively on race. They were more concerned with basketball issues and, for all his Southwest strangeness, their coach never made much of their racial differences.

"I know it's hard for people to believe now, but we were just kids. Just kids who played basketball," said Worsley. "'Black' didn't enter our minds. We were concerned about getting playing time and about getting through practice because that man was working the hell out of us. That was my priority. Playing time. I'm a ballplayer. I was used to playing thirty-two minutes in high school. I always had the ball in my hands. I was the main man. Now I was surrounded by eight other main men."

■ ■ ■

That afternoon's practice—at which Haskins had worked them as sternly as any Fort Bliss sergeant—had ended only a few hours before. It was too hot in the rooms for cards and they had missed dinner again. Pretty soon they were outside shooting baskets. These games, away from Haskins' confining demands, reminded them of how much fun basketball could be.

Shed, a transfer from North Carolina A&T, recalled one of his first days at a Haskins practice. He broke free on a break and was shouting for the ball. The player who had it ignored him. The run-and-gun style was not the way Haskins' teams played. "Coming from New York City, it was a fast pace," said Shed. "You know, run and gun, run and gun. Not a nice neat passing game. [Now it was] bounce, bounce, bounce, bounce. Pass, pass, pass. And some more bounce, bounce. . . . I remember Coach Haskins saying, 'Son, in this program we pass the ball. You're not back there in one of them city-slicker places. We pass the ball.'"

The El Paso temperature climbed over ninety degrees that day and it was even hotter inside Memorial Gym. They ran up and down the steep steps and through the same few defensive sets over and over. Players didn't carry excess weight for long. And Haskins, employing an old Iba technique, refused them water breaks. When at last he would relent, players sprinted to the gym's lone fountain.

"We used to run there to get to the front of the line," said Hill, who got there first frequently, "because the water got warm in a hurry. . . . Man, we used to pray for those games to get here. The practices were killing us."

Haskins' system was so plain that it held little interest for these players, most of whom had come from high school teams where they shot when they wanted to shoot. Behind the coach's back they called it a "junior high offense." Defense was even worse. At a lot of practices, the starters played defense exclusively. Often those drills would consume two hours.

"We played man-to-man and never switched," said Baudoin. "If you switched, you came out of the game. I remember one time a kid came out of the game and was sent to the locker room to change his clothes because he switched on defense. It was very serious. . . . But that discipline was exactly what we needed because we were eighteen-, nineteen-year-old kids who all came from a variety of cultures, neighborhoods, and families. We had to have one unifying thing to keep us going and that was it. It was simple and straightforward and there were very few rules. You were on time and you didn't miss class."

Haskins sensed early on that he would have difficulty holding this team's interest. Five of them—Hill, Flournoy, Shed, Baudoin, and David Palacio—were left-handed and Haskins felt left-handers were a little odd. They did not like to practice and it showed. "What he was trying to instill we just couldn't see," said Artis, a senior that year. "We were there just for fun, you know. We thought practicing was for people who couldn't play."

As early as October, Haskins knew his team needed to be knocked down a level or two. So he sat his perspiring players on a bench for one of his high-volume lectures, punctuated with obscenities, threats, malaprops, and down-home Oklahoma expressions.

"I'm going to tell you a story about when I was at college," he began. "They had this thing where they used to shave freshmen's hair off and I was not about to have this done to me. What I went and did, I found the biggest football player on the team and kicked the hell out of him. So anytime you feel a little salty and you feel that you cannot do as I say, I'm welcome to oblige you."

Haskins' poker buddies will tell you that nobody bluffs better. He had his players' attention.

"I don't know about the other guys," said Shed, "but I got the message loud and clear and when he said, 'Shed, get on the floor' . . . my feet were moving before they'd hit the floor."

Intimidation was essential in any contest of wills, Haskins knew. Make the other guy a little afraid of you, a little wary. Plant a little seed of doubt, of fear.

"He had this Texas drawl but he'd try to intimidate you New York City style," said Worsley. "He'd look you up and down and my heart was pumping chicken blood. He'd come at you in his kind of way. Bang! And if that didn't work, he'd try another way. He was tough and it rubbed off on us."

Haskins continued: This team had a lot of work ahead—not just basketball, but conditioning. He pointed to the gym's steps, angled on a forty-five-degree rise to the ceiling. Players would soon be very familiar with them.

"He said—and I can almost remember like it was yesterday," said Shed. "He said, 'Just look at y'all. You're far and none the worst bunch of athletes I ever had. Just look at y'all. With the way y'all look, I doubt if we'll even win half our games. Just a pitiful bunch of athletes.'"

There were guys with glasses. Guys carrying several extra pounds. Guys like Shed who "weighed about 100 and nothing soaking wet." Worsley was not much taller than 5-6. Still Haskins believed this might be a pretty good team. Maybe not as good as the 25-3 bunch he had in 1964, Barnes' senior season, but certainly better than the previous year's 18-9 team.

Six letter-winners returned from the '64–'65 Miners, which went ten deep. Shed and Hill, plus leading scorer Artis (11.2 points per game) and Harry Flournoy, the top rebounder (11.8 rebounds per game), were the best of them. The freshman team had gone 18-2 and now its three stars, Lattin, Worsley, and Cager, were moving up to varsity.

"I don't think we actually knew how good they were going to be, but we knew they had a chance to be good," said Iba. "Our freshman team the year before was better than the varsity. Once we started practicing and played a few games, we saw that they were awfully good. They were awfully athletic and defensively they were very, very good. They had a good mix between great rebounders and enough shooters to keep everybody honest. And they were very good one-on-one players. You always look back and say, 'Could that team have played today?' Well, that team could have played today."

Racially, the previous year's varsity had been split almost evenly between white and black players. But Haskins always had one of three whites—Bobby Dibler, Steve Tredennick, or sophomore Jerry Armstrong—in the lineup. "That's just the way the chemistry worked out," he explained. "Didn't have nothing to do with what color they were."

This year, however, Haskins and Iba had no doubt that their top seven players were blacks. "Coach Haskins was playing who he thought were the best," said Dick Myers, a white junior on that team and now an executive with Coach leather products. "The fact that they happened to be black was just the way it was. And the other five ball players on the team . . . understood it that way, and we never really had any friction along those lines. And I really don't remember it ever being discussed that much here in El Paso."

Haskins didn't care much about getting bench players time. If it happened, it happened. He had a rule that unless a reserve was inserted before there was a minute left in a game, he wouldn't put them in then. "He didn't want to embarrass anyone," said Baudoin.

The best of the nonblack Miners—maybe the most forgotten reserves in national championship history—was Jerry Armstrong. The

6-4 senior, a bruising Missouri farm boy, was a tough defensive player and Haskins turned to him in twenty-four games that year.

Baudoin, the second-most-used of the Miners' bottom five, played in sixteen games, averaging 2.2 points. At 6-7 and 200 pounds, the bespectacled New Mexican was a good rebounder and low-post player and a good foil for Lattin in practices. "There's complete acknowledgment from the regulars that without the contributions of the second five in practice, it would never have happened," said Baudoin.

David Palacio, a hometown Hispanic youngster who would go on to become a vice president for Capitol Records, had been an important member of the freshman team a year earlier, but Haskins could not work him into the rotation that championship season. A 6-2 guard, he would play in fifteen games and average less than a point.

Myers, a 6-4 jump shooter from Peabody, Kansas, would play in only fourteen games, and average less than a point. The twelfth man, El Paso's Togo Railey, was a junior guard with a bad case of nerves. He played in only four games, and scored just one point. During the first half of the title game, he passed out from the excitement.

"It's kind of funny, but things worked out the opposite of how they did everywhere else then," said Worsley. "But whatever has been said, and I hope I can say this correctly, we could never have been where we were if it wasn't for the five other players on the team. They were our competition in practice, our buddies off the floor.

"In all the years we were together and all the years since, we never talked about race," said Worsley. "We never had an argument. We had some battles, just like two babies playing in the same pen. But we didn't know black or white. Ask any of the black players and they'll never say anything bad about our white teammates. They wanted to get playing time, but that was normal. They partied with us. They played cards with us. They joked with us. We had water fights with each other."

■ ■ ■

Haskins can still tell you the telephone number—he readily reels it off. "I'll never forget that one." The coach had called David Lattin's home in Houston hundreds of times.

He had driven there to watch the senior center play for Worthing High School. The player's physique and toughness impressed Haskins. Strength and intimidation were what the coach prized above all else. That was what eventually would make the big center his pet. "He loved David," said Worsley. "David and Bobby Joe [Hill]. They could do no wrong."

In Lattin's senior year, Haskins sent Moe Iba to Houston to wrap him up. When the assistant arrived at Worthing, he couldn't find Lattin and telephoned Haskins in a panic. The coach asked how Iba could lose someone as big as Lattin and told him to go back the following day. He did. This time Lattin, who had been absent with an illness, was there.

Both men thought they had him locked up, until Lattin said he'd come to El Paso only if four of his Worthing teammates came too. "I said, 'David, I'm just recruiting you,'" recalled Haskins. "So he went to Tennessee A&I (later Tennessee State) and his four buddies went down there with him. Those other four kids couldn't play, and that would have caused me a hell of a problem."

Early in his freshman year at the Nashville school, Lattin was suspended for disciplinary reasons. The reason never has been explained fully. Harold Hunter, Tennessee A&I's basketball coach at the time, called the incident "minor" and Lattin agreed with that characterization. Apparently, he was the player Rupp later claimed had been recruited from a Tennessee penitentiary. There is no record of Lattin having been charged with any crime during his stay at the Tennessee school. Regardless, he soon decided to transfer. And at 3:00 A.M. one morning, he telephoned Haskins.

"He said, 'Coach, this is Dave. I'm gonna transfer. Send me a plane ticket,'" said Haskins. "I told him I wasn't allowed to do that, but I must admit I thought about it the next day. Anyway, the next day I get another call from him. This time he was at the bus station here in El Paso."

In 1964–65, Lattin led the freshman team in scoring and rebounding. And he adapted immediately to El Paso's bicultural atmosphere. A jazz lover, he soon was hosting his own show, *The Big D Jazz Session,* on a local FM radio station. A sharp dresser who didn't smoke or drink, Lattin enjoyed Juárez. When a recruit needed convincing, he escorted him around the Mexican city.

"Lattin was Daddy Cool," laughed Worsley. "He was big and baldheaded and all the ladies loved him. We called him Lattin the Latin Lover."

That shaved head and his style of play lent Lattin the look of a modern-day NBA player. In fact, he was a prototype for the power forward—big, strong, a determined rebounder and defender, and a good outside shooter. And he loved to power-dunk. "I never saw anyone dunk with that kind of force," said Hill.

Surprisingly Haskins, who banned behind-the-back dribbles and passes, encouraged dunking. He recognized its ability to intimidate and humiliate. "Coach was always telling me to flush it, that's what he called it, whenever I got the chance," said Lattin.

That image of mean, muscular manliness was essential in Haskins' physical system. When he wanted to wound his players, he would challenge their manhood, calling them "girls" or "sissies." They in turn took it out on their opponents in the same fashion. When Kansas's 6-11 Walt Wesley had a dunk blocked by the 6-5 Flournoy in the regional final, Flournoy called the big center a "sissy." Anyone who drove the lane on this defense, with the daunting Lattin as its last line, had to possess courage.

"First you had to get by Bobby Joe and Orsten out front," said Shed. "Then you got to Flo and me. After that, you met the man [Lattin]. If anyone drove the lane on us, we'd knock his lights out. For the brave ones, it used to get cloudy in there real fast."

Every game opened the same way. Haskins would study the opposing team for a few trips up and down the floor. Then the hustler in him identified the mark. "He'd call out some poor player's number and we'd just nail him," said Baudoin. "We'd score off him until their coach took him out. Haskins might not have had a degree in psychology but he knew his stuff."

At the other end of the floor the intimidation came even earlier. "We'd waste the first foul," said Baudoin. "We always had a history of big bruisers in the middle so maybe the first time they came down on offense, we'd pick up some dancing guard and turn him into the middle. Someone like Lattin would take his head off. The rest of the team and their bench would see it and that would set the tone."

Consequently teams shot terribly against the Miners. Opponents hit only 40 percent of their shots that season. With more room to operate inside, the Miners, never great outside shooters, converted 45 percent and outrebounded teams by more than 12 a game.

Haskins knew he had his center for the 1965–66 season. "David will be a first-round pro draft choice," he predicted that preseason. Haskins also had supreme confidence in his point guard Bobby Joe Hill.

"Hill was good out front. He was as good as Nate Archibald was in college—every bit as good, plus he was a great defensive player. He did what I wanted him to do," said Haskins.

Hill grew up in Detroit's racially mixed Highland Park neighborhood, where his father worked in a Dodge factory. He was All-City as a senior, averaging better than 23 points a game for Highland Park.

Though Hill was intelligent—"He would not look at a book until an hour before a test and still get an A or a B," said Worsley—his high school grades kept him out of the bigger colleges. He ended up at Burlington Junior College in Burlington, Iowa. One of his teammates was 7-footer Mel Daniels, and it was while watching Daniels that Haskins and Moe Iba really fell in love with Hill.

"Don had seen him play in the national [junior college] tournament when he was a freshman there. He was quick and fast and we decided to keep an eye on him," said Iba. "In what would have been his junior year, Don asked me, 'Whatever happened to that Bobby Joe Hill?'"

Hill had quit school after his freshman year and returned to Detroit. Haskins reached him by phone and asked him if he'd like to come to El Paso. Haskins and Nolan Richardson met Hill at the airport in the winter of 1963 and the coach was shocked. "He had been this little old bit of a kid when I saw him and here he was now, weighing about 220," said Haskins. "I told him he'd lose that in a hurry."

Haskins said that in the early and mid-1960s he had a recruiting budget of about $5,000. Iba made most of the trips and Haskins usually limited his involvement to phone calls from the tiny trainer's room at Memorial Gym.

One particularly fruitful trip the head coach made was to Gary, Indiana, in 1962. It resulted in his signing two future starters on his championship team, Flournoy and Artis. A former Oklahoma A&M teammate had told him about the players and Haskins was intrigued enough to want to see them himself.

Flournoy, a 6-5 leaper, was walking home from Emerson High when he noticed a strange white man following him in a car. Haskins stopped the car and introduced himself to the player. He asked if he could meet his mother. She gave Haskins a cup of coffee and a slice of homemade apple pie that the coach told her was the finest he ever had. Not long afterward, Flournoy signed with Texas Western.

Orsten Artis, a 6-1 guard, was a star at Gary's Froebel High. He was a superb shooter. "He was the only guy on that [1966] team who could really shoot," said Haskins. Artis had been recruited by such big schools as UCLA and Oklahoma but Haskins had been the only head coach to visit personally and that convinced him.

"Earlier Don had had Al Tolen and Danny Vaughn and a couple of other kids from Indiana," recalled Iba. "Harry and Orsten were both on my first freshman team and they were very, very good. And they were both really nice kids, really fine people."

Shed, who played at Morris High School in the Bronx, had heard about Texas Western from Hilton White. Originally though, the lean 6-8 son of a Pullman porter attended all-black North Carolina A&T. Suspended for a curfew violation, he left after a year and returned to New York. Not long afterward Haskins phoned him. "He said, 'Butch—which is my nickname—do you want to go to a Texas school?' Without any reservations I said, 'Yes. When do I leave?'"

Once Willie Cager got into school, he was diagnosed with a bad heart murmur. In a strange way, it made the talented low-post player the ideal sixth man. "We would play him about four minutes at a time and that would make him so damn mad," said Haskins. "His mother wanted him to play but we didn't like putting him on the floor too much. Cager could score. He was not a great shooter but he'd figure out a way to get it in the basket. He was a great sixth man. Sometimes we'd put him in there and say, 'Willie, make something happen.'"

These players, along with the mercurial Worsley, gave Haskins a nucleus that excited him. And though he wouldn't admit it to them, he liked them too.

"They were real good kids," said Iba. "Don does such a great job of coaching but the other thing he does, that all good coaches do, is he really handles people well. And he handled these kids. There were no petty jealousies. They played very well as a team. There were no problems with them in the community or on the floor. They were perfect to work with. They'd come in the office and he was very open. If they had a problem, they could talk to him about it. They knew where Don stood on every situation. They knew that if they stepped over the line, on the basketball floor or whatever, he wasn't going to put up with it."

■ ■ ■

The Miners had left the Border Conference after the 1961–62 season, but in 1965–66, their independent schedule still included many of that league's member schools. Their season began on December 4 with an 89–38 rout of Eastern New Mexico. With Haskins mixing and matching starting fives from among his top seven, the Miners ran off a string of easy victories.

The only early scare came on December 17 in a 75–73 win over Fresno State at home. The following night, in the same location, the two teams met again. This time Texas Western won handily, 83–65.

Haskins always points to the championship game of El Paso's Sun Carnival Tournament as the moment his eyes were opened. The Miners played Iowa, then ranked number six nationally. And before the December 30 game, Haskins let his players know that Iowa coach Ralph Miller was looking past them. "He told us their coach was talking about how tough the teams they were gonna play in January were," said Cager. The Miners ran out to a 34–4 lead and their bench finished up with an 18-point win.

"After that I thought we might be pretty good," said Haskins, "but there was no way I was thinking about a national title."

The players insist they knew they were good long before that Iowa game. They sensed immediately how uncomfortable opponents were with their aggressive, physical style.

"I know Haskins has this great story about us beating the snot out of Iowa," said Baudoin. "Well, we beat the snot out of each other in practice every day and we knew we were a pretty good bunch of players. And the kind of basketball we played, nobody else played. We'd play Arizona State and they'd be averaging 105 points a game and they'd score 50 against us. We were getting cockier with each win."

They routed a good Seattle team by 22 in El Paso on January 6. After a three-week break for exams, they beat Arizona State in Tempe by 17. By early February they were 15-0 and in the top ten when they embarked on a stretch of three road games against solid opposition—Colorado State, Arizona, and New Mexico.

Hill hit a 35-foot buzzer-beating jumper at Colorado State to give the Miners a 68–66 victory on February 4. Six days later they beat Arizona easily. But New Mexico, led by 7-footer Mel Daniels, jumped all over them in the first half of their February 12 game at Albuquerque's "Pit," and it looked as if Texas Western's unbeaten streak would come to an end.

The deficit was 37–21 at the half and the Miners were down 20 with 14:03 left. Thirty-five seconds later Lattin fouled out. But Daniels soon followed him to the bench with his fifth foul and Texas Western fought back to tie the game with half a minute remaining. They won in overtime, their first of three OT victories that season.

Each dramatic victory not only broadened their appeal in El Paso but chipped away at the notion that blacks folded under pressure. "These kids were intelligent, they played hard, and they had composure," said Baudoin. "And that's all you can ask out of a basketball team."

"We were down a ton," said Iba of the New Mexico game, "and that was a very, very tough place to play. But nothing seemed to rattle these kids and they came back. They just kept playing hard all the time."

El Paso was getting excited now. The Miners and Kentucky were the only unbeaten major-college teams. Texas Western's home games were sold out. Sometimes their road games would be televised on an old movie screen set up in the gym and students and townspeople would fill the place.

"I can remember sitting in my car in the driveway during that New Mexico game, not wanting to get out until it was over," said professor Gladstein. "You can't believe how terribly excited everyone was about that team. Their games became *the* thing in town. It seemed like every one of them came down to the last shot."

They moved to 19-0 with another last-minute victory, this one at home against Arizona State on Valentine's Day. On February 22, Haskins got word that the Miners had been awarded another NCAA bid, his third in five seasons. They would play Oklahoma City in Wichita in a first-round Midwest Regional game.

When they traveled to Seattle for their final regular-season game on March 5, the Miners were 23-0 and ranked number two behind Kentucky. Since they would not be returning to El Paso before Monday's NCAA opener, Texas Western students had formed a caravan of horn-honking autos that escorted the unbeaten team on its journey to the airport Friday morning. For the players, the noisy send-off and the knowledge that they already were in the tournament encouraged them to look past Seattle.

"They just couldn't get themselves prepared for Seattle," said Haskins. "They were looking ahead to Oklahoma City. That's the one that mattered to them."

If Haskins hoped to focus his players on Seattle, he realized that would be impossible when on the afternoon of the game they learned Kentucky had lost for the first time that season, at Tennessee. "We knew then that if we won, we'd be number one," said Hill. But Tom Workman scored 23 points and Seattle, which had lost to the Miners in El Paso earlier that season, upset them, 74–72.

Haskins would later call the loss the wakeup call his team needed for the NCAA tournament. That cold and rainy night in Seattle, though, he was angry and he told them curfew would begin as soon as they returned to their hotel. "We had never had a curfew be-fore," said Artis.

But Hill had friends in the city and they had planned a party for that night. Most of the players planned to go. They decided to meet in the lobby after Haskins' bed check. The coach soon discovered them missing. Learning that Hill was the ringleader, he decided his star point guard would not start in the NCAA opener. "He put a scare into us," said Artis. "He told us that he wasn't going to help us anymore."

■ ■ ■

The team flew from Seattle to Wichita on Sunday morning. The cur-few-breaking players tried to sleep on the long flight but Haskins kept them awake with constant questions and lectures. The Miners worked out at Wichita State's Levitt Arena and Haskins ran them into the ground. That night they got to bed early.

Oklahoma City, offensively at least, gave them a little taste of Kentucky-style basketball. Like Rupp's teams, Abe Lemons' Chiefs liked to push the ball up the court. Because of their style, Oklahoma City was usually among the nation's high scorers. They weren't huge, but forward Jerry Ware played a lot like Pat Riley—aggres-sively athletic. Ware was a leaper who led the country in rebounding with more than 21 a game. Haskins warned his players that the Chiefs could score in bunches and that the last thing they wanted to do was fall behind early.

As the coach promised, Worsley started in place of the benched Hill. And as he feared, the Chiefs jumped right on his Miners. They leaped to an 11–2 lead, and after six and a half minutes, were ahead by 11. Haskins called a timeout midway through the opening half and pointed at Hill. "Get your ass in there," he told him. The tactics worked. Hill, who would lead both teams with 24 points, was inspired on offense and defense.

Soon the Miners tied the score, 25–25. From there the Miners gradually pulled away for an 89–74 win. Hill was the story, but it was Lattin, who collected 20 points and 15 rebounds and stifled Ware, that Lemons discussed afterward. "Without Lattin," he said, "Texas Western is just a good team." Typically, the Miners limited Oklahoma City to 44 percent shooting and outrebounded them, 55–32.

In the next round, Texas Western faced Cincinnati in the Midwest Regional at Lubbock, Texas—as close to El Paso as an NCAA tournament game was ever likely to be. The Miners had played Texas Tech there in the past and the city was not one of their favorites.

"The tournament was actually a little easier for us because having to travel so much we didn't have to practice as hard as we normally did," said Baudoin. "We were excited about possibly getting to see some other places. So we were kind of disappointed when we got sent to scenic Lubbock for our first game. Lubbock was a tough place for black players to go. It was a pretty racist place then, and still is. But we knew we'd be getting a chance to play some real good teams there. No more Eastern New Mexicos. Finally we were going to play somebody that could challenge us."

Just how great the challenge would be they had no way of knowing.

"I think Don thought we could beat Oklahoma City in the first game and we did," said Iba. "But when we were in Lubbock, we didn't know if we could get out of there. And we had two tough, tough ball games."

Because of Lubbock's proximity, more than 2,000 Texas Western fans were in attendance in Municipal Coliseum for Friday night's regional semifinal. Cincinnati had been among the first teams to use black basketball players extensively and this year's team was

integrated. Its star, Don Rolfes, who was white, immediately provided Haskins with some mental ammunition.

Rolfes had played for Kentucky and started as a sophomore in
the 1962–63 season before transferring to Cincinnati—just after
landing in Rupp's doghouse by getting married. One newspaper
story quoted the native Kentuckian as saying, "Playing against Kentucky for the national championship is something I have dreamed
about."

Texas Western targeted Rolfes immediately and the Cincinnati
star didn't back down. With less than five minutes played, Shed and
Rolfes jostled under the basket. The Cincinnati star clutched Shed's
shorts and the Texas Western player responded by popping him in
the nose. Shed was ejected. "Haskins went wild," Shed recalled. "He
said . . . 'You're through.'"

The incident prompted several black-white jokes among the
spectators, who were somewhat astonished by Texas Western's
lineup. "My gosh, that Shed is in trouble," one anonymous coach
told the *Dallas Morning News.* "Did you see? He [Haskins] made
him go sit with the white boys." But the incident also affected
Rolfes. He would score only 10 points and Texas Western would
win in overtime, 78–76.

Cager, who had missed a free throw with eleven seconds left in
regulation, redeemed himself by scoring 6 of the Miners' 9 overtime
points. Lattin (29 points and 8 rebounds) was again a dominating
force. "I just saw one smart guy from Cincinnati," said Texas Tech
coach Gene Gibson afterward. "He was the one that saw Lattin coming and got the heck out of there."

The Miner center was attracting national attention now and the
white press didn't quite know what to make of this big, physical, extremely confident black man. Many of them, believing there were
only so many personality niches blacks could occupy, thought him
another Sonny Liston, the scowling, trouble-prone ex-heavyweight
champion. One sportswriter mentioned his "treacherous strength and

coldblooded tactics." Another described him as the "scowling Lattin, a huge and awesome specimen." Those descriptions didn't bother Haskins at all. He hoped his center would scare the daylights out of every team they played.

In the region's other semifinal, number four Kansas, behind black stars Jo Jo White and Walt Wesley, defeated SMU. Kansas coach Ted Owens, having witnessed Texas Western's intimidating tactics, immediately began lobbying the officials. "We'll be all right," he said, "unless we get a loosely called game."

Officials Rudy Marich and Bill Bussinius would call 46 fouls in the Texas Western–Kansas Regional Final, but that didn't help Owens. Flournoy fouled out, but so did Wesley, White, and teammate Ron Franz in the long and memorable game.

"Kansas was the deepest, best-balanced team we played that year," said Baudoin. "But we also shocked them. They weren't ready for that kind of basketball. Nobody was. When you face a team that plays that kind of tough-nosed ball, that turns you away time after time from getting good shots when you're used to getting them, you get weary running your offense. And our opponents would have to run their offense five, six, seven times to get a good shot. And when they'd finally get one, they'd never get a rebound. Four or five minutes into the second half, teams would just be pooped. It wasn't from running. It was from the frustration of never getting good shots and never getting the ball back once they did."

With Kansas leading by 2, 55–53, in the second half, Owens switched to a stalling offense. Texas Western was too quick. A steal and layup by Hill put the Miners in front, 57–55, and with 1:17 to play they had a seemingly safe 69–64 lead.

But after a Lattin dunk was disallowed—the big center hung on the rim afterward and was whistled for a technical—Al Lopes hit 2 foul shots with 1:02 left to pull Kansas within 3. With thirty seconds left, White turned a steal into a 3-point play and tied the game at 69.

Texas Western set up for the final shot but Hill's 20-footer, over Wesley's long, outstretched arms, bounced off the rim.

Each team scored only 2 points in the first overtime until, with seven seconds left, White threw up an off-balance 35-footer as he was stumbling out of bounds. It swished through the net and Kansas's fans and bench went wild. Lattin went after Hill. "How could you let him shoot it?" he asked. "Why didn't you smack him in the head?" But Marich was standing just a few feet from White and the referee immediately dropped to one knee. He pointed to the spot where the Kansas star's left foot had stepped out of bounds. "That was probably the most important moment in Texas Western's history, right there," said Worsley. "God bless Rudy Marich."

The call seemed to deflate the Jayhawks. Texas Western hit a series of free throws in the second overtime to build a 6-point lead with thirty-five seconds left. Five late points by Kansas, the last two at the buzzer, were not enough. Texas Western won, 81–80.

"We tried to give the game away," said a relieved Haskins, "but at least we looked good doing it."

This time Lattin accumulated 15 points and 17 rebounds while Hill added 22 points. Shed came off the bench to contribute 12 and shut down Wesley, who still ended up with a game-high 24 points. The All-America White added 19. "Shed did a great job," said Haskins "[Wesley] only got the ball four or five times in the second half."

Haskins, in just his fifth year as a college coach, appeared somewhat stunned to be heading to the Final Four. "I guess I never realized we'd get this far," he told a Texas writer. "But I thought from the first, we'd be a lot better than people were giving us credit for. We weren't in the top twenty at first but I felt there weren't twenty teams that could beat us."

Owens agreed with him. "We felt the two best teams in the country had played that night," he said. "We didn't feel Kentucky had enough size."

■ ■ ■

In 1966, the NCAA Final Four was still evolving into the monster event it would soon become. The culmination of the tournament—played on Friday and Saturday—normally attracted only supporters of the four schools and residents of the area in which it was played. Most other college basketball fans were content to stay at home, follow the results in the newspapers, and maybe watch the title game on TV.

It was obvious that television still viewed college basketball as a relatively minor sport. Rights were awarded for modest fees and that year's rights-holder, Sports Network, was powerless to alter the Saturday night championship game's awkward 10:00 P.M. EST starting time.

Even though the game would end far after the big deadlines of most major Eastern dailies, newspaper interest in the game had exploded. A record 150 sportswriters requested credentials, so many that the media headquarters had to be moved from the Shoreham Hotel in Washington to a larger facility near Dupont Plaza.

Campus arenas still could host the event and Maryland, where Cole's capacity of more than 14,000 made it one of the largest on-campus basketball facilities, was awarded the finals when labor problems forced Chicago Arena officials to cancel their contract.

In Lexington, Baltimore, Washington, and particularly El Paso, where there had been virtually no experience with national sporting events, the Final Four created tremendous excitement.

At 9:00 A.M. on March 17, a sold-out American Airlines 707 lifted off the runway at El Paso International Airport. The chartered flight was bound for Baltimore's Friendship Field. Texas Western's team was on board as were a pep band, cheerleaders, and scores of fans and civic leaders. El Paso businessman Robert Blum carried a native cactus plant to give to William Elkins, the president of the host University of Maryland, who had been Ray's Texas Western predecessor.

The college's allotment of 250 Final Four tickets had sold out in minutes on Monday, although Rupp had telephoned the athletic department offering to purchase all their leftovers. Those who couldn't travel to College Park were cheered by the news that KROD would be televising the games, live and in color. One local reporter at the El Paso airport asked Haskins if he thought his physical Miners would get a fair shot from the officials. "I thought the officiating at Lubbock was pretty strict and we won," he said.

In Baltimore, the plane was met by El Paso Congressman Richard White, who announced that he had arranged Friday White House tours for anyone interested. The players hustled off to the Interstate Inn in College Park and by 3:00 P.M. were practicing on the floor of Cole Field House.

The practice was, said Haskins, their worst workout ever. They obviously were distracted by all the reporters and photographers, and all the friends and relatives that had come down from New York City to see Worsley, Cager, and Shed.

"All I was thinking right then is 'I'm back on the East Coast. I'm a couple of hours from home,'" said Worsley. "My people can come to see me play. My father, who I hadn't seen in years, was there. Lots of friends. I was probably thinking more about how I was going to sneak home than I was about Kentucky."

Iba had not accompanied the team. The assistant had flown to a junior college tournament and was planning on joining them Friday afternoon. When Iba telephoned Haskins Thursday night, the Bear, as he was known, was growling. He groused about how bad practice had been and how unconcerned his players appeared to be. This time his concerns were justified.

"There really wasn't a lot of hype among our guys," said Worsley. "Maybe we were just old for our age because of our life experience. And remember in my high school career, I had played before

18,000 people in Madison Square Garden. Being from New York City, and being MVP in the city championship game, playing in the Garden was my greatest thrill. After that, everything was anticlimactic."

Much of the national press had its first look at Texas Western during that practice, only the first fifteen minutes of which were for public display. Many had not realized the Miners included seven blacks; soon the whispered jokes began. When reporters matched up the players with their listed hometowns, suggestions were made that Texas Western was not playing by the rules.

"Some Texans," wrote James Doyle in the Cleveland *Plain Dealer.* "Texans from the wide-open spaces of New York City, Detroit, Gary, Ind."

Some were surprised at how harshly Haskins treated the players during their drills, calling them "lazy" and "worthless." Others, like Charles Heaton, also of the *Plain Dealer,* couldn't resist noting that the Miners "have those springs for leg muscles."

Texas Western would be playing unranked Utah in the second semifinal Friday night. That was an advantage. Haskins knew Utah coach Jack Gardner well, having attended some of the veteran coach's clinics. In fact, in November of 1965, Haskins had gone to Utah to watch a Texas Western–Utah football game. While there he asked Gardner if he could watch some of his preseason practices. "Sure," said Gardner. "Why don't you stay a week?"

Utah had finished near the bottom of the Western Athletic Conference in 1965, but this season the Utes were 23-6. One of their best players, George Fischer, was out with a broken leg, and another, Lyndon McKay, was bothered by a sore knee. Their star was Jerry Chambers, a black 6-4 forward from nearby Washington. "Chambers is the best forward in the country," said Haskins. He had scored 73 points in Utah's two West Regional games.

Actually no one appeared very interested in this matchup. It was widely assumed that the national champion would emerge from the other semifinal, pairing number one Kentucky and number two Duke. "If Kentucky can beat Duke," said UCLA coach John Wooden, whose Bruins had won the previous two national titles, "it would have to win the tournament."

The snubs annoyed Haskins, but as always he would use them to his advantage. Pregame pep talks would not be a problem that weekend. He would employ the "no respect" clause before the Utah game and then, should the Miners win, he could turn to lily-white Kentucky or Duke for inspiration.

"Here were number one and number two playing each other and right away the talk was the winner was going to be champion," said Worsley. "Right away that was very distressing. It showed us no respect at all. Coach Haskins played on that and that played on our minds. We were number three and we ought to have gotten our just dues. The papers were filled with stuff about Duke and Kentucky and their All-Americas. We didn't have any All-Americas. We felt a little left out. Pat Riley was from the East and so were some of us, but guess who got all the ink?"

At Thursday's news conferences, Haskins told reporters his team would have to slow Utah's fast break. Asked about the Miners' easy schedule, he bristled. "We don't worry about that talk," he said. "We play a lot of teams like ourselves . . . ones without a name."

Like other coaches of Texas Western opponents that year, Gardner issued a not-so-subtle plea to the officials. "They're like a pro team around the boards," he said. "They throw their weight around and they're all leapers. All we have is a bunch of skinny little kids."

Bussinius officiated this game too, along with Lenny Wirtz. The two of them called 47 fouls, 27 on Texas Western. The most significant came early in the second half when Lattin picked up his fourth and had to sit down. "They called it like a girls game," Lattin said later.

The Miners led, 42–39, at the half but when Chambers dunked over Shed, Utah pulled to within 1, 54–53. At that point Haskins inserted Armstrong and the white forward shut down the Utah star. Soon the Miners' lead was 11, 68–57, and Utah never challenged again. The final score was 85–75, in Texas Western's favor.

Chambers finished with 38 but none in the final minutes. "He's the best player we faced all year," said Haskins. "No one has ever scored 38 points on us." Afterward everyone credited Armstrong with turning the game around.

"I had a big advantage since I had been watching from the bench," said Armstrong. "So when I came in I had a good idea of where Chambers was going to move and what he would try to do."

The contribution by Armstrong, the Missouri farm boy who said he never had seen a black until he arrived in El Paso, was the most significant by a white Miner that year.

"I guess a lot of people think that we might have started something because you see so much of that now, black guys," Artis recalled. "But I remember that Utah game where it was a black guy who was almost beating us singlehandedly. . . . Armstrong, who is white, did a hell of a job and if it wasn't for him playing that good, we might never have gotten to that championship game."

And history might never had gotten its perfect matchup. In less than twenty-four hours, on a college campus below the Mason-Dixon Line, five blacks would be lining up opposite five whites for a war. Just how civil it would be, no one could predict.

8.

Rupp's Runts

"That's a good little team. [But] when it runs into a big boy, it's going to have trouble."
—Hardin-Simmons University coach Lou Henson, after Kentucky beat his team in the season-opener

When it was stuffed with 11,500 screaming fans and Kentucky was pulverizing an opponent, Memorial Coliseum shook like a crystal in an earthquake. Visitors to the campus arena frequently likened the game night atmosphere there—tinged with so much noise and formidable tradition—to a spiritual force. Opponents found it nearly impossible to win. After the Wildcats moved there from Alumni Gym in 1950, they did not lose a home game until 1955.

Empty, however, there was something cold and lifeless about the old facility on Euclid Avenue. Perhaps it was its concrete drabness and its size. Or maybe it was because it had been built to honor nearly 10,000 Kentuckians killed in World War II, their names inscribed on bronze plaques that hung like stars on the gloomy corridor walls. The basketball court itself, unadorned but for a modest blue "K" at its center, was surrounded by a half-dozen rows of folding chairs. Above it, tier after tier of plain wooden benches rose on an angle like stairways to the darkness.

On autumn and winter afternoons, when the building was otherwise black and hollow, a lone rectangle of light shone on its floor. As they walked toward that illuminated court on October 15, 1965, the first day of workouts for the season that would begin forty-seven days later, Kentucky's fourteen varsity basketball players resembled commuters arriving at the office. Silent, unsmiling, dressed alike in white gym shorts and shirts, they portrayed more dread than enthusiasm. The season about to begin, most of them believed, could be one from hell.

The boss, Adolph Rupp, was waiting. The old man's matching khaki workshirt and pants were stiffly pressed, a whistle dangled from his neck, and he wore an expression that, if possible, seemed even less pleased than usual. The Wildcats' 15-10 record the previous season had been Rupp's worst in thirty-five years at the school. That team often had played selfishly, violating one of Rupp's grand coaching principles. "The first thing you have to do is curtail the individual desire of the boy in the interest of team play," Rupp liked to say. All through the off-season, the sixty-four-year-old coach had heard and read suggestions that he was now as much a basketball relic as the set shot. He was too old, too unyielding, too concerned with his farm.

Someone, his players knew, was going to have to suffer. "He realized he was toward the end of his career," said Larry Conley, a senior in 1965–66, "and because he had been so embarrassed that previous season, he was bound and determined it was not going to happen again."

Rupp viewed his critics with disdain. As the 1965-66 season began, he wanted to prove them wrong. But revenge wouldn't be easy. Though he had four very experienced players back from a mediocre team, none was taller than 6-5.

Tommy Kron, a senior guard, was perhaps alone among his teammates in anticipating a successful season. "A lot of people were saying we were dog poop," he said, "and we were getting tired of hearing that. I can't say I knew it was going to end the way it did, but I really thought it was going to be a much better year than everyone was expecting. The year before had been so bad, a miserable year. We had a lot of injuries, even Coach Rupp had missed some time with phlebitis. We never really got our act together. But I thought we had started playing a lot better by the end of the season, and we had pretty much the same team."

Several of the upperclassmen, including Kron, had stayed in Lexington that summer and a bond had developed, especially among the top four players. There were no athletic dormitories at Kentucky and Kron and fellow senior Conley roomed together, as did Louie Dampier and Pat Riley, a pair of talented juniors. "We all spent so much time together," said Kron, "practices and study halls. And we did a lot of stuff together off the floor, going to movies, that kind of thing."

They gathered for pickup games three or four times a week that summer, and began to talk about a new weight-and-running program Joe B. Hall, one of Rupp's young assistants, had planned for them. The program would be strenuous and different from anything they had been used to. "We'd been in school three years and all of a sudden a new assistant comes in and says we're going to have a running program," said Conley. "He damn near killed us. I think maybe seven of the first ten days I absolutely lost my lunch. We started running the first week of school. Mondays, Wednesdays, and Fridays we ran. Tuesdays and Thursdays, we worked with the weights. But on October 15, when practice started, we already had the stamina. We were ready to play."

Privately, Rupp liked this team, though he never would consider telling them that. "They listen and do what they're supposed to," he told an out-of-town reporter, before adding an important distinction in those rapidly changing times, "and they're all regular." Individually, those four returnees were strong-headed, but together they meshed well. Each recognized the other's strengths and weaknesses.

Riley, a 6-3 forward, was a natural leader. Raised in the factory town of Schenectady, New York, he had a street toughness that set him apart from his Southern and Midwestern teammates. He shot pool at the student center, was a fastidious dresser, and had a certain charm with the ladies. One of seven kids, Riley possessed the sort of inner strength one develops growing up in a large family with a domineering, emotionally distant father. "He could withstand intimidation," said Hall. Having watched Kentucky win a national title in 1958, Riley decided that's where he would play in college. And even when Alabama offered him a football scholarship, he never wavered.

But the Rileys were not well off financially, and in his freshman year Pat considered transferring to Syracuse to be closer to them. "Not once did my family come to see me play when I was at Kentucky," he said. "There were six other kids and they just couldn't afford it." Riley was a terrific baseline jump shooter, a versatile athlete who could leap as well as anyone Rupp had ever coached.

The 6-5 Kron was lanky, smart, and a great defender, particularly at the top of the 1-3-1 zone Kentucky had begun to employ in his sophomore season. He grew up in Tell City, a tiny town in southern Indiana. His high school coach had told Rupp about him. Kron had a cocky streak and a temper, two potentially dangerous traits around Rupp, who could provoke rage in the mellowest of players. "Those things he said to us, like calling us 'sons of bitches' or saying our moms and dads wouldn't be proud of us, it was banter," said Kron. "You had to forget those things and go on. As long as he played me, we had no problems."

Rupp had known Larry Conley since he was ten when the boy's dad, George Conley, a college referee in Kentucky, brought him to the Coliseum to meet the legendary coach. Conley, a skinny, blond 6-3 swingman from Ashland, Kentucky, had the perfect attitude for Rupp's tightly disciplined system. He was smart, unselfish, and obedient. And unlike his cowed teammates, he knew how to talk to Rupp. Once, after a victory at Vanderbilt, he grabbed the aloof coach and hugged him, shocking his teammates. "It was just a feeling of the moment. There were days I hated him as much as anybody else," said Conley, "but I had a lot of respect for him." It was mutual. Rupp later would call Conley one of the finest boys ever to play for him.

Louie Dampier was another Indianan and the team's best shooter, maybe the best in Kentucky history. The 6-foot guard from Indianapolis used the Wildcats' famous screening system to perfection, running off picks to find open floor and open jumpers. He had led Kentucky in scoring in 1964–65 with 17 points a game and along with Riley was named to the All-SEC team as a sophomore. "Pat was like Superman," said Dampier. "Me, I was more like Robin." Dampier was the quietest of the four. "He just seemed like a sad person," said Riley of his friend. No wonder. His mother had died suddenly when he was sixteen, and a year after that, his father passed away.

These four could shoot, pass, play defense, and, despite their size, rebound aggressively. The fifth man, whoever that might be, was going to have to add some bulk. Had circumstances been different, Wes Unseld might have filled that spot perfectly.

One of the candidates was a 6-5 sophomore from Lexington named Thad Jaracz, whose father had played football at Kentucky. "Thad Jaracz played out here at Lafayette [high school in Lexington]," said Rupp. "He was about 6-5 . . . he had too much weight and was kind of lazy. But I kept telling Harry [Lancaster], 'Get that boy for me.' He said, 'He can't play.' I said, 'Get him anyway. We've got to have somebody [and] that guy's got some possibilities.'"

It eventually came down to a battle between two sophomores, Jaracz and 6-8 Cliff Berger, a gritty, self-made player. Jaracz, at 230, was heavier and surprisingly agile and he won the job. "People discount how important Jaracz was to us . . . he gave us something a lot of people didn't have," said Conley. "He was very, very quick and while he had difficulty guarding people on one end, he weighed 230 pounds and was really tough to guard on the other end. He had this little running left-handed hook shot nobody could stop."

Berger and sophomore Bobby Tallent, like Dampier a superb distance shooter, quickly established themselves as the top reserves.

Tallent was a born gunner from the Kentucky hills and he and Rupp never coexisted easily. In fact, an in-game shouting match between Tallent and the coach the following season caused Rupp to dismiss him from the team. Even diehard Kentucky fans were stunned that Rupp would take such an action so quickly and so cavalierly. But the aging coach would not relent. "No boy talks back to me," he said.

Berger provided a big body for a team that sorely needed one. He played adequate defense and rebounded well, but his lack of quickness made him a bad fit for this limber team.

So, very early into practice, Rupp's top seven had been set. The coach rarely went deeper than that. The reserves knew their roles and—not that they had any choice—quietly accepted them. The dissension over playing time that contributed to 1965's failures would not be a problem.

Those first seven would combine to play 5,407 minutes and average better than 84 points a game that memorable season. The next seven—Jim LeMaster, Brad Bounds, Steve Clevenger, Tommy Porter, Gary Gamble, Gene Stewart, and Larry Lentz—would total less than thirteen minutes of playing time a game.

"Battling for position is important, but there wasn't anybody that could beat us four out," said Conley, "and everybody accepted that. The only question we had was in the middle, and Jaracz won that spot in the first two weeks of practice."

■ ■ ■

Kentucky's first practice of the year began at 3:15, as they always did. Players shot free throws for 15 minutes, then worked on positional shooting for another half-hour. Rupp stationed himself on one side of the floor, assistant Harry Lancaster on the other. Players called the intimidating arrangement "The Crossfire." "You could almost see the sergeant's stripes on their arms," said Vern Hatton, a Kentucky star in the 1950s.

The sessions were indeed much like boot camp. Players could get a drink or towel off but never loiter. Talking was prohibited. "No one is to speak unless he can improve on the silence," Rupp told them. There was no improvisation, and no mistake went unnoticed or uncriticized. Foul up and Rupp was going to chew you out on the spot. He didn't call a player aside, wrap an arm around a shoulder, and quietly correct him.

"Sarcasm greeted every error," said Lancaster. "He went after them right there. We put so much pressure on the kids that some folded or transferred." Two of the best players on the outstanding freshman team of 1962–63 that Conley and Kron had played on, Mickey Gibson and Jimmy Rose, had transferred without ever getting a letter.

"The man was genius," said Ralph Beard, a Fab Five star. "He won with little players, big players, and middle-sized players. He won with talented players and untalented players. . . . [But] I don't say I didn't hate him as a teenager. He could be scathing in his criticism and he broke some guys down. But his philosophy was that you'd break down in games if you broke down in practice."

After the shooting drills, the team gathered at midcourt to listen to Rupp. One photograph from the era shows him, hands in his pockets, making a point during one of those lectures. Almost all of the fifteen players surrounding him are staring at the floor. None are looking him in the eye. Those talks were strictly monologues and, for many, the only noncritical words they would hear directly from Rupp.

"This was a man who did not communicate well with you," said Conley. "It was the type of coaching that was done by fear. It was like, 'Here's your job. You're supposed to do it. We're going to train you to do it. Now get your ass out there and do it or get out of the way and let somebody else do it.'"

Rupp expected a lot from them and would not bear any backtalk or childish behavior, just the way his parents had raised him. "If I had wanted to be a father to all of you boys," he told them once, "I would have adopted twenty boys and moved to the farm and raised white-faced cattle."

Except for the criticism, he left the personal stuff to Lancaster. "That's just the way he was. He did not want to get close to his players," said Kron. "Coach Rupp ran it like a corporation. He was the man. I'm in management now and I've come to realize that sometimes you can get too close to the people working for you. And whether the university liked it or not, we were working for him."

His talk concluded, players worked intensely for another hour on various drills before Rupp would dismiss them. "It was always one hour and forty-five minutes and every minute was taken up," said Kron. Rupp believed basketball was a game of rhythm and the only way anyone could improve was by constant repetition. "They practice everything so much," he said, "[so] there's no stuttering around during a game."

It was a cold and harsh system but it worked. Rupp's players, wherever they came from, usually were far better when they departed. In 1953 alone, Red Auerbach drafted three of them for his

Boston Celtics—Frank Ramsey, Cliff Hagan, and Lou Tsioropoulos. "Just knowing they played for Adolph Rupp," said Auerbach, "told me they were motivated and fundamentally sound."

This season, in addition to the weight-and-running program, Rupp would add a few new twists. For the first time, he would conduct two-a-day practices, standard procedure in football but unheard of in basketball. During November and December, the Wildcats practiced twice every Tuesday and Thursday, the first session from 3:15 to 5:00, the second at night, from 8:00 to 9:00 or 9:30.

"One of the other things we worked on was installing a new offense," said Conley. "Anybody who followed Kentucky knew all about our plays. The '6,' '7,' '8,' '9,' and '10.' So Coach Rupp decided to put in a whole new offense, something we could use if we ever came up against a defense that put a lot of pressure on us." Oddly, when that moment arrived five months later, Rupp never used it.

On that first day, Rupp watched his players more closely than usual. He looked particularly long at Kron and Riley. Their bangs, in keeping with mainstream mid-1960s fashion, dipped far down their foreheads. These would soon be considered conservative haircuts, but at the time, in Lexington, Kentucky, they brought to mind the slightly defiant moptops of the early Beatles—hip, stylish, but just long enough to set them apart. Rupp despised the long hair he was starting to see on campus, "damned hippie stuff," he called it. Long hair, mustaches, blue jeans, there would never be any of that on his teams.

Once, not long after he took the Kentucky job, he had sent his team home to change after they showed up at the railroad station in casual clothes. Since then, whenever they traveled, Kentucky players wore blazers bearing the university's crest. And if he were the university's president, Rupp thought, no one would dress sloppily on campus either. And there wouldn't be any of those SDS meetings or antiwar protests. That was all President Oswald's fault. He was one of those Northern liberals for whom anything went. He was even bothering Rupp, pushing him to integrate his team. Didn't he know there weren't many black kids he could get into school? And even if he could, how many would want to travel to Mississippi or Alabama?

Rupp couldn't see it, of course, but Kentucky and the nation were straddling two worlds that autumn. The surface serenity and passion for conformity that lingered from the 1950s was about to give way to Vietnam, marijuana, and social unrest. "Culturally, Kentucky had been a be-bop, rock-and-roll, fraternity-type school," said Kron. "You still had sock hops and the frats had beer parties. It was that whole lighthearted image. But things were starting to change in 1966. The stuff that was starting then was the stuff you see about the '60s in movies now," said Kron. "But we were living it. We'd be sitting in the grill and some SDS guys would walk by and one of the fraternity guys would yell, 'Bomb Hanoi!' If anybody in the frat house had long, shaggy hair they would have been ostracized. . . . Civil rights issues weren't huge then, probably because we didn't have a huge minority population on campus."

Basketball players at Kentucky were hardly affected by the growing ferment. It was as if they were enclosed in a glass bubble. They could view outside events with amazement, but those same events rarely intruded on their world. "It was an eerie feeling," said Conley, "to be in a sport that demanded discipline during an era that we think of as having had no discipline. I had one world I lived in with Coach Rupp. And then I'd leave practice and enter that other world. I'd see Lyndon Johnson signing the Civil Rights Act in 1964 with Martin Luther King standing behind him and I'd think, 'This is a good thing.' And then I'd go back into that other little world of basketball and discipline."

Elsewhere on that little island of basketball, however, the real world was making inroads and Kentucky's players couldn't help but notice. They saw increasing numbers of black players whenever they traveled North. They saw how their speed and power were changing the game. They saw integration taking hold and, occasionally, they'd wonder how Kentucky fit into that larger picture. The haggling between Rupp and Oswald took place out of public view, but the players understood what was happening.

"I'd played against black players from junior high on up. So had all of us," said Conley. "We pretty much knew there was some discussion about bringing black players in. But for the most part we were removed from all that. I did, in my sophomore year, go down to Louisville to try to get Wes Unseld to come to Kentucky. Wes would have been an ideal guy to break the color line. He was such a class guy. A tremendous player. Wes just didn't want to be the first black player at Kentucky. I understood that."

Rupp asked Kron to make a similar visit a year later to Butch Beard's home in Breckenridge County. It was typical recruiting strategy for the coach, who did not like to involve himself too personally in the process. The problem was, if blacks were going to be convinced to attend Kentucky, they were going to need a lot of personal persuasion from Rupp.

"We really weren't aware of everything that was going on in that regard," Kron said. "and I really don't know what kind of effort Coach Rupp expended to get Wes or Butch. Did he have the same feelings that a lot of sixty-year-old men had about blacks back then? Very probably so. But so did my dad and a lot of other people. There was so much misinformation going on back then, and it was easy to paint a picture of a program that had never *had* a black player as a program that didn't *want* a black player."

As familiar as they said they were with black players, however, Kentucky's players actually had almost no experience with them that season. Of all the players they faced in twenty-seven regular-season games, sixteen of them against eight SEC opponents, fewer than a dozen opponents were black.

■ ■ ■

However Rupp and his players felt about the prospects for 1966, Kentucky's fans entered that season with their typical optimism. Memorial Coliseum was always sold out, and for the previous few years, season-ticket sales had been closed to the public. Unless some students failed to show up in their allotted spots, seats were never available for home games.

Ironically, Kentucky's first game, against Hardin-Simmons on the night of December 1, 1965, would be a sort of preview of their final game in that the opponents were a little-regarded team from Texas. In thirteen previous games against Texas clubs, the Wildcats had lost just once, to SMU at Dallas in 1957. Despite Hardin-Simmons' lack of stature, 1,500 fans bought standing-room tickets.

Before that season-opener, Rupp had talked with reporters about the changes he had seen coaching basketball at the school since 1930. As usual, the present came up lacking in his assessment. "The boys in those days were more eager to play," he said. "They weren't on scholarships. They wanted to play. They wanted an education. . . . The boys in those days played for the love of playing."

Fans began filling Memorial Coliseum an hour before the opening game. They were mostly students and alumni, with a smattering of businessmen from Lexington and Kentucky mixed in. Not long before game time, Kentucky's cheerleaders appeared. Their attire, like the megaphones they carried and the all-white team they cheered, soon would be obsolete. The girls wore long blue jumpers with long-sleeved white blouses. The men were in long white pants and blue letter-sweaters.

There were boos when Hardin-Simmons came out for warmups and a great roar when, for the first time, the 1965–66 Wildcats ran onto the floor. Rupp, tremendously superstitious, was in the corridor, from where he never emerged until just before game time.

Kentucky blew out Hardin-Simmons, 83–55. Afterward, losing coach Lou Henson rated his opponents in terms they would hear all season. "That's a good little team," said Henson. "[But] when it runs into a big boy, it's going to have trouble."

Trouble was a long time coming. That same week, with Jaracz scoring 54 points, they won easily at Virginia (99–73) and Illinois (86–68). The Wildcats then returned home to defeat another Big Ten school, Northwestern, 86–73. As usual, they captured their Kentucky Invitational at Christmas, routing Air Force, 78–58, and Indiana, 91–56. They were on a remarkable run. No one even challenged them. Kentucky had won its first six games by an average margin of more than 23 points.

"We started out winning games so easily," said Kron. "We were kicking people's butts big-time. We'd take a 15-point lead and extend it to 30. It seemed we got stronger as the games wore on and part of that was our new conditioning program, the weights and especially the running."

By then their already adoring fans in Lexington were in a frenzy. The Wildcats were running up whopping point totals with an entertaining style that combined unselfish passing, phenomenal perimeter shooting, and a devastating fast break. "Kentucky plays a lot like Loyola of Chicago," said Northwestern coach Larry Glass. "They all handle the ball well, run with excellent speed, and they all shoot well." And, as the coeds on campus liked to point out, they were cute too. That season, said a *Louisville Courier-Journal* sportswriter, Kentucky's players were bigger than the Beatles. "I don't think I've ever seen the kind of excitement the fans had that year," said Kron.

But Coach Rupp, believing interviews could distract players and occasionally get them in trouble, limited the media's access to them. He kept the attention focused on himself—not an unpleasant task for the man. "In a lot of ways we were very insulated," said Conley. "Of course, Coach Rupp loved the notoriety. He ate it up. He was toward the end of his career and had one of his best teams ever. And he was taking full credit for it."

The Kentucky media struggled to find an alliterative nickname for this undersized team. Great Wildcat teams always had one—The Fab Five, The Fiddlin' Five. Finally, before the Kentucky–Notre Dame game at Louisville's Freedom Hall on December 29, a wire-service writer came up with one that stuck—Rupp's Runts. Then they went out and beat the bigger Irish by 34 points.

Unbeaten, the Wildcats assumed the number one spot in national polls. It wasn't until their eleventh game, a 69–65 double-overtime win at Georgia, that an opponent came within 10 points of them.

"It was about then that we started to say to each other, 'Hey, we're really playing well together,'" said Kron. "Every one of us was on a roll. All five of us knew who was going to take the shot if all of us were open—Louie or Pat. Everybody knew that when the ball went up certain people would go get it. Everybody knew that when there was a tough guy to guard, he was mine. . . . Everybody knew if we were running a play, I'd start it so that Louie could end up on the shooting end of it. Before long we were 10-0 and it had a sort of mushroom effect."

The Runts were a talented offensive team, one that like most Rupp teams looked to run at every opportunity. "If we had to go to a half-court game, we knew we'd be in a lot of trouble because teams were bigger than us and we couldn't pound it inside," said Conley. "We had to get shots from the outside or get it off the break. So as soon as we got the ball it looked like an all-out blitz. Five guys running to the other end. But we almost always got it into the hands of the right people."

Kron and Conley were able to sublimate their egos, making sure that Riley and Dampier got the bulk of the scoring opportunities.

"They [Kron and Conley] were the real leaders—the spirit and the glue," said Riley. "Louie and I were just the finishers." And this out-sized team was better on the boards than almost all its opponents. Only five times that season did Kentucky get outrebounded.

Still it might have been their defense that made this team special, particularly the 1-3-1 zone they saved for just the right moments. Rupp had always disdained a zone, perhaps because his teams usually attacked them so easily with their quick passing and good outside shooting. "Nobody has yet shown me a zone defense that I'd trade for my man-to-man," he often said.

In the mid-1960s, however, Lancaster saw the 1-3-1 trap at a summer clinic and was impressed by its disruptive elements. He soon began using it with his freshman team. One night, as Rupp watched the freshmen play, the old coach recognized it. "Harry," he said, "you were running a goddamned zone out there tonight. You're just wasting our kids' time."

Eventually Lancaster convinced Rupp the 1-3-1 could confuse bigger opponents. The Wildcats began working on it at practice and finally, as they were getting blown out at Georgia Tech on January 4, 1964, Rupp ordered them to play it. "He wanted to see what it looked like and he put me in, and for the first time we used it," said Kron. Rupp liked what he saw in the 76–67 loss and began practicing it more frequently, telling his players not to reveal its existence to anyone. Then, at Tennessee, they sprung it on the hated Volunteers and coach Ray Mears. "We baffled them with it," said Kron. "For some reason they responded by holding the ball and we beat them down there [42–38]."

Kentucky played it a little more in 1965, but by 1966, Rupp felt his quick starting five was ideally suited to the defense. Kron, with his long arms and reach, was at the point. Riley roamed the baseline. Dampier and Conley were on the wings and Jaracz in the middle. "It allowed us to take advantage of our speed and quickness. We had pretty good anticipation and we could see the whole floor," said Kron. "I would chase the ball and people would gamble and make bad passes. They'd try to dribble into it and that was a mistake."

Lancaster called the zone pivotal to the Runts' success, but surprisingly, though they remain associated with that defense in people's minds, they used it sparingly. "A lot of people thought the zone was our key but I would guess we didn't play it a total of sixty minutes that entire season," said Kron. "Once teams saw it seven or eight times down the floor, they'd recognize how to attack it. You can really tear up a 1-3-1 if you know how." Occasionally, Kentucky would set up in a man-to-man and then spring the trap on opponents when they arrived downcourt. It was a defense that served as an antidote to their lack of height.

"The only time we went to it was when we had real problems," said Conley. "We played a game in Lubbock [against Texas Tech on December 22] and they were real big up front, like 6-7, 6-8, 6-8. We were having a hard time guarding those guys. We were down at halftime as I recall and Coach Lancaster said, 'Let's break it out.' Coach Rupp agreed. We came back out and I don't think they scored for the first nine and a half minutes. That was when I began to realize that maybe we'd have a good year." Dampier was hurt that game but Tallent scored 13 in the 89–73 comeback win.

After the double-overtime scare at Georgia, no opponent came within 10 of the Wildcats until their 73–69 win at Mississippi State on February 19. Kentucky won its first 23 games and clinched the school's twenty-second SEC title. Then on March 5, they traveled to Tennessee. Kentucky had beaten the archrival Vols, 78–64, a week earlier. This time Mears, who relished his ability to irritate Rupp, wore one of the old coach's trademark brown suits. "Rupp was not amused," recalled Russell Rice.

Tennessee handed the Wildcats their first defeat, 69–62, spoiling a perfect regular season and a campus rally planned for the following day in Lexington. Only Riley showed up for the event and he apologized to those fans who had anticipated celebrating the school's first unbeaten season since 1954.

"There was a lot of disappointment after that game because they were our biggest rivals," said Conley. "We had played a near perfect game against them earlier that week in Lexington, only two turnovers. It was absolutely amazing. Then we went to Knoxville and lost and felt awful because we had a great season going and we pretty much knew we were going to beat Tulane in the last game."

They did, on March 7 at the Coliseum, by a 103–74 score, the sixth time they had reached 100 points that season.

The news that Kentucky would play in the Mideast Regional at Iowa City the following weekend created tremendous excitement in the state. Western Kentucky, which was 23-1 and ranked tenth in the country, was one of the regional's other three teams—along with Dayton and Michigan.

Rupp had always ignored in-state schools like Western Kentucky, Louisville, and Eastern Kentucky. In his forty-two years at Kentucky, he never played a regular-season game against any of the three colleges. For one thing, he could always find a less-challenging patsy somewhere else, and, for another, he didn't want to help them get any publicity that might aid their recruiting. He disparaged them whenever possible. Years earlier, when someone pointed out that Ed Diddle, the kindly old coach at Western Kentucky who was in many ways the anti-Rupp, was close to him in lifetime victories, Rupp snidely responded that none of Kentucky's wins had come against YMCAs.

Actually, these schools were just beginning to take advantage of Rupp's failure to recruit the state's best black athletes. Louisville already had Unseld (a sophomore) and Beard (a freshman) and this Western team started three black Kentuckians, Clem Haskins and brothers Dwight and Greg Smith. Now Western's fans and players were aching for a chance to play the ballyhooed Runts in the regional final. Especially the black players, who felt personally shunned by Rupp.

"Dwight Smith, Greg, and me wanted Kentucky so much we probably overlooked Michigan," said Clem Haskins. "We all wanted to get Michigan out of the way and play Kentucky."

Kentucky did its part, dispatching Dayton—with some difficulty. The Flyers were led by forward Donnie May and 6-11 center Henry Finkel. Finkel's size bothered the Wildcats early. He would finish with 36 points, but, once again, the 1-3-1 turned the game around. "Henry had a good first half and so did Donnie," said Conley. "Henry was really tough for us. We kept having to drop off our men and try to help inside when we were in our man-to-man. In the second half, we ended up going to the zone to stop him because we couldn't stop him inside. But they were having trouble on the other end containing us." Dayton led by two at halftime but behind Dampier's 34 points and Riley's 29, Kentucky won, 86–79.

That win was the 747th of Rupp's career, moving him past the record total of his old Kansas mentor, Phog Allen.

In the regional doubleheader's second game, Western Kentucky and Michigan played it close throughout. Michigan had two black stars, Player of the Year Cazzie Russell and Oliver Darden, a muscular banger. Kentucky's players watched the first half from the stands, then returned to their motel, where most saw its dramatic conclusion on TV. "Coach Rupp never wanted his teams to stay around and watch a team that they were going to play in a tournament," said Conley. "He thought you would end up getting bad thoughts and bad ideas. He felt like, 'Let the coaches do the scouting and I'll tell you what you need to do to win.'"

With seconds left in a tied game, a play took place that Clem Haskins would call "the worst call in the history of basketball." That play prevented the much-anticipated in-state matchup and set off decades of complaints from Hilltoppers fans.

"There was a jump ball between Cazzie Russell and Greg Smith," said Conley. "Steve Honzo tosses the ball in the air, not straight up but toward Cazzie. Greg jumps across to try to tip the ball and he jumps into Cazzie. Honzo calls a foul. On a jump ball! The ball was never in play. All Greg was trying to do was tip the ball. Anyway, Cazzie hit the free throws and Michigan won. It was incredible but it really didn't matter to us. We didn't care who we were going to play. Western, though, they really wanted to get us."

They would have to wait another five years for the chance.

■ ■ ■

Somewhere in Iowa City a flu bug was circulating. Conley began to experience a heaviness in his chest the day of the Michigan game. Jaracz was sneezing and so were a few other players. "Iowa City is one of those really cold places and that weekend it was just freezing out there," said Conley. "The wind was blowing and out there there's nothing to keep that wind off you."

Michigan had been to the Final Four in each of the last two seasons, losing by 91–80 scores each time—to Duke in a 1964 semifinal and to UCLA, which won both years, in 1965's championship game. Cazzie Russell was a senior now and though coach Dave Strack's team was only 18-7 and ranked ninth, many people anticipated that this might be the Wolverines' year.

Like most of Kentucky's opponents, Michigan tried to get the ball inside, to Darden. Smaller bodies bounced off the big center all afternoon and that opened things up for Russell on the perimeter. "Darden was tough inside, very similar in size and style to David Lattin," said Conley. "But Texas Western had no one like Cazzie. He was something else." Kentucky led, 42–32, at the half but with twelve minutes to play, Michigan went ahead, 53–52. Riley and Dampier then got hot and Kentucky held on for an 84–77 triumph.

At that point, having won twenty-six of twenty-seven games,

even Rupp had to marvel at how this team had overachieved. "Nobody could have foreseen this," he said. "You could only dream about it. [It] is a simply unbelievable record when you stop and think about it."

The team returned to Lexington on Sunday night. By then several of them had scratchy throats, the chills, and sniffles. "That Monday I just felt awful," said Conley. "I went to the doctor and I had a temperature. I knew something was wrong. That week I practiced maybe two times."

On Thursday morning, Kentucky flew to Baltimore and bused to its hotel, the Sheraton Motor Inn, in Silver Spring, Maryland. They worked out that afternoon at Cole, the floor of which some players felt was extremely slippery.

The prevailing attitude in College Park was that Friday night's Duke-Kentucky semifinal would produce the national champion for 1966. "I think the finals are going to be played Friday night," said Syracuse coach Fred Lewis. George Minot of the *Washington Post* called it the "game the nation has been squirming for."

Duke, with Mike Lewis, Bob Verga, and Steve Vacendak, had played at Cole once that season, rallying from a 15-point deficit to defeat Maryland on February 19. The Blue Devils' staff didn't need much time to prepare for Kentucky.

"Kentucky's only got six or seven plays," said Duke assistant Chuck Daly, the future NBA coach, "and you can read about them in Rupp's book. But stopping them is another matter. They run those plays with precision. They make few mistakes and they've got outstanding shooters."

Conley felt terrible on Friday but he assured Rupp he could play. Verga was ill with the flu as well. Duke's coach, Vic Bubas, had sent him back to the hotel during a walk-through earlier in the day. But unlike Rupp, the Duke coach was reluctant to discuss his star's illness. "I don't want to be making excuses," he said. Both coaches planned to rest the two players when and if they got a comfortable lead. Each had several.

Kentucky led, 23–14, and out came Conley. But Jaracz got in foul trouble and Duke went up, 40–35. Kentucky moved ahead again in the second half, 53–46.

Six times between 61–61 and 71–71, the game was tied.

Conley hit a pair of free throws, and baskets from Riley and Dampier put Kentucky ahead, 77–71. They held on, winning, 83–79.

"We were both very familiar with each other's personnel," said Conley. "That game was close throughout and neither could get the jump on the other. But you know I occasionally look at tapes of that game and it looks like we were in slow motion. I guess that's another way the great black players changed the game."

The pace wasn't all that looks odd in retrospect. In the stands that night, Johnson mentioned to Oswald that they were probably witnessing the last significant NCAA game between two white teams. He was right.

9.

March on College Park

*"It was a violent game. I don't mean there were any fights—but
they were desperate and they were committed and they were more
motivated than we were."*
  —Pat Riley

Haskins' heart was thumping like a basketball on a fast break. He
had been guzzling black coffee since daybreak and all that caffeine
aggravated the gruff restlessness that led others to call this imposing
man "Bear." Nervous, sleepless, and deprived of his cigarettes in an
arena that had banned smoking for the tournament, Haskins' head
pounded with pain.

He had paced a corridor nonstop, glancing out at his team as
they warmed up, sneaking a look at his opponent, watching the Cole
Field House stands fill up. He was behaving, a friend would remark
later, "like a big bird with ten-foot wings and no feet." Then he
checked the clock. It was almost 10:00 P.M. on Saturday night.
"Let's get going," he grumbled to himself. "Let's get this damn
game started."

This level of agitation was nothing new. Texas Western's coach thrived on it. He had hustled his way through college shooting pool and that was how he had supported himself and his wife when they were newlyweds. He liked cards and high-stakes golf. "He's got to have action," said Earl Estep, "action all the time."

But even by those standards, Haskins had been unusually jumpy all week. On Tuesday, he had interrupted a telephone interview with Houston sportswriter Mickey Herskowitz to run to the bathroom. "Nervous tummy," he explained. Part of the reason, he knew, was a nagging self-doubt. Whenever anyone suggested that maybe this little-known Texas Western team with its little-known coach didn't belong in the Final Four, Haskins' temper bubbled. Yet, at some level, he too found this sudden good fortune bewildering. "I'm just a young punk," he said more than once that weekend.

He had needed pills to sleep on Thursday night. And on Friday, after his Miners beat Utah, he sat up much of the night in his room at the Interstate Inn, drinking beer and reliving the win with friends. The combination of the victory and the all-night bull session, interrupted at one point by noisy college students in the parking lot, briefly relaxed him but did little to ease his doubts. "I kept telling myself that no matter what happened in the championship game against Kentucky, we had a good season," Haskins said. "But I couldn't convince myself."

Though he would never admit it, Haskins was a little cowed at the prospect of playing Kentucky and the great Rupp. He assumed his team would feel that same trepidation. "Going into that ball game, playing for the national championship and playing Kentucky, he was concerned that we might not play at the same level we played at throughout the year," said Iba.

That morning, his stomach was churning acid again. When he met with his players early in the afternoon for a team meeting and shootaround, they seemed typically unconcerned. ("They never got uptight," Haskins recalled.) Hands folded behind their heads, they twirled toothpicks in their mouths and cracked wise. Irritated, Haskins walked out. "I ended up getting mad because I'm trying to tell them how good Kentucky is and they're all just looking at me, like, 'You've gotta be kidding me.' Bobby Joe Hill is in the room and he's got a toothpick hanging from his mouth and I'm telling him how good Louis Dampier is. And he gets this smile and just looks at me. I left . . . thinking that they needed to get their butts kicked."

They were so relaxed, in fact, that when sports information director Eddie Mullens walked into their locker room not long before the championship game, he found the lights off and the players napping. "It was just business with us," recalled Hill. "It was one of the highlights of my life, but I knew that even if we lost, the sun was still going to be shining when I woke up the next morning—especially in El Paso."

Later they reconvened for a pregame dinner (steak, baked potatoes, and peas) at the motel's restaurant. There, Hill's shimmying rendition of the Miracles' "Going to a Go-Go" told Haskins his players remained apparently unaffected by what confronted them. "They were nowhere near as shook as I was."

"Sure, we might have been cocky," said Worsley. "But we were all from places—New York, Detroit, Indiana, Chicago—where you had to be cocky to survive. We knew Kentucky was a good team, we weren't going to overlook them. But we felt we could beat them. If you would have seen us that afternoon, you'd have thought we just had a pickup game that night. You would have thought that we thought we could walk on water."

After the meal, Texas Western's twelve players, two coaches, cheerleaders, pep band, president, sports information director, trainer, and assorted fans boarded a bus for the short ride to the arena. Someone sat down beside Texas Western president Joseph Ray and tried to reassure the nervous administrator. "He said to me, 'Don't worry, Dr. Ray, we're going to win.' I said, 'How do you know we're going to win it?' And he says, ''Cause those niggers there won't let those white boys beat 'em.'"

Friday night's losers, Duke and Utah, were preparing to play in the 8:00 P.M. consolation game when the Texas Western entourage arrived at the arena. That meaningless preliminary didn't interest Haskins any more than it did its participants and he told trainer Ross Moore to escort the team to its locker room. He and Iba walked to a nearby restaurant for a hamburger. Later, back inside Cole, he peeked out at the court. "I'm tired of looking at the players," he explained to the cluster of reporters outside his locker room, "and they're tired of looking at me."

All that he could later recall about that preliminary game was that late in its first half, Kentucky's players and coaches had entered the Field House. They looked rested and poised, Haskins thought, a team that appeared deserving of its number one ranking.

Although both teams were 27-1, virtually all of the big-time coaches surveyed believed Kentucky was going to win even though few had seen Texas Western play before Friday night. "I don't think Texas Western can contain . . . Kentucky's outstanding shooters and fast break," said Tennessee's Ray Mears. "And if Conley is healthy, I know it will be UK. I don't know of many teams that can beat them on a neutral court." Only one of the polled coaches, Providence's Joe Mullaney, gave Texas Western a chance. "They're big and they play pretty good defense," Mullaney said.

None of them mentioned it, of course, but an article of faith among most of the era's coaches was that an all-black team could not beat a talented, disciplined, well-coached white squad. And Kentucky was the epitome of all those things.

The logical converse to that thinking, of course, was that Texas Western was not. "Texas Western is even bigger and rougher than Duke," read an Associated Press preview that typified the prevalent thinking. "But that may be the downfall of the Miners against a team with the finesse and discipline of Kentucky."

The Eastern writers never bothered to seek the opinion of coaches from the Southwest, coaches who had seen the Miners play

more than once. Basketball and Texas just didn't seem to fit together
in their minds. It was like New York and hillbillies. No Texas team
had ever been much good, so what could those coaches possibly
know?

Quite a bit, as it turned out.

"Kentucky can't play Texas Western man-to-man," West Texas
State coach Jimmy Viramontes predicted to a Dallas writer. "They
have no one who can stay with Bobby Joe Hill."

SMU coach Doc Hayes had a similar opinion. "I said from the
first I thought Texas Western would win," said Hayes. "It has the
strongest defense, a great driver and ball handler [Hill], a good outside shooter [Artis], a tough rebounder [Lattin], and is tremendously
well disciplined as a team."

Most of the spectators and tournament administrators, like
everyone else outside of Texas, also believed the championship
game would be a mismatch in Kentucky's favor. And so, apparently,
did some of the referees.

"Hanging around the hospitality rooms and what not hardly anyone gave Texas Western a chance," said Jimmy Rogers, a friend of
Haskins' who was in College Park that weekend. "I can even remember hearing some of the officials who were hanging around the
lobby talking like Texas Western didn't have much of a chance. I
thought, 'What are they doing talking about that? That's not right for
them to be doing that.'"

Haskins couldn't shake a sense that this was his life's grand opportunity. "Mr. Rupp is sixty-four, and he's made it lots of times,"
Haskins said, when asked if he thought this might be the first of
many championship games for him. "It's probably going to be just
once in a lifetime for me."

While Haskins fidgeted, he glanced at his counterpart. To Haskins, the Kentucky coach appeared serene on the sideline. And why
not? Rupp had won 749 games, 644 more than Haskins, and he
didn't seem to think getting number 750 was going to be much of a

problem. In Rupp's narrow view of the world, Texas Western was some tiny desert reformatory. How could such a remote institution, one whose basketball team had played Eastern New Mexico, East Texas State, and Pan American, for God's sake, possibly compete with his glorious Kentucky program? "I wonder," Haskins thought to himself as he looked again at Rupp, "if he even knows who I am."

If Rupp didn't know who Haskins and his players were, he knew *what* they were. Some in the Texas Western party had heard that Rupp had boasted on a Kentucky radio station that week that five blacks would never beat his Wildcats. Haskins, recognizing some potentially useful motivation, tucked the comment away. Earlier, just before the Miners left their locker room, he had called aside some of his black players and told them how the opposing coach felt. "We figured it was just talk," said Lattin.

"Coach Haskins before the game quoted Rupp . . . that he had never played five black guys before and that five black guys would never beat his team," said Flournoy. "And we kind of thought that Coach Haskins was just trying to hype us up, you know. And we weren't sure if he said that or if it was just Coach Haskins talking."

Whether they all believed him or not, it produced a spark. Minutes later, Haskins fanned it. Grasping the arm of Lattin, Texas Western's 6-6, 240-pound center, he told him, "The first chance you get, flush it. Flush it as hard as you can."

Haskins watched his players warm up. The diminutive Worsley dunked the ball during layup drills and 14,253 fans stirred.

■ ■ ■

When that historic Saturday dawned, Rupp, having downed two bourbons before putting on a pair of red pajamas, was sleeping comfortably in his room at the Sheraton Motor Inn. In the superstitious Rupp's successful three and a half decades at Kentucky, bourbon and red pajamas were as much a part of his game-day ritual as brown suits, lucky-pin hunts (hairpins were the luckiest), and socks. On multigame road trips like this, he wouldn't change socks unless Kentucky lost. "I know darn well that when we won, he washed them and had them ready for the next night," said Lancaster.

An NCAA title game was nothing new for Rupp. The Kentucky coach had been in four of them previously and each time his Wildcats emerged as champions. This Rupp team came to the Final Four geared to beat Duke in a matchup the *Washington Post* called "the perfect end of the long season." Once that was over, Rupp believed his title game record would soon be 5-0. "Kentucky," said Flournoy, "thought they had a pushover."

Texas Western was, in fact, as unlikely a foil as the great Rupp and his ballyhooed Kentucky team could have imagined. Few among the then 183 Division I teams were as obscure. Though they were ranked number three, the Miners entered the NCAA tournament having played only one team then in the top ten. Their schedule was crowded with other schools from the Southwest, a region where basketball was still a long way behind football.

Rupp's program was still the most successful in college basketball history. (But it wouldn't be for long. Lew Alcindor was in his first year at UCLA and when his freshman team beat the UCLA varsity by 15 points in a scrimmage that season, it was assumed that the Bruins would win the next three national titles. They went on to win the next seven.) Rupp's Wildcats had won NCAA championships in 1948, '49, '51, and '58 and might have won several more had the tournament been in existence before 1939.

It had always been easy for Rupp. But now eight years had passed since his last national title and people were starting to whisper about his age and outside interests. He wanted this fifth NCAA title to shut them up.

"They said we were a little old," he told reporters after his team beat Duke. "They said we used old-fashioned coaching methods, that we went to the bank too often and worried more about our farm and cows than the ball team. I think we showed them."

The only remaining obstacle, it seemed to him, was an insignificant one.

■ ■ ■

Haskins, the pool hustler, knew you sometimes could beat an opponent just by the way you carried yourself, or by what you showed him on your first few shots. He figured Kentucky had never played against anyone quite like Lattin—so big, so strong, so black.

"David didn't score a lot of points but the one thing he did," said Iba, "was he could be very intimidating inside. He was like 6-6, 240, and a great jumper. And I don't think Kentucky had ever played against anyone like him, someone that could dominate them."

That's what Haskins hoped to exploit. He just hoped the officials, Steve Honzo and Thornton Jenkins, allowed it. "We didn't know if they were going to let us win," said Iba. "Would they let us play?" Against Utah, the Miners had been called for 27 fouls to Utah's 20.

So as he gathered his team around him that night, Haskins again told Lattin to dunk the ball as quickly as possible. "There's a big guy on the bottom [of their defense]. Even if you draw a foul," said Haskins, "I want you to take it to the guy and show him something he hasn't seen."

Haskins loved the early dunk. It was an in-your-face challenge to an opponent, like running your first rack of balls in pool. "He was very strict about some things," said Artis. "You couldn't go behind your back, or between the legs. But he loved the dunk."

Lattin, Hill, Artis, and Flournoy were starting. The fifth man, Haskins told them in the locker room, would be "Willie." The 5-6 Worsley assumed he meant Cager and patted his taller teammate on the back. "Coach said, 'No, little man, you,'" Worsley recalled. Worsley was starting in place of Shed, a forward, and would be guarding Conley. Hill was on Dampier, Lattin on Jaracz, Flournoy on Riley, and Artis on Kron.

"We gave up some size for speed because they had damn quick players," said Iba of the three-guard lineup. "Don was trying to match up with their shooters. We played a man-to-man. The only time I ever remember Don playing a zone was when he'd get mad at them and make them stand there in a zone until they got mad enough and decided they wanted to play man."

Pound the ball into Lattin, Haskins told them, and pressure the hell out of them. Rebounding would be essential, he reminded them, because if the Wildcats controlled the boards, they might run all night. And definitely make it ugly because Kentucky prefers pretty.

If Rupp was concerned as he gave his team its final instructions, it was only about his players' health. Conley's fever had broken at about 3:00 A.M. but he was still weak. The other players hit by the flu were improving. In the years that followed his most disappointing loss, Rupp would state that he had spoken to a doctor after Friday night's game, believing his team was at last healthy. "After I told the doctor they'd be stronger tomorrow, he said, 'Adolph, I don't want to kill you but you're through,'" said Rupp. "He said, 'You shot your load.' He said, 'Your kids tomorrow are simply not going to be strong.'"

The Kentucky players told Rupp they were fine. They certainly weren't overly worried about their opponents. "The only thing I knew about Texas Western was that they were ranked third," said Conley. "We watched the first half [Friday] and they were beating Utah pretty good. We knew we were going to get a lot of pressure, particularly outside. They had Lattin in the middle, which presented a problem for us."

Rupp sent them out in a man-to-man defense and told them to be patient. Sooner or later, he said, Texas Western would self-destruct.

"They thought they could outsmart us," said Worsley. "They

thought if they slowed it down, we would get impatient and commit stupid fouls. If they passed instead of dribbled, they thought they'd beat our press. We wouldn't be able to stand the pressure. We were from the ghetto. We were on national TV so we'd get a big head and become selfish.

"Well, Coach didn't allow us to be selfish. We were too scared of Coach to be scared of the other team. What could they do to us that Coach hadn't already done to us?"

■ ■ ■

The players broke from their huddles and lined up for the center jump, beneath a huge American flag and around a red "M" in the middle of a floor gleaming with reflected lights. Lattin looked for the biggest opponent he could find.

"Hey," he called to Jaracz, "I'm going to break your neck."

Riley, who had won 40 of 48 jumps that season by subtly sticking an elbow in his counterpart's stomach, went up against Lattin and tried the same trick. This time, the referee whistled him for a violation.

Thirty years later, watching it on film, the game appears to have been played at half-speed on an oversized court. It resembles, in many ways, a Princeton game today. The emphasis was on defense, a controlled pace, and passing. Ball handlers stood straight up, with their knees seldom bent. Defenders kept their distance. Picks and weaves were run constantly and many of the shooters pushed the ball toward the basket rather than flicking it one-handed.

But there were moments—when Lattin leaped high for a strong rebound or Hill flashed out of nowhere for a steal, or Dampier rose up for a quick jumper—when you could almost see the future.

"It does look like slow motion," said Kron. "And the floor seems so much bigger. The players today are so much faster and quicker and stronger. Look at Conley and Shed. They probably didn't weigh

200 pounds between them. But Lattin was a big, strong guy, a sort of prototype of the modern power forward. And Hill had the kind of quickness you see now."

The only defensive concern Haskins had involved Worsley. Despite his quickness, he was six inches shorter than the Wildcats' smallest player, Dampier. And Haskins wanted the quicker Hill on Dampier. The Wildcats' other guard, Kron, was 6-5. That meant he had to stick Worsley on the 6-3 Conley. On Kentucky's first timeout, Conley told Rupp he could post up his defender. Rupp called plays that allowed that, but Conley's shots didn't drop.

"They spent so much time trying to get Conley into a position to shoot that it took them out of what they were trying to do," said Haskins.

Worsley had developed a method for guarding bigger players and he used it successfully. "I would go up for my shot and he would tip the bottom of my elbow," said Conley. "On one shot, the ball went flying over the backboard. I looked at Honzo and said, 'Come on, Steve. I'm not that bad a shot.' But I remember Honzo had this kind of glazed look on his face, like he really wasn't there. I went back to the bench and said, 'Coach, he's not in the game.'" But the issue of Honzo's state of mind never arose again.

On Kentucky's first possession, Lattin, as he had all season, delivered a forceful message. He swatted Riley on a drive, fouling him in the process. The second time Texas Western had the ball, Hill saw Lattin flash open beneath the basket. He whipped a pass down the spine of Kentucky's defense and the muscular center, the San Francisco Warriors number one pick a year later, jammed the ball through Riley's outstretched arms and down into the basket. Lattin turned and barked at Kentucky's junior All-America before walking to the foul line.

"I was right below the dunk, and the Texas Western player said, 'Take that you white honky,'" recalled Riley. "It was a violent game.

I don't mean there were any fights—but they were desperate and they were committed and they were more motivated than we were."

To Riley and others, it appeared Kentucky was intimidated. They had never played against five blacks at once and weren't entirely sure what to expect.

"They were playing for something a lot more [important] than I think people realized at the time," said Riley. "I mean it wasn't written about much back then, but it was basically five black players, or so the perception was, against five Southern white guys. Now, I'm from New York so I sort of resented that."

Worsley recognized that there clearly was something defensive about Kentucky's play, something that was causing them to perform much more tentatively than usual: "They either had a lack of respect for us because we were black, because their coach had told them derogatory stuff about us, or they were scared because they knew we were 'better athletes,' or they were cocky and thought they would kick our butts. They might have had two or three athletes on the team who felt comfortable and two or three who didn't."

Perhaps Kentucky's backing off was due to something else. Perhaps it was an example of what DePaul coach Ray Meyer observed about that period when blacks were becoming a major presence in college basketball. "At first," said Meyer, "the whites seemed afraid to play against blacks."

Whether it was due to racial factors or not, the Wildcats, said Kron, were thrown off their game by Lattin's dunk. "We were all just kind of standing there and he soared up and it seemed to be a real exclamation point," said Kron. "It really picked their team up and I think we were intimidated by their quickness and power. We didn't quit playing, but I think we were intimidated to the extent that we didn't go to the boards as hard as we could. I kept going, but I was always late. They were already up there."

Conley saw it all differently. "That never bothered me. People had dunked on us all year," he said. "[Vanderbilt All-America] Clyde Lee used to do it to us all the time. And Lattin was nowhere near the player Lee was. I don't think we were intimidated."

Neither team was shooting well and it was 9–9 when, with 10:18 left in the half, Shed put Texas Western ahead—for good as it turned out—with a free throw. About that time, Flournoy signaled to Haskins that he needed to come out. The knee he had injured the previous night was limiting his motion. "I was afraid I might hurt the team defensively," said Flournoy. "I could run forward but I had no lateral movement."

As Kron brought the ball upcourt following Shed's foul shot, he attempted to avoid Artis by turning left. When he did, Hill reached around him for a steal. A breakaway layup resulted. Next time up, Dampier had the ball stolen by Hill. Another layup made it 14–9. "Those two steals, that had never happened to them before," said Iba. "It just forced them to the perimeter."

Decades later, when participants were asked about the game, it was that quick sequence of plays, Hill's two steals, that they invariably mentioned first. "I wish I could forget those two steals," said Dampier. "I wish I could say that he fouled me, but he didn't. I was changing directions, dribbling with my left hand . . . and then it was gone. I can never forget it."

A minute later, when another Lattin dunk made it 16–11, Rupp uncrossed his legs, leaned back in his chair, popped to his feet, and called a timeout. Neither the man-to-man nor the 1-3-1 was working.

"I sat at a table near our bench and after he jumped up and called timeout, as they were coming off the court, he confronted his two guards about the steals," said Mullens. "[He said] 'You stupid sons of bitches.' He just couldn't take it."

Though his team did not appear confused against the 1-3-1, Haskins was surprised by it. Not having scouted Kentucky that season until Friday, he had assumed Rupp's teams always played man-to-man. That was the conventional wisdom in college basketball. "They didn't play it the night before," he said. "I sat there and watched the game and they played man-to-man all night. When they got into that zone, we took a timeout. There was no clock then, fortunately, and we handled the ball two or three possessions and moved it around and felt it out. I had a smart point guard and they picked it up real quick. We didn't do much. It was pretty simple. We kind of spotted up and moved the ball and drove some gaps. We practiced against it for three possessions and you'd have thought they practiced against it for a couple of hours."

The teams sparred with each other through the next several minutes until jumpers by Dampier and Riley and Jaracz's layup off a Conley feed pulled Kentucky to within 3 points, 32–29, with just under two minutes left in the half. Baskets by Lattin and Riley in the final minute left the halftime score 34–31.

Now the Miners not only were convinced they could play with the Wildcats, they were sure they could beat them. Some of that cockiness was visible to those who watched each player closely. "You probably couldn't see it," said Artis, "but after we'd score a basket, we made a habit of deliberately going down the Kentucky sideline. We'd wave, point, smile at Rupp."

Back in the locker room, Haskins told his team they had played well but that they ought to be ahead by more. As usual, he blamed their defense for keeping Kentucky in the game. "You've got to keep covering them," he said. "Stay on top of them or that break is going to burn you." It was something he had learned from Mr. Iba. Offense would even itself out, but no matter how good the defense was, it could always be better. He told them to be patient on offense, that the longer they held the ball the less time Dampier and Riley would have to get hot.

In the other locker room, Kentucky's players now had a different opinion of Texas Western. "They had the best defense we saw all year," said Conley. "They really came after you." Haskins had played the race card before the game, informing his team about Rupp's remarks. Now, with his team gathered in the tiny locker room, it was Rupp's turn. The Kentucky coach told them they would never be able to show their faces again in Lexington if they let five blacks beat them.

Sports Illustrated's Frank Deford, invited into the locker room for some off-the-record observations, said Rupp used the word "coons" in referring to Texas Western. Rupp's son, who also was there, contends he never heard his father use that derogatory term. Conley and Kron also don't recall hearing it, but both said they wouldn't have been surprised if they had.

"I never heard it, but I know Frank Deford real well and Frank is honest. If he said it happened, it happened," said Kron. "[Rupp] said so many things that was banter. He was not in good health and he was a cantankerous old guy."

"Was he a bigoted or prejudiced man? For a man in his sixties, perhaps he was," said Conley. "I will tell you this. I never heard him utter a derogatory word or a bigoted word in my presence. Never. I'm not going to say he didn't do it, but in my presence, never. Frank may remember that, I don't."

■ ■ ■

Perhaps because of the 10:00 P.M. starting time and the lateness of the games the previous night, neither team had looked particularly sharp the first half. That was more of a concern to Rupp than Haskins. Texas Western's game plan had been to force Kentucky out of its fast-breaking rhythm and that had been accomplished. The Wildcats were frustrated.

"It was a game of keepaway," said Baudoin. "Kentucky was lost. They were so frustrated and it never got any better for them. We could have played poorly and come back but not Kentucky. They didn't get a chance to run a whole lot. Bobby Joe's steals broke their backs. They looked like, 'This is silly. Let's go home.' I think we probably could have beaten them by a whole lot more. Like I've heard Pat Riley say, if we had played three times, we'd have beaten them three times."

The Miners were terrific rebounders, collecting an average of 13 more a game than their opponents in the regular season. But despite the size disadvantage, Kentucky stayed with them on the boards. "People don't realize that we had a lot of guys who could get up," said Conley. "Four of the five could dunk. The only one who couldn't was Dampier. Riley was a tremendous rebounder as were Jaracz and Kron." (Curiously, though, Kentucky's leading rebounder in that game would be Dampier with 9.)

The second half might have been one of the least memorable in NCAA history. Kentucky twice got to within a point—at 37–36 and 46–45 with about twelve minutes remaining—but whenever the Miners needed a big basket or free throw, they got one, often from Artis, the quiet senior. "People talk about Hill and those steals," said Conley, "but the guy that really killed us was Artis. Every time we got close, he would hit a big shot."

At 46–45, Artis connected on a jumper and a free throw and Worsley added 3 free throws to stretch Texas Western's advantage to 52–45. Riley and Dampier baskets made it 52–49 with 8:42 left.

As Kentucky grew more desperate and Texas Western's quickness became more of a factor, the Miners got to the foul line often. On the season they had hit 69 percent of their free throws, while Kentucky made nearly 75 percent. Now the Miners couldn't miss. They would convert 28 of 34 foul shots, with Hill accounting for 3 of the 6 misses. "Everybody on that team could shoot them," said Iba. "Don worked very hard on it. At that time, most teams shot free throws pretty good. Now they just throw them up."

Later Rupp would complain about the officiating, particularly

the discrepancy in fouls, 23–12. "Well, I don't know why we had
[23] personal fouls playing a 1-3-1, a defense that's supposed to
eliminate fouls, and they had only 12 fouls playing a man-to-man."

Most of them, noted Conley, came when Kentucky was franti-
cally trying to get back in the game. "There were a lot of fouls called
on us but I really can't complain about any of the calls," he said.

It was 54–51, Texas Western, when the pull-away burst came.
An Artis jumper, another Hill steal and jumper, and another em-
phatic Lattin dunk built the Miners' lead to 60–51 with 6:54 left. The
Miners stretched it to 68–57 in the next three and a half minutes. A
minute later, the score was the same as Worsley dribbled in the front
court. Conley reached in for a steal, gathered in the ball, and took off
for the basket. But Honzo's whistle stopped him. The Kentucky captain had been called for a foul, his fifth. He slumped his shoulders,
walked to the bench, and buried his head in his hands.

The outcome was inevitable now and as the clock ticked off the
last seconds, Texas Western's fans stood and screamed and counted
them down. "Oh, how I can remember those last seven seconds,"
said Shed. "When that clock started ticking off it seemed like the
whole world just stood still. . . . Five, four, three . . . I could feel my
heart beating. We were going to beat Kentucky. We were going to
win the national championship."

Haskins smiled for the first time all day as Iba reached for his
hand. Texas Western's players, cheerleaders, and fans rushed onto
the court and gathered beneath their second-half net.

"We didn't have any stepladder or anything," said Worsley. "I
just got on Cager's shoulders to cut it [the net] down. People ask me
if the Kentucky players or Rupp shook our hands afterward. I don't
remember because I was up at the net." (Some recall Riley and
Dampier coming into their locker room to shake hands. Others remember only Dampier.)

The Kentucky bench was stunned as they waited for the trophy
presentation ceremony. Riley cried. Conley couldn't watch. Rupp

stood there with Lancaster, looking as if he'd rather be anywhere else. "We had never had a game like that," said Kron. "It could have been pressure. We could have choked. We were just twenty-two-year-old kids."

To make matters worse for them, they had to watch Shively, Kentucky's athletic director and the head of the tournament committee, present the trophy to Ray, Haskins, and Texas Western's players.

Throughout the game, the racial taunts from a few Kentucky fans had been audible. Future Maryland coach Gary Williams, then a student at the school and an up-close spectator at the game, heard them. Now, in the aftermath of the shattering defeat, these same fans gathered behind the defeated Wildcats. Many were angry about what had happened, or what they believed had happened.

"There were definitely some racist comments made about all their players being recruited from places like Chicago and junior colleges," said Oswald's son, John, who stood there with his father. "Kentucky fans wanted to know how these kids ended up in El Paso. The inference was that they must not be very bright, that they must not be very good students. Some people said this wasn't fair. They said the rules should be changed against players like that."

Hill scanned the stands for his older brother, Virgil. Later that night, at a team party in College Park's Fireside Beef House, Virgil mentioned to Hill that Texas Western's win was a historic one.

"What do you mean?" Hill asked.

"Virgil said, 'It's the first time five blacks have beaten five whites in a game like this.'"

"I hadn't thought about that until then," said Hill. "All I could do was smile. And say, 'Wow.'"

10.

"Our Reward Will Be in History"

"Everyone got it wrong. That's the thing. The story is messed up. It was Kentucky that was different, not us, not Texas Western. We didn't make it white against black. We didn't even think about it that way. To us it was just a game. We always started five black players."
—Bobby Joe Hill

It was after midnight when Rupp emerged from his locker room to meet with the reporters crowding Cole Field House's dark corridor. He was upset, humiliated, and angry. "The pressure got to us," he told them, letting loose with a litany of excuses. "Riley was as tight as a drum. Jaracz didn't play much of a game. Kron wasn't feeling well and he gave out. We didn't shoot well and we didn't handle the ball well either."

In other words, Texas Western didn't win the title, Kentucky lost it.

"Rupp was the most ungracious guy in the world," said Mullens. "He went to his grave never forgiving. After that game, I was running around like crazy but I stopped and listened to Rupp and the reporters. Somebody asked him the question, 'What did you think of Hill?' And he said, 'Ah, he was a good little boy. But everybody's got a good little boy.'"

Kentucky's coach left the arena that night, Riley recalled, clutching a fifth of bourbon. His players, equally devastated, returned to their hotel. More than thirty years later, they could not recall much of how they spent the rest of that terrible night.

"We went back to the hotel," recalled Kron. "I think we had some beer iced down. We were extremely tired and extremely worn out. It was like we were experiencing an out-of-body experience. 'Am I really going through this? Did we really play that bad? Did we really not win this after going this far?'

"But you get over it. You start thinking about getting married, graduate school. We did try. We just came up short and got beat by a good team. It wasn't a fluke. Everybody always said if we played them ten times, we'd win nine. If I've heard that once, I've heard it a thousand times. It's Kentucky people trying to justify what happened. Kentucky people have a tough time losing. Well, it's never going to happen again. We played them once and we got beat."

Conley, a senior, said the most difficult thing he had to deal with in the game's aftermath was the realization that he was never going to win a national championship.

"I didn't get it because we played a team that was really prepared to play us," said Conley. "That's all that mattered. Whatever was created, was created without us being involved. We were simply the pawns. We were the pawns of the game. If the African-American community wants to use that as something to better their cause, I don't have a problem with that. If that is a watershed in their history, something vitally important to them, then they can use that. That's fine."

Rupp, on the other hand, would blame everything but UFOs for the defeat, insinuating that Texas Western recruited outlaws, that the referees favored the Miners, that the Wildcats would have won easily if not for their debilitating illnesses.

"Don't let anyone tell you any different," said one longtime Rupp acquaintance who did not want to be identified, "Adolph hated each and every loss in his career. But that one hit him like a ton of bricks. And the reason ought to be obvious. The man was under pressure for not recruiting blacks, he was being criticized for that even by people at his own school. Then he goes and loses an NCAA championship game to an all-black team. Think of how humiliating that was for him. He was repudiated. That's why it stung the man."

It stung much of Lexington too. After the team arrived back in Kentucky the following day, there was a gathering for them at Memorial Coliseum, an event originally planned as a championship celebration. Now it became a farewell to the Runts, perhaps the most beloved team in Kentucky's history, and more than 5,000 fans attended. Many described the mood of the ceremony as funereal.

The most touching moment occurred when Conley, his eyes downcast, his voice made soft by the illness, told a now-hushed crowd: "I'm sorry. We did the best we could."

Then Rupp spoke, using the opportunity to offer more excuses. "It was regrettable that we got so far and were not up for the game. Our shots just would not drop," he said. "The boys provided us with a wonderful winter of entertainment. I don't believe any team in history received as much publicity as they did."

On Monday, a snide editorial in the *Lexington Herald* explained the Runts' loss as an unfortunate fait accompli and reflected the thinking of many in the state. "There is no disgrace in losing to a team such as was assembled by Texas Western after a nationwide search that somehow escaped the recruiting of the [Harlem] Globetrotters," it read.

The notion that Texas Western somehow had cheated Kentucky

lingered in Lexington for decades. "Not long ago I rode on a bus at a national educators conference with a guy from Kentucky," said Baudoin. "I just couldn't believe the things he was saying about that game. He didn't even know that I had played on that team. Just absolutely asinine statements about stuff he knew nothing about. I just waited until he was finished and then started back at the beginning and corrected him."

Haskins sat back and listened to this criticism without response. He never complained in public, never felt it necessary to answer Rupp. But he nearly snapped one night in the spring of 1966 when he and the Kentucky coach showed up at the same banquet in Columbus, Ohio.

"We were both co-coaches of the year or something . . . and at this little banquet he just coolly looked at me," said Haskins. "Rupp didn't bother me a damn bit. I was not the least bit intimidated. I played for Henry Iba and if he was still alive he'd still intimidate me. But Rupp didn't. He was cool and I was damn cool to him. I had been listening to all this damn crap out of him and it's a wonder I didn't say something to him about it. But I didn't."

On March 24, 1966, Kentucky held its basketball banquet at a Lexington hotel. Oswald and Johnson were there, both of them scanning the room for the two black high-schoolers—Perry Wallace being one—that Rupp had assured them would be there. "He told us all of his recruits, including the two black youngsters, would be there," said Johnson. "But for some reason, while the white recruits were there, the two blacks were not."

Oswald and Johnson virtually came out of their chairs when the banquet's master of ceremonies, *Herald* sports editor Billy Thompson, a close friend of Rupp's, said the Wildcats should not be ashamed. "At least," said Thompson, "we're still America's number one white team."

"God, were Jack [Oswald] and I mad," recalled Johnson. "Jack called the paper's publisher the next day and really let him have it.

I'm sure the very fact that Billy Thompson said that reflected some people's views, certainly some people at the paper. Nothing appeared in that paper that the publisher didn't approve. I remember at the time of the Watts riots, nothing appeared in the Lexington paper until a few days later when the publisher editorialized about it."

Despite the continuing pressure and the constant prodding of Johnson, and, to a lesser degree, Hall, it would be more than three years before Rupp finally signed his first black player. On June 9, 1969, Tom Payne, a 7-footer from Shawnee High School in Louisville, agreed to come to Kentucky. The announcement was made in the player's living room, where the coach posed uncomfortably with the family.

Payne sat out his freshman year with academic problems. But on December 1, 1970, more than forty years after Rupp became Kentucky's coach and more than four years after the Wildcats' loss to Texas Western, he became the first black to wear a Kentucky basketball uniform, playing in a road victory over Northwestern.

The sophomore center averaged 17 points and 10 rebounds as the Wildcats went 22-6 that 1970–71 season and lost their first-round NCAA game to Jim McDaniels' Western Kentucky. (Rupp had not mellowed by then. This was his assessment of the Western Kentucky loss: "Not one of our boys would do what I wanted him to.") The next year Payne would declare hardship and depart for the NBA. His life slid downhill from there and he eventually served time in prison for rape.

The 1971–72 season would be Rupp's last, though he had to be coerced into retiring by administrators who threatened to invoke the school's mandatory "retire-at-seventy" policy. Payne's premature departure meant that once again school officials were embarrassed by Rupp's all-white Wildcats. By then, Auburn and Florida had four blacks each on their teams, Vanderbilt three, Mississippi and Tennessee two, and LSU one.

So Hall found two black football players who had been basketball players in high school, Darryl Bishop and Elmore Stephens, and convinced Rupp to add them to his team. While they played sparingly, they at least gave the Wildcats a more contemporary racial look. Rupp, however, soon dismissed both from the team when they were late for a team plane. "I can't really say he was a racist," Stephens said in 1997. "He treated all his players tough when I was there."

Rupp won his final home game, beating Auburn, 102–67, on March 6, 1972. After the pregame national anthem, a spotlight was directed at the bench, and to a thunderous ovation in Memorial Coliseum, Rupp walked into it. On March 18, in the Mideast Regional final at Dayton, Ohio, all-white Kentucky was beaten by Florida State, 73–54, in Rupp's last game.

Fate had provided an appropriate setting for the farewell. Florida State's starting five was all-black.

Hall replaced Rupp and on February 23, 1979, two years after Rupp's death, he started Dwane Casey against Vanderbilt instead of Kyle Macy. That switch gave Kentucky its first all-black starting five. Gradually, especially under Rick Pitino, the Wildcats made inroads in the state's black communities. "We've totally changed the image of Kentucky basketball," said Pitino. And when Pitino left for the NBA's Boston Celtics after the 1996–97 season, Kentucky replaced him with the first black head coach in its history, Tubby Smith. "Daddy would have applauded the choice," said Adolph Rupp, Jr.

■ ■ ■

In what must have been one of the great mergers of egos in sports history, Rupp went to work for Charles O. Finley not long after his retirement. Finley owned the Memphis Tams in the struggling American Basketball Association and assumed the legendary coach's stature in the region might help attendance. He hired him to the largely ceremonial position of president.

"I told him that if he had hired me for my knowledge of basketball, he should use that knowledge," said Rupp. "He just laughed and told me to come on down to Memphis and have a good time."

Rupp apparently took him at his word.

"Charlie Finley would have Adolph Rupp sit at the press table for a game," recalled Ron Grinker, then just beginning his career as a sports agent. "It was a $90 round trip from Lexington to Memphis so it didn't cost Charlie much to bring in Adolph and Charlie was always very big on saving money. Once I was on a flight with Rupp and sat with him in the first-class section. He had about six Kentucky bourbons in less than an hour and was about halfway to the wind. I told him I was an attorney who represented some basketball players. Now I had never met the man and the first significant thing he said to me was, 'The trouble with the ABA is that there are too many nigger boys in it now.'

"I sat there just stunned. That just killed my image of Adolph Rupp, the great coach. Maybe it was because he had too much to drink, but even so. . . . He asked me to sit with him during the game that night. I spent the first half with him and then left. I couldn't stand listening to him anymore."

Rupp quit in June of 1974, calling the ABA "a bush league." Three months later he took a spot on the board of directors of the league's Kentucky Colonels.

Rupp never admitted it, of course, but he missed coaching terribly. On his last trip to Madison Square Garden, as he sat watching a Kentucky-Niagara game in 1976, New York writers approached him. They waited nearby for a break in play that would permit a brief interview with the retired coach. As they waited, they watched Rupp watch the game. At one point, the Wildcats appeared puzzled by a new defense as they brought the ball upcourt. Rupp immediately sprang from his seat a few rows behind their bench and held three fingers aloft. Old habits die hard. It might have been the last play the old coach ever called.

When he learned he had cancer, Rupp accepted the news gracefully. During interviews with Russell Rice for his biography, he informed the author about his recently diagnosed illness and asked him to keep it quiet. He was ill when Rupp Arena, a new 23,000-seat facility downtown, was dedicated in December of 1976, but attended a ceremony in his honor as well as a Lawrence Welk concert there. On November 9, 1977, he entered the hospital for the final time.

Not long before his death, Rupp and a visitor discussed his career. The old coach's gruff voice was barely a whisper when he brought up the Texas Western game.

"I often wake up in the middle of the night," the dying coach said, "wondering what I could have done to turn the tide."

As the 1966 title game's significance grew, Rupp's reputation diminished. His reluctance to integrate overshadowed all his accomplishments. Even when in 1997, North Carolina coach Dean Smith surpassed his record victory total, most mentions of Rupp noted his reputation as a segregationist.

The stark contrast provided by Texas Western, the subsequent overwhelming change in the sport's racial demographics, and his own history made him an easy and legitimate target. In the complex story of basketball's integration, Rupp had become George Wallace, the bigot blocking the gymnasium door. And, regardless of what his true feelings were, he fit the role perfectly.

But had fate played out differently, had all-white Duke, with genial coach Vic Bubas, beaten Kentucky in that 1966 semifinal, Rupp might have escaped more easily into history's shadows. The Kentucky coach still would have won no NAACP awards, but the Bull Connor comparisons might have been more difficult.

Much of the taint attached to Rupp is justifiable. On racial matters, the record shows him to be, at best, insensitive, patronizing, and backward-looking. Yet it is tantalizing to imagine how differently he might have been regarded had Texas Western not struck Rupp in his oversized Achilles' heel.

Friends and relatives continue to defend him. They contend Rupp was a man of his times. It is an argument they are not likely to win. Rupp will never shake the legacy of Texas Western. And maybe he doesn't deserve to.

"No one will remember him without remembering us," said Harry Flournoy. "And I guess there is a certain justice to that."

■ ■ ■

El Paso's church bells rang as if it were Easter morning in the aftermath of Texas Western's victory over Kentucky. As soon as the game ended late that Saturday night, students, soldiers, and permanent residents began pouring into the streets. Most of them congregated on campus or at San Jacinto Plaza downtown.

A "We're No.1" banner replaced the American flag on the college's flagpole. Fire hydrants were opened up, a caravan of more than 100 honking cars formed quickly, and someone started a bonfire near the intersection of Hawthorne and College Streets. Like the celebration itself, the bonfire grew so intense so quickly that firemen were summoned to protect nearby buildings and lawns. When all the wood that could be collected had been fed into the blaze, students began tearing limbs off trees. One falling branch struck a fireman, sending him to the hospital. Soon shirts, caps, and other articles of clothing were being tossed into the flames. It was the wildest party in El Paso's history, and, after a respite to greet the team at the airport the next morning, it resumed Sunday night.

"I'll always remember those church bells," said Robert Seltzer, an El Paso native and a sportswriter. "There had never been anything like that celebration in El Paso's history. When the game was over, people just went outside. And the parade from the airport the next day was amazing."

Thousands waited at International Airport for the arrival of the plane carrying the new NCAA champions. They already had been feted at a postgame party in a College Park restaurant. Haskins and others hadn't stayed long, preferring to return to the motel for a more private celebration.

"After the game, I'm naturally the last guy to leave and by the time I got back to the motel they were already gone to this impromptu dinner," said Mullens. "I didn't know where everybody was, but it was terribly quiet. All of a sudden Haskins' door burst open and he picked me up and started swinging me around. There was a roomful of people. I don't know where we confiscated the booze, but there was plenty of it. After a while I just happened to look out the window and, hell, they were loading up the buses. It was time to go already."

By the time their flight left Friendship Field at 5:45 A.M. Sunday, most of the players were asleep in their seats. At about 8:45 A.M. in El Paso, as the jet approached the city's airport, Shed looked out a window to the sight of a massive crowd below. He shouted to his teammates. The crowd was so large that the pilot took an extra pass to allow his passengers a better view. "The plane did a little dip as it circled around, you know," recalled Shed. "And we saw all these little tiny ants of people waiting to greet us. . . . It was fantastic."

The first off were the cheerleaders, then came Cager hoisting the championship trophy over his head. One fan carried a sign that read, "Bobby Joe Hill for Capitol Hill," but Hill was not there. He had gone back to Michigan to be with his father, who was dying of cancer.

"To tell you the truth," Haskins told the cheering crowd, "I can't yet believe it's reality."

The coach seemed emotionally spent. After the airport ceremony, Haskins got into a car with campus police chief Ralph Coulter. Thousands more, some estimates were as high as 10,000, lined Montana Street between the airport and Texas Western's campus. But Haskins hardly noticed. "I sure expected he'd be jumping up and down, or at least be a little bit excited," said Coulter, "but all he said was, 'Take me home, will ya, Ralph?' and nothing else the whole way."

Almost immediately, the letters began. Haskins said he received maybe 40,000 of them in the months following the game. "It started like a week to ten days after, and all of a sudden we were just flooded with mail," he said. "It was just all 'nigger lover' stuff, all from Southern states. One in particular I got the biggest kick out of was from a professor at Alabama. He wrote this neat letter saying they'd never have a 'black nigger' on their team. It wasn't too many years later when I saw Alabama play and eleven of their twelve were black. All I could think of was that letter. Times change.

"I got letters from black leaders too calling me an 'exploiter,'" he said. "Those pissed me off more than some dumb-ass in Georgia. . . . The next year was about the toughest of my life. There were death threats. One guy called and said he'd shoot me if the 'niggers' stepped on the floor for a game in Dallas. A lot of days I wished I'd finished second."

■ ■ ■

In 1967, Kentucky endured its worst year under Rupp, going 13-13. Riley was hurting and their lack of size caught up with them. Texas Western went 22-7 but was not invited to either the NCAA or NIT. In the next few years, as the presence of black starting fives became much more commonplace, memories of the game faded.

Black leaders, embroiled in the era's civil rights battles, made little mention of what ought to have been a heartening victory. But Bill Nunn, Jr., a columnist for the black-run *Pittsburgh Courier,* hinted immediately that the game might have been the last stand for the notion of white athletic supremacy. "[Kentucky] missed out on the opportunity of proving that there are schools who can still win the big title without Negro players," Nunn wrote that week.

Once El Paso's weeklong celebrations concluded, the Texas Western players fell back into their routines. It wasn't, they said, until Olsen's 1968 *Sports Illustrated* series that people really began to view the game in a racial context.

"People on both sides, black and white, began making a big deal of it," said Worsley. "It got all confusing for us."

By then people were searching for something to explain how and why blacks had come to dominate basketball. That night in College Park, with its striking racial contrast, was a convenient place to look for answers.

No one has ever studied the effect Texas Western's victory had on integration, nor would such a thing be entirely measurable. Clearly, the number of black athletes at major colleges surged immediately afterward, and within twenty years twice as many blacks were playing major-college basketball. But the greatest change wrought by Texas Western's victory took place in hearts and minds. Basketball began to be linked almost exclusively with blacks. No discussion of the sport, it seemed, was possible without racial issues being raised. The game altered one set of stereotypes about black teams but gave rise to another. "Okay, maybe blacks are tough enough and smart enough to beat whites," this new thinking went, "but that's only because their bodies are so well suited to the game. They can run faster, jump higher. What do you expect?"

Basketball, which had always been linked with sweet-shooting country boys from places like Indiana and Kentucky, became the "City Game." For a while at least, that triggered white backlash. Many college and professional teams assumed that unless rosters included a few whites, even if they just decorated the bench, attendance would suffer—a philosophy that endures on many campuses for reasons that are as much financial as racial. One 1994 study by social scientists in Texas suggested fans were "willing to pay a premium of over $100,000 in annual home gate revenues just to have an additional white player on the team's roster." Only a few coaches, like Georgetown's John Thompson, were strong enough to buck this trend toward reverse quotas.

In later years, many black athletes—emboldened by the passage of time and no longer fearful of speaking out—began to reveal the psychological impact the Texas Western game had on them. Bob McAdoo, a North Carolina All-America and NBA star, said he never would have considered North Carolina if not for Texas Western's eye-opening victory. Superstars like Bill Russell and Julius Erving spoke of its significance. Before long, a championship that originally was viewed as an oddity came to be seen as a monument.

"It took time for people to turn around and look back," said Baudoin. "There was a time when everyone just said '66 was a down year in basketball nationally. People made all kinds of excuses. But eventually, when black kids started showing up at places where they'd never been welcomed before, its importance became clear."

Several months after the game, Hill received a letter from a young basketball player in New England. "He said he was short and black like me and that after that game Boston College called and said they wanted him," said Hill. "He even got a few letters from the ACC."

When Haskins suffered a heart attack in 1996, one of his visitors was ex-NFL star Chuck Foreman, who had never met the coach previously. "All of us who were young saw that '66 game and felt like there was hope for us. . . . The man gave black people a chance," Foreman told a reporter at the hospital.

"We all led up to Texas Western," said Jerry Harkness, one of four blacks on Loyola of Chicago's 1963 national champions, "and Texas Western knocked almost all of those stereotypes about black athletes right out the window. And they're still constantly going out the window. We couldn't run long distances. Now the Africans dominate those sports. We couldn't compete at mental games like golf. Now you've got Tiger Woods. This is a great era for me to live in. I saw the stereotypes from the beginning and now we're just knocking them out the door.

"History has a way of doing things right," said Harkness. "When Texas Western's point guard turned the game around with those two steals, that was kind of ironic. Point guard was a position we weren't supposed to be able to play."

Even Haskins, loath to read too much significance into anything, saw it eventually. "It took me a few years to figure it out, watching what was happening around the country," said Haskins. "Two or three years later the All-Southwest Conference team was all-black. It happened very quickly and I guess we played a part in that. But I wasn't trying to be a pioneer. I was starting the best five players and they happened to be black."

If, as the *Sports Illustrated* stories suggested, the players resented their El Paso experiences, those feelings appeared to vanish when, in 1976, El Paso held the first of many emotional reunions for the championship team.

"I didn't really think about it until ten years later," said Worsley. "I thought we were dead and forgotten. Out of sight, out of mind. All of a sudden these people from El Paso called and said they'd like me to come out this weekend. They wanted to give us a ring and honor us. Then some writers called and it started to snowball.

"There was a packed house that first night," he said. "Coach cried. It was beautiful. The ring they gave us was so beautiful. I still won't wear it. I've worn it three times. I keep it in a vault. Then ten years later they had us back and the story got a little bigger. We were telling bigger lies to each other. The people down there love us and we all love them back.

"But the funny thing was a lot of us went to watch the practices, to see if Coach was still the same. But Coach just didn't seem to have that same fight. He became very loose on offense. Guys were averaging 30 points a game, taking 15, 25 shots a game. Shoot, I didn't take 25 shots in three games. He lets people show a little more individuality now. It's not always, 'I want it this way and that way.'"

Now they return regularly to a city where they have become legends. "The city of El Paso has a remarkable allegiance for this bunch of guys," said Baudoin. "There are always thousands of people at the reunions and now there are grandchildren who want autographs."

■ ■ ■

In his modest North Nashville home, a black teenager whose parents had left rural Tennessee decades earlier to find work as servants watched that 1966 NCAA championship with friends.

As he did, Perry Wallace, a reserved 6-5 high school senior, never realized his name one day would be linked forever to its outcome. All he understood then, watching Texas Western frustrate Kentucky, was that this was a wonderful moment.

"I can't confess to having had any great insight into the game's sociological importance at the time," Wallace recalled, "but watching it, we were all so very excited—even if we still were unsure as to what it all meant."

Wallace and his equally excited buddies compared the game to a recent historic victory by their own Pearl High. The all-black school also had confounded white expectations earlier that month, winning the championship in Tennessee's first integrated state basketball tournament.

"We just about went crazy," said Wallace. "Being black in the South, you had grown up watching games, usually from behind a fence, involving white athletes. You always knew that, given the chance, you could be as good or better. So when we got that opportunity for the first time and won, it was a tremendous feeling."

In just a few weeks, Wallace would become the first member of his race to agree to play basketball in the SEC (at Vanderbilt), America's last segregated basketball conference. Following him, in ever greater numbers after Texas Western's upset, young blacks would break ground at overwhelmingly white colleges everywhere. Within four years, 80 percent of Division I basketball teams were integrated. Within six years, blacks played at every school in the recently segregated Southwest, Southeastern, and Atlantic Coast Conferences—even in places like Starkville, Mississippi (Mississippi State), and Anniston, Alabama (Auburn).

For many of these pioneers, the experience would be more painful than they could have imagined on that heady Saturday night in 1966. Many young black athletes discovered an environment at these white schools that, in the words of sociologist Harry Edwards, could be "brutally dehumanizing."

Universities that commended themselves on integrating their athletic teams often failed to look past that hurdle once it was crossed, as if they never considered these youngsters might have lives divorced from sports. Beyond athletics, much of normal campus life remained closed to them. Many never adjusted to this strange new world. Their graduation rate was abysmal, their alienation total. "In a way," said Wallace, "it was like life at the old plantation house."

Educators at traditionally black colleges, finding it increasingly difficult to attract the same caliber of athlete, watched this trend with regret. "Until there is complete integration into every phase of college life," warned Jake Gaithers, the football coach at Florida A&M, "it's not going to be a healthy situation for our boys."

In this context, Wallace's experience would be both typical and unique. Like a lot of them, he wanted to quit. Like a lot of them, he needed someone to understand him. Ultimately, many of these black players disappeared or were discarded. Some, like Wallace, persevered.

"It was a fight," he said, "and I had to win it."

■ ■ ■

History has drawn a straight line from the 1966 NCAA championship game to Wallace's integration of SEC basketball a month later. Actually, some of the conference's northernmost members had been trying to find the right black—one with no discernible flaws—for at least two years.

"There's no question that SEC basketball teams were making plans to integrate before that game," said Wallace. "But the reason Texas Western is so important is that its victory underscored those efforts. It underscored points that were already being made and underscored them in a truly dramatic way."

That spring, Tennessee, Vanderbilt, and even Kentucky were recruiting Wallace, the valedictorian of his class of 441 and a high school All-America. No black ever had played basketball at these schools, but that didn't concern him nearly so much as how the representatives of these schools chose to approach him. Tennessee's Ray Mears and Vanderbilt's Roy Skinner impressed him during visits to his home. Kentucky sent two assistants, Lancaster and Joe B. Hall. Rupp's absence, as it would for many other black players and their families, sent a clear, negative message.

Wes Unseld, another well-rounded high school All-America who was Wallace's role model, had received similar treatment from Kentucky before signing with the already integrated University of Louisville in 1964. So when Wallace saw the sad looks on the faces of Rupp and his players after that championship game defeat, he couldn't help but think that maybe Kentucky had brought this doom on itself.

"Looking back, that game was absolutely a watershed," Wallace said. "It broke open the old safe rules that teams had always followed about how many blacks you could have on a team. It revised the thinking about an all-black team's supposed vulnerabilities."

Many whites, not surprisingly, saw it differently.

"It reinforced some of their stereotypes," Wallace said. "Bobby Joe Hill's speed and Big Daddy Lattin's raw strength were the kind of attributes people expected from black players. In their minds, if blacks succeeded in the sport, it was because of those traits and not because they might be smarter or better-conditioned or more focused than the white players. They pointed to Haskins and said, 'Sure you can win if you get kids like that off the streets.'"

Wallace, who throughout his recruitment had refused to rule out black schools like Grambling or Tennessee State, keeping them in mind as a kind of psychic insurance, now quickly made his decision. In April, he signed with Vanderbilt, in his hometown.

"I was very interested in going to a school where I could get a top-quality education," said Wallace, who would graduate with a double major in engineering mathematics and electrical engineering. "Vanderbilt didn't have any physical education department and that was a plus."

If Wallace arrived on the lovely Nashville campus that next September with any illusions that his experiences might be different than those of other blacks at other schools, he rapidly discarded them. Vanderbilt students ignored the two dozen blacks among them. It was at nearby Fisk University, a well-respected black school, that most of the blacks' social life took place.

"Vanderbilt was a school where most of its students came from an upper-class Southern background and it replicated a lot of Southern society," he said. "It did that through the fraternity system. Most of the people who counted belonged and the social life took place there. If you were black, or a foreign student, or a poor white, you got left out and you felt like outsiders. Fisk gave us a place to go where we could round out our lives and have a certain social acceptance."

Knowing he would be watched closely by other schools and other blacks, Wallace kept silent about his troubles. On the court, he worked at staying composed and unemotional. "The last thing I wanted," he said, "was for people to be able to accuse me of playing 'Nigger Ball.' I didn't want to reinforce those kinds of stereotypes about black athletes. That inhibited me, I think, made me play a more cautious, conservative game."

No amount of self-control, however, would help him on the night of February 27, 1967.

More than anything else, Wallace had been dreading his first games at Mississippi and Mississippi State. He knew about the 1964 murders of the Freedom Riders in Philadelphia, Mississippi, and the state's history of lynchings, the most recent of which had occurred only two years earlier.

Wallace won a brief reprieve when Mississippi, rather than play against an integrated opponent in Oxford, canceled its freshman game with Vanderbilt, citing "scheduling conflicts." Mississippi State, whose basketball team three years earlier had had to defy state officials to play against an integrated team in the NCAA tournament, surprisingly did not. So on February 27, Vanderbilt's freshman team boarded a bus for Starkville, a primitive and desolate place that even Rupp feared.

During the conference's thirty-five segregated seasons, Starkville fans had won a reputation for mistreating opponents, particularly Rupp and Kentucky. They mocked opposing coaches and pummeled any visiting player who passed too close to the stands in old Maroon Gym. Wallace, the first black athlete ever to compete there, wondered what was in store for him. He found out quickly.

At halftime of that historic freshmen game, as he and Godfrey Dillard, a Detroit black who had signed shortly after him, sat in the drafty visitors locker room, they held each other's hands and silently prayed.

The torment had been nonstop. Even as they waited to run onto the court for pregame warmups, Wallace and Dillard could hear the racist chants. "These people are crazy," Wallace whispered before the two embraced and walked into view. Fans taunted them, laughed at them, threw coins and cups at them. Frightening Rebel yells echoed through the old gym and dozens of Confederate flags unfurled. One spectator waved a noose as if threatening them with a lynching.

So in the welcome quiet of halftime, shaking from fear, the two black nineteen-year-olds clutched each other's hands and tried to focus on coach Roy Skinner's mundane instructions.

"It was terrible," recalled Wallace. "At that time, Mississippi State played in an old airplane hangar that had been converted into a gym and the crowd was right on top of you, extremely close. You could hear everything they yelled very clearly there. This was Mississippi State, a state school, where the fans were more blue-collar, more wild and woolly than even at Mississippi. It was depraved. Nightmarish."

And it was what Wallace, Dillard, and many of the next wave of blacks who followed them into the SEC had to endure at many conference road games. "It was very hard," Wallace said. "You were anxious and nervous about these games months in advance." What might have helped, he said, was some sense that his teammates understood.

"No one said anything. Nothing. And you got to thinking that maybe there was something wrong with you," said Wallace. "You wanted just one of these guys to say, 'Look, you're not crazy. I hear those people calling you "nigger" and threatening your life.' But they didn't say anything, not even when I made a bad play. They were usually nice. But in their world and their parents' world, blacks were people you talked to only when you were giving orders."

He never really forgot the mental anguish. And a few years later, there was a moment when he actually *felt* it again, a visceral reaction that was frightening in its rebirth. It happened when he heard about Henry Harris' suicide.

"I thought to myself, 'Wait a minute. I know that guy. I played against him.' In fact, he was the only black from the Southeastern Conference I played against in my four years at Vanderbilt. It just dredged up all those feelings."

Harris, two years after Wallace, had been the first black to sign with one of the SEC's Deep South schools, Auburn. If Vanderbilt had wounded Wallace with its aloofness, he could hardly imagine what torment Harris must have suffered in Anniston, Alabama.

"Going down to Auburn then was like going to hell. Going straight to hell," said Wallace. "I know what it was like for me and I can only imagine what he must have endured down there. I've never been one to try to decipher the psychological cause behind every action, but if I were going to hypothesize about Harris' suicide, I would wonder about those experiences at Auburn and what damage they might have done."

One day in 1974, without offering a reason, Harris leaped off a New York City building.

Somehow Wallace survived. He averaged 13 points and 12 rebounds for his career and was drafted by (but never played for) the Philadelphia 76ers in the fifth round of the 1970 draft. He earned a law degree from Columbia, worked for the Justice Department, and became a college professor, presently at American University's Washington School of Law.

"There were times when I felt close to a nervous breakdown," he said. "They weren't the worst four years any black man ever had experienced, but it took me a while to learn to deal with the pain.

"The fact that I did is a credit to my parents," said Wallace. "They had eighth-grade educations and they worked as servants and what not. But they emphasized education, decency, and morality. I grew up poor but with strong values. My parents wouldn't let me hate back. They used to say, 'No matter what is done to you, you don't get the chance to hate back.'"

■ ■ ■

Less than a year after Lattin's dunks so forcefully punctuated Texas Western's championship, the NCAA Rules Committee banned the shot.

The all-white committee at first portrayed the move as an attempt to prevent injuries and equipment damage, citing 1,500 cases in the previous few seasons. Then they called it an effort to preserve basketball's integrity.

"The feeling was that this was a game of skill and the dunk was not a skillful offensive maneuver," said Ed Bilik, the athletic director of Springfield College who was then a Rules Committee member. "That [1966] game was just one of many games that led the Rules Committee to decide that a dunk was not a legitimate try for a goal."

But it was hard to view the ban as anything but an attempt to diminish the impact of black stars like Lattin, and, particularly, 7-footer Lew Alcindor, who as a sophomore that year had led UCLA to the NCAA title—and who would win two more championships without the benefit of the shot.

"I don't think there's any question that some of those rules were racially motivated," said Purdue sociologist Randy Roberts. "They were like the anti-celebration rules in football now. I think in part they were attempts to get back to the world in which these coaches grew up in, a white-bread world."

It wasn't the first time the NCAA had taken actions that appeared to be aimed at a big, strong, threatening black man. A decade earlier, the rule book was rewritten when Wilt Chamberlain and Bill Russell emerged. The NCAA eliminated several of Chamberlain's pet ploys. Inbound passes over the backboard and offensive goaltending were banned. Players had to remain stationary on free throws, and the defending team had to station two men under the basket on foul shots. And to limit the impact of shot-blockers like Russell, the lane was widened to twelve feet.

"I think along about the time we won, they were seeing that people of color were dunking, jumping higher, and running faster," said Worsley. "They were thinking, 'That's not how the game's played. Let's see if these "athletes" can shoot.' I know it was intended for Kareem [Alcindor], but I'm sure we had some input in that decision."

Committee members noted that similar measures had been enacted when George Mikan, a 6-10 white man, was at DePaul, but they were neither as numerous nor as dramatic as the no-dunk rule.

"I'm not one to buy into conspiracy theories, because for the most part they are nonsense, but I did find it curious that this action came a year after the Texas Western game," said Wallace. "I know people view this rule as anti-Alcindor, but that game had provided this powerful image of Big Daddy Lattin dunking over Pat Riley and getting in his face. Dunking, in a way, typified what a lot of people felt about blacks in basketball. It was threatening."

During a freshman game at Kentucky that preceded the ban, Wallace once slammed home a rebound over future Wildcat superstar Dan Issel. "For some reason, Rupp was in the stands watching the game and he just threw a fit. Maybe he just figured that it wasn't good fundamental basketball," said Wallace.

The ban was one of the first volleys in the battle between the freer, more improvised style of play many blacks favored and the more controlled game that white coaches like Rupp had been demanding for decades.

"If you saw the black-college teams play in the 1950s and early 1960s, you saw that more wide-open style," said Sonny Hill, a former black-college player who has established several influential summer leagues in Philadelphia. "I always say that people who saw those games got to see basketball the way it's being played today."

Amazingly the dunk stayed banned for a decade, until the 1976–77 season. But as professional players like Julius Erving turned it into a kind of art form that thrilled and attracted fans, the pressure on the NCAA Rules Committee increased. It reached a boiling point just before the shot was reinstated.

And there was one more aspect to the anti-dunking rule that raised the suspicions of blacks. Though he gave up his seat on the committee after the 1966 season, longtime member Adolph Rupp still had considerable influence on the panel.

"Rupp had been a powerful member of that committee for a long time," said Wallace. "I'm not saying the decision was racially inspired, but I would love to have been able to hear the discussions that took place on the day dunking was outlawed."

■ ■ ■

Willie Worsley sat in his office at the Harlem Boys Choir High School one afternoon in the summer of 1997. Young boys passed in and out. All of them were black, and all were talented singers, which is how they ended up there. He asked one lanky teenager what he knew about Texas Western and the boy looked at Worsley as if he were an alien. Someone asked Worsley if young blacks approached him often and thanked him for the contributions he and his team had made. He laughed.

"Kids today don't know what 'thanks' means," Worsley said. "They have no clue what we did. I never tell them my background. Very few kids in this building know my background. Now sometimes men in their forties will say thank you for giving us someone besides Jackie Robinson that was important in sports history. But how many people know who Willie Worsley is? How many black coaches making these millions and jillions of dollars know what we did? We didn't do it all. It would have happened eventually, but we helped speed it up.

"I'm not comparing us to Jackie Robinson, because he stands alone," said Worsley. "But I feel we are definitely a part of history. There's very few things people have in life. They have their word, their family, and their legacy. Our legacy is we were a part of history. How many others can say that? The truth will shine through any smoke screen. We were true. We were good and we were bad, but we were true."

If Worsley and his teammates, now all men in their fifties, have any lingering regrets about that championship, it is that, to an extent, they felt ignored by the world beyond El Paso.

"We may never have gotten our just due," he said, "but, see, history will give us our just due. People say your reward is in heaven. Our reward will be in history."

And if they could all do it over again, if they could be young and hopeful and champions again, there is just one thing they would change.

"*The Ed Sullivan Show*," said Shed. "All the other champions used to get on *The Ed Sullivan Show*. But they never asked us."

■ ■ ■

In April of 1998, on the night before black coach Tubby Smith led Kentucky to another NCAA championship, Rupp's ninety-five-year-old widow, Esther, died. Some observers, recalling the circumstances of Rupp's death, noted that the family certainly had dramatic timing. They also couldn't resist mentioning the irony inherent in the Wildcats' eighth national title. The Kentucky that Rupp had kept all-white now was winning championships with a black-dominated team *and* a black coach.

"That 1966 championship game," said Smith, who as a Maryland teenager watched it with glee, "was the first step toward this."

By then, thanks in large part to Texas Western, the sport had changed. Today's basketball—its speed, grace, and racial makeup—might have been unrecognizable to 1966 eyes. The world had changed too. Racial barriers remained, some of them sizable and spiked with bitterness. But there were far fewer walls than three decades earlier and even those were tumbling down all the time.

Maybe only Don Haskins had remained the same. On the 1998 night when he got his 700th victory, the coach wore a bad sport coat, a cheap shirt, and a clip-on tie. He still didn't want to talk about himself or the milestone. And the reporters surrounding him didn't want to discuss the game at hand. Only one of his 700 victories interested them.

"I can't really believe it yet, even all these years later," said Haskins, "but it looks like maybe that game is never going to go away."

Instead, it continues to stand out in any discussion about the birth of modern college basketball. Perhaps it is destined to be recalled like that memorable scene from *The Wizard of Oz,* the moment when everything changed from drab black and white to unforgettable color.

Appendix

1966 NCAA Championship Game

Texas Western

Name	FG	FT	RB	PF	Pts
Hill	7-17	6-9	3	3	20
Lattin	5-10	6-6	9	4	16
Artis	5-13	5-5	8	1	15
Worsley	2-4	4-6	4	0	8
Cager	1-3	6-7	6	3	8
Shed	1-1	1-1	3	1	3
Flournoy	1-1	0-0	2	0	2
TOTALS	22-49	28-34	35	12	72

Kentucky

Name	FG	FT	RB	PF	Pts
Riley	8-22	3-4	4	4	19
Dampier	7-18	5-5	9	4	19
Conley	4-9	2-2	8	5	10
Jaracz	3-8	1-2	5	5	7
Kron	3-6	0-0	7	2	6
Berger	2-3	0-0	0	0	4
LeMaster	0-1	0-0	0	1	0
Tallent	0-3	0-0	0	1	0
Gamble	0-0	0-0	0	1	0
TOTALS	27-70	11-13	33	23	65

Bibliography

Books

Althouse, Ronald, and Dana Brooks, eds. *Racism in Collegiate Athletics: The African American Athletic Experience.* Morgantown, W.Va.: Fitness Information Technology, 1993.

Ashe, Arthur. *A Hard Road to Glory: A History of the African-American Athlete.* New York: Amistad, 1993.

Branch, Taylor. *Parting the Waters: America in the King Years (1954–63).* New York: Simon & Schuster, 1988.

Bryant, Paul, and John Underwood. *Bear: The Hard Life and Good Times of Alabama's Coach Bryant.* New York: Little Brown, 1974.

Chalk, Ocania. *Black College Sport.* New York: Dodd, Mead, 1976.

Chamberlain, Wilt, and David Shaw. *Wilt.* New York: Warner Books, 1973.

Chandler, Dan, and Vern Hatton. *Rupp: From Both Ends of the Bench.* Chicago: Basic Books, 1972.

Clark, Thomas D. *A History of Kentucky.* Ashland, Ky.: The Jesse Stuart Foundation, 1988.

Coakley, Jay. *Sports and Society: Issues and Controversies.* St. Louis: C. V. Mosby, 1978.

Craver, Rebecca, and Charles H. Martin, eds. Diamond Days*: An Oral History of the University of Texas at El Paso.* El Paso: Texas Western Press, 1992.

Douchant, Mike. *Encyclopedia of College Basketball.* Detroit: Visible Ink Press, 1995.

Dunnavant, Keith. *Coach: The Life of Paul "Bear" Bryant.* New York: Simon & Schuster, 1996.

Edwards, Harry. *The Revolt of the Black Athlete.* New York: The Free Press, 1969.

Embry, Mike. *Basketball in the Bluegrass State: The Championship Teams.* New York: Leisure Press, 1987.

George, Nelson. *Elevating the Game: Black Men and Basketball.* New York: Harper Collins, 1992.

Gergen, Joe. *The Final Four.* St. Louis: The Sporting News, 1987.

Gowdy, Curt. *Seasons to Remember.* New York: Harper Collins, 1993.

Hall, Joe B., with Russell Rice. *Joe B. Hall—My Own Kentucky Home.* New York: Strode, 1981.

Hamilton, Nancy. *A Pictorial History of the University of Texas at El Paso.* El Paso: Texas Western Press, 1988.

Harrel, Kenneth E., ed. *The Public Papers of Gov. Edward T. Breathitt, 1963–1967.* Lexington: University Press of Kentucky, 1984.

Haskins, Don (as told to Ray Sanchez). *Haskins: The Bear Facts.* El Paso, Tex.: Mangan Books, 1987.

Heisler, Mark. *The Lives of Riley.* Los Angeles: High Top Sports Productions, 1994.

Henderson, E. B. *The Negro in Sports.* Washington, D.C.: Associated Publishers, 1969.

Herskowitz, Mickey. *The Legend of Bear Bryant.* New York: McGraw-Hill, 1987.

Hoose, Phillip M. *Necessities: Racial Barriers in American Sports.* New York: Random House, 1989.

Hu, Evaleen. *A Level Playing Field: Sports and Race.* Minneapolis: Lerner Publications, 1995.

Isaacs, Neil D. *All the Moves: A History of College Basketball.* New York: Harper Collins, 1984.

Lancaster, Harry (as told to Cawood Ledford). *Adolph Rupp: As I Knew Him.* Lexington, Ky.: Lexington Productions, 1977.

Lapchick, Richard, and John Brooks Slaughter. *The Rules of the Game: Ethics in College Sports.* Indianapolis, Ind.: Macmillan, 1989.

Lapchick, Richard, ed. *Fractured Focus: Sport as a Reflection of Society.* Lexington, Mass.: Lexington Books, 1986.

Laudeman, Tev. *The Rupp Years: The University of Kentucky's Golden Era of Basketball.* Louisville, Ky.: Courier-Journal Press, 1972.

McGill, John. *Kentucky Sports.* Cambridge, Mass.: Jim Holt, 1978.

Metz, Leon C. *El Paso Chronicles*. El Paso, Tex.: Mangan Books, 1993.

Meyer, Ray, with Ray Sons. *Coach*. Chicago: Contemporary Books, 1987.

Michener, James. *Sports in America*. New York: Random House, 1976.

Nelli, Humbert. *The Winning Tradition: A History of Kentucky Wildcats Basketball*. Lexington: University Press of Kentucky, 1984.

Noverr, Douglas, and Lawrence E. Ziewacz. *The Games They Played: Sports in American History (1865–1980)*. Chicago: Nelson-Hall, 1983.

Oakley, Ronald. *God's Country: America in the '50s*. New York: Dembner Books, 1986.

Olsen, Jack. *The Black Athlete*. New York: Time-Life Books, 1969.

Packer, Billy, with Roland Lazenby. *50 Years of the Final Four*. Dallas: Taylor Publishing, 1987.

Padwe, Sandy. *Basketball's Hall of Fame*. Washington, D.C.: Associated Features, 1970.

Peterson, Robert W. *Cages to Jumpshots: Pro Basketball's Early Years*. New York: Oxford Press, 1990.

Pluto, Terry. *Loose Balls*. New York: Simon & Schuster, 1990.

Rader, Benjamin G. *American Sports: From the Age of Folk Games to the Age of Spectators*. New York: Prentice Hall, 1983.

Ray, Joseph. *On Becoming a University*. El Paso: Texas Western Press, 1968.

Rice, Russell. *Adolph Rupp: Kentucky's Basketball Baron*. Champaign, Ill.: Sagamore Publishing, 1994.

——. *Kentucky Basketball: Big Blue Machine*. New York: Strode, 1976.

——. *The Wildcat Legacy*. Virginia Beach, Va.: JCP Corp. of Virginia, 1982.

Riess, Steven A. *City Games*. Champaign: University of Illinois Press, 1989.

Roberts, Randy, and James Olson. *Winning Is the Only Thing: Sports in America Since 1945*. Baltimore: Johns Hopkins Press, 1989.

Rosen, Charles. *Scandals of '51*. Austin, Tex.: Holt, Rinehart and Winston, 1978.

Rupp, Adolph. *Championship Basketball*. 2nd ed. New York: Prentice Hall, 1957.

Russell, Bill, with Taylor Branch. *Second Wind*. New York: Random House, 1979.

Rust, Art, Jr., and Edna Rust. *Art Rust's Illustrated History of the Black Athlete*. Garden City: Doubleday, 1985.

Rutherford, Glenn. *Tracking the Cats.* Louisville, Ky.: Courier-Journal Press, 1984.

Salzberg, Charles. *From Set Shot to Slam Dunk.* New York: E. P. Dutton, 1987.

Sanchez, Ray. *Basketball's Biggest Upset.* El Paso, Tex.: Mesa Publishing, 1991.

Smith, Ronald A. *Sports and Freedom: The Rise of Big-Time College Athletics.* New York: Oxford Press, 1988.

Stanley, Gregory K. *Before Big Blue.* Lexington: University Press of Kentucky, 1961.

Stern, Robert. *They Were No. 1.* New York: Leisure Press, 1983.

Talbert, Charles G. *The University of Kentucky: The Maturing Years.* Lexington: University Press of Kentucky, 1968.

Thelin, John R. *Games Colleges Play.* Baltimore: Johns Hopkins Press, 1994.

Tuell, Gary. *Above the Rim: A Pictorial History of Basketball at the University of Louisville.* Louisville, Ky.: University of Louisville Athletic Association, 1987.

Twombly, Wells. *200 Years of Sports in America.* New York: McGraw Hill, 1976.

Vaught, Jamie H. *Crazy About the Cats.* Kuttawa, Ky.: McClanahan Publishing, 1992.

Vecchione, Joseph, ed. *Book of Sports Legends.* New York: Random House, 1991.

Walker, Chet, and Chris Messenger. *Long Time Coming.* New York: Grove Press, 1995.

Williamson, Joel. *The Crucible of Race: Black-White Relations in the American South Since Emancipation.* New York: Oxford Press, 1984.

Windhausen, John D., ed. *Sports Encyclopedia of North America.* Gulf Breeze, Fla.: Academic International Press, 1989.

Young, A. S. "Doc." *Negro Firsts in Sports.* Chicago: Johnson Publishing, 1963.

Scholarly Papers and Journals

Beghorn, F. J., Norman Yetman, and F. R. Thomas. "Racial Participation and Integration in Intercollegiate Basketball, 1958–1980." *Journal of Sports Behavior* 5, no. 1 (1988): 44–56.

Brown, Robert W., and R. Todd Jewell. "Is There Customer Discrimination in College Basketball?: The Premium Fans Pay for White Players." *Social Science Quarterly* (June 1994): 401–13.

Grundman, Adolph. "The Image of Intercollegiate Sports and the Civil Rights Movement: A Historian's View." *Arena Review* 5, no. 3 (1980): 77–85.

Martin, Charles H. "Jim Crow in the Gymnasium: The Integration of College Basketball in the American South." *The International Journal of the History of Sports* 10, no. 1 (1993): 65–86.

———. "Racial Change and Big-Time College Football in Georgia: The Age of Segregation, 1892–1957." *Georgia Historical Quarterly* 30, no. 3 (1996): 532–62.

McCormick, Richard. "A Winning Tradition, a Losing Tradition: The Integration of University of Kentucky Athletics." Unpublished, 1995.

Paul, Joan, Richard McGhee, and Helen Fant. "The Arrival and Ascendance of Black Athletes in the Southeastern Conference, 1966–1980." *Phylon* 45 (December 1984): 284–97.

Report of the Visiting Committee to Texas Western College, 1965.

Sandiford, Les, and Mimi Gladstein. "Sad Story: UTEP's Cage Dilemma." *El Paso Times,* 19 March 1978.

The Socio-Cultural Characteristics of El Paso's Poor. Community Research Project, El Paso Department of Planning and Research, 1971.

Spivey, Donald. "The Black Athlete in Big-Time Intercollegiate Sports, 1941–1968." *Phylon* 44 (June 1983): 116–25.

Archives

Lexington Public Library, The Kentucky Room: Adolph Rupp files.

Special Collections, University of Kentucky: President John W. Oswald's papers; Adolph Rupp files and tapes; the University of Kentucky Athletic Association papers; the University of Kentucky Oral History Project.

Special Collections, University of Maryland.

Special Collections, University of Texas at El Paso: President Joseph M. Ray papers; the University of Texas at El Paso Oral History Project.

Index